ASIAN PERSPECTIVES ON INTERNATIONAL SECURITY

By the same author

CHINESE COMMUNIST POWER AND POLICY IN
  XINJIANG, 1949–77

ASIAN PERSPECTIVES ON INTERNATIONAL SECURITY

Edited by
Donald Hugh McMillen

St. Martin's Press   New York

© Strategic and Defence Studies Centre 1984

All rights reserved. For information, write:
St. Martin's Press, Inc., 175 Fifth Avenue, New York, NY 10010
Printed in Hong Kong
Published in the United Kingdom by The Macmillan Press Ltd.
First published in the United States of America in 1984

ISBN 0-312-05643-5

Library of Congress Cataloging in Publication Data

Main entry under title:
Asian perspectives on international security.
Revised versions of papers presented at a conference held at the Australian National University, Apr. 11–14, 1983.
Includes index.
1. National security—Congresses. 2. Asia—Strategic aspects—Congresses. 3. Security, International—Congresses.
I. McMillen, Donald Hugh, 1944–
UA10.5.A73 1984   335'.033'047   83-24576
ISBN 0-312-05643-5

For Dini, Damon, Santi and Ashley,
our larger family in America and Indonesia,
and the cabin amidst the aspen –
may our world know peace

Contents

List of Tables	ix
Foreword R. Gerard Ward	xi
Preface	xiii
List of Acronyms and Abbreviations	xvi
Notes on the Contributors	xviii
Map	xxiii
Introduction: Asia in the Global Balance T. B. Millar	1
1 A South Korean Perspective: Implications of the Eroding Superpower Balance in East Asia Sang-woo Rhee	9
2 Japan's Security and the International Environment in the 1980s Fuji Kamiya	28
3 ASEAN Perspectives on International Security: an Indonesian View Jusuf Wanandi	40
4 Vietnamese Perspectives on International Security: Three Revolutionary Currents Carlyle A. Thayer	57

5	Arab and Israeli Perspectives on International Security *Robert Springborg*	77
6	Perspectives from the Gulf: Regime Security or Regional Security? *Mohammed Ayoob*	92
7	Afghanistan and International Security *Zalmay Khalilzad*	117
8	Pakistani Perspectives on International Security *Pervaiz Iqbal Cheema*	135
9	An Indian Perspective on International Security *K. Subrahmanyam*	151
10	Chinese Perspectives on International Security *Donald Hugh McMillen*	168
11	The Soviet Union's Security Outlook *Paul Dibb*	195
12	Concluding Thoughts *Donald Hugh McMillen*	215
	Appendix: Military and Socioeconomic Profile of Selected Asian States	221
	Index	223

List of Tables

1.1 The US–USSR military balance in Northeast Asia (to end 1965) 19
2.1 Changes in Japan's defence-related expenditures (after 1965) 35
2.2 World's ten biggest defence spenders 36
6.1 Typology of politics in Gulf states 95

Foreword

Each year the Strategic and Defence Studies Centre organises a major international conference as one component of activities which embrace research, debate and publication on important strategic, defence and peace issues. Naturally, the tendency is for discussion in these conferences to give emphasis to Australian interests and views. But the Centre, like the rest of the Research School of Pacific Studies, has a research region which embraces much of Asia and the Pacific Islands. The organisers of the project which provided the thematic focus for the 1983 conference and this volume recognised that through this diverse region perceptions of security vary greatly and that as 'security is international and indivisible' an understanding of regional, national, and often local security cannot be divorced from global issues. The contributors are all authorities in their field, and the majority can speak as insiders. Many have had experience in government and policy areas as well as in academic circles and, although they do not write as representatives, they quite properly bring out the place and time of specific perceptions of security issues.

The volume's emphasis, therefore, has been placed on Asian perspectives on security at all levels of scale. As one author notes, 'any country's perception of reality will always be different from reality'. As each country views reality from a different location, a different level in a hierarchy of power, and a different set of ideological or cultural norms, it is not surprising that the authors in this volume present widely different national views of security issues at all levels. Some states see a need for the shelter of a superpower; others feel it desirable to keep away from the edge of all superpower umbrellas. States on either side of an ideological, military or economic frontier may each feel themselves under great threat from the other, neither perceiving the same reality. If 'the Western intelligence community does not have a particularly good record when it comes to the analysis of the USSR', one can have little faith in the Soviet intelligence community having a much better understanding. The same seems equally true in the other areas of tension dealt with in this volume – in the Arab–Israeli conflict; between North and South Korea; between Vietnam and China (or Thailand); and even between the adversaries in areas of internal insecurity. Lack of understanding of the perceptions of others, and unwillingness to accommodate to them, is a continuous underlying base of much of the insecurity in the Asian region. If the authors of the excellent essays in this volume can help even a few of their readers to recognise, and endeavour to consider, this dangerous gap, then this project and its products will have had an additional and much wider influence.

Politicians and national leaders naturally seek to minimise risks to themselves and their constituents. Inadequate information and poor understanding of the views of others greatly increase risks in the security area. This is well illustrated in cases described in this book. At the same time, the book should increase understanding of different viewpoints. It is a volume which deserves wide and thoughtful readership.

26 September 1983 R. GERARD WARD

Preface

The claim to universality which inspires the moral code of one particular group is incompatible with the identical claim of another group; the world has room for only one, and the other must yield or be destroyed. Thus, carrying their idols before them, the nationalistic masses of our time meet in the international arena, each group convinced that it executes the mandate of history, that it does for humanity what it seems to do for itself, and that it fulfills a sacred mission ordained by Providence, however defined.

Hans Morganthau*

This volume of essays has been conceived on the belief that there is a continuing need to air, and thus, it is hoped, understand better, Asian perspectives of the world, and in particular of the crucial issues related to contemporary international security. It is further felt that the scholars treating these perspectives should not merely identify and describe them, but should also dissect and analyse these views so as to discover what factors have shaped them and will probably continue to do so in the future. It is recognised that in some Asian states more than a single, dominant perspective may be extant, and that 'variable' outlooks also should be identified and assessed whenever possible. The discovery and analysis of linkages between perspectives and foreign and defence policy-making is also deemed to be of concern in our efforts here, as is the importance of the interplay of domestic and external affairs. The authors have sought to explore these complex issues at the global, regional and local (national) levels of security interaction, with commentary on how the 'superpower balance' is seen to impinge upon the Asian region as a whole and on each Asian state in particular and, conversely, on the degree to which the region and its individual states influence the 'superpower balance' and global politics

* *Politics Among Nations*, 4th ed. Alfred A. Knoff, New York, 1967, p. 249.

generally. Also, where possible, each Asian state's conception of its 'ideal' world or regional order is to be treated.

The planning and preparation for this volume has taken nearly two years. I was assisted in the initial stages of sharpening the focus and shaping its structure by Professor Mohammed Ayoob and Dr Robert O'Neill, and by my colleagues in the Strategic and Defence Studies Centre and the Department of International Relations, Research School of Pacific Studies, The Australian National University. Most of the authors were invited at that time to prepare initial drafts of their chapters for presentation at a conference at The Australian National University from 11 to 14 April 1983. In the light of that conference, as well as previous and subsequent discussions, these essays took the form in which they now are presented. It has been a guiding principle throughout that the purpose of the conference was to assist in the shaping of the book rather than for the book to be merely a record of the conference proceedings. Moreover, it was not our intent that any of these essays should constitute an official statement by any government.

This project could not have gone ahead without the continuing support, both financial and otherwise, of the Strategic and Defence Studies Centre and the Research School of Pacific Studies, The Australian National University. Several other institutions also provided financial support for the conference, including Boral Limited, CRA Limited, Ansett Transport Industries Limited, the Japan Foundation and the Japanese Ministry of Foreign Affairs, the Australian Development Assistance Bureau of the Australian Department of Foreign Affairs, and the United States Information Service.

I must also warmly acknowledge gratitude to the following for their assistance with the organisation of the conference and the production of this volume: Dr T. B. Millar, Head of the Strategic and Defence Studies Centre, for his advice and constant encouragement; Mr J. O. Langtry, Executive Officer of the Strategic and Defence Studies Centre, who bore the main burden of the conference administration; Mrs Billie Dalrymple, Mrs Patrya Kay, Ms Claire Nipperess, Mrs Dawn Langtry, Mrs Lynne Payne, and, especially, Mrs Elza Sullivan who provided essential secretarial and other administrative assistance; the Rt Hon. Ian Sinclair, Shadow Minister of Defence and Member of the Parliament of Australia, for his address at the conference dinner; Professor R. Gerard Ward, Director of the Research School of Pacifc Studies, for his many contributions to this project; the scholars and public officials who took time from their busy schedules to chair the conference sessions and make useful comments on each paper; the SOCPAC Printery in the Research School of Pacific Studies for its usual fine job in reproducing the conference papers; Mr John Fitzgerald and Ms Antonia Finnane who proofread the manuscript; and Ms Anne-Lucie Norton of Macmillan Press, London, who helped us to achieve a smooth and rapid publication. I am particularly indebted to the authors of the essays for their efforts both in preparing presentations for the conference itself (and travelling so many miles to attend the gathering) and for their ready cooperation in revising their drafts in light of discussions there and in response to editorial suggestions. Any editorial errors or shortcomings remain my responsibility.

Most of all, I must pronounce my deepest appreciation and continuing loving affection to my family, especially my wife, Dini, and our three children, Damon, Santi and Ashley, without whose constant encouragement and sacrifice this volume could not have been prepared.

Canberra DONALD H. McMILLEN

List of Acronyms and Abbreviations

ASEAN	Association of Southeast Asian Nations
ASW	Anti-submarine warfare
C3	Command, control and communications
CENTO	Central Treaty Organisation
CIA	Central Intelligence Agency
CMEA	Council for Mutual Economic Aid (COMECON)
DEF	Division equivalent forces
DMZ	De-militarised zone
EEC	European Economic Community
GATT	General Agreement on Tariffs and Trade
GCC	Gulf Cooperation Council
ICBM	Intercontinental ballistic missile
INF	Intermediate range nuclear forces
IRBM	Intermediate range ballistic missiles
IRP	Islamic Republican Party
LDC	Late-developing country
NAM	Non-Aligned Movement
NATO	North Atlantic Treaty Organisation
OAPEC	Organisation of Arab Petroleum Exporting Countries
OECD	Organisation for Economic Cooperation and Development
OPEC	Organisation of Petroleum Exporting Countries
PLO	Palestine Liberation Organisation
PRC	People's Republic of China
RD(JT)F	Rapid Deployment (Joint Task) Force
SEATO	Southeast Asia Treaty Organisation
SLBM	Submarine-launched ballistic missile
SLCM	Sea-launched cruise missile
SLOC	Sea lanes/lines of communication
SRV	Socialist Republic of Vietnam

SSBM	Surface-to-surface ballistic missile
START	Strategic Arms Reduction Treaty
UAE	United Arab Emirates
UN	United Nations
US(A)	United States (of America)
USSR	Union of Soviet Socialist Republics
VCP	Vietnamese Communist Party
ZOPFAN	Zone of Peace, Freedom and Neutrality

Notes on the Contributors

Professor Mohammed Ayoob is Associate Professor, Department of Political Science, National University of Singapore. His previous positions include: Lecturer, Indian School of International Studies, New Delhi, 1967–9; Research Associate, Institute for Defence Studies and Analyses, New Delhi, 1969–70; Associate Professor, School of International Studies, Jawaharlal Nehru University, New Delhi, 1970–8; Senior Research Fellow, Department of International Relations, Australian National University 1978–82. He has published widely on the politics and international relations of the Middle East and South Asia, including three edited books: *Conflict and Intervention in the Third World* (London, 1980); *The Politics of Islamic Reassertion* (London, 1981); and *The Middle East in World Politics* (London, 1981).

Dr Pervaiz Iqbal Cheema is Assistant Professor, Department of International Relations, Quaid-I-Azam University, Islamabad, Pakistan, and was a Visiting Fellow in the Strategic and Defence Studies Centre, Australian National University, in 1979. He has been Lecturer in History and Political Science, Government College, Lahore, 1962–6; Director/Course Co-ordinator, Foreign Office Training Courses, Pakistan Administrative Staff College, 1975–6; Chairman, Department of International Relations (1976–8) and Chairman, Department of Strategic Studies (1978–81), Quaid-I-Azam University. He has authored three books and 'Conflict and Cooperation in the Indian Ocean: Pakistan's Interests and Choices', *Canberra Papers on Strategy and Defence, No. 23* (Canberra, 1980).

Mr Paul Dibb is Senior Research Fellow, Department of International Relations, Research School of Pacific Studies, Australian National University. His previous positions include: Head, National Assessments Staff, National Intelligence Committee, 1974–8; Deputy Director, Joint Intelligence Organisation, 1978–80; and Assistant Secretary, Strategic Policy Branch, Department of Defence, 1981. He is editor of *Australia's External Relations in the 1980s* (Sydney, forthcoming), and is writing a book for the International Institute for Strategic Studies, London, about the limits to Soviet strategic power over the next decade.

Professor Fuji Kamiya received his LL.D. from Kyoto University. Besides being Professor of International Relations at Keio University, he has also been Visiting Professor at the East Asian Institute, Columbia University, and is a member of the board of directors of Japan's leading academic and advisory bodies in international law and relations. Of his many published books, the most recent is *The Security of Korea: US and Japanese Perspectives on the 1980s* (1980). His articles have appeared in leading Japanese and Western journals such as *Survey* and *Asian Survey*.

Dr Zalmay Khalilzad is Assistant Professor of Political Science and a Member of the Institute of War and Peace Studies at Columbia University, New York. Besides co-authoring a book on Iran (New York, 1983) and a monograph on the security of Southwest Asia (London, forthcoming), Dr Khalilzad's writing has appeared in *Survival, International Security, Bulletin of the Atomic Scientists, Political Science Quarterly, Survey, Orbis, Current History, Asian Survey,* and *Problems of Communism*.

Dr Donald Hugh McMillen is Senior Research Fellow in the Strategic and Defence Studies Centre, Australian National University (where he is on secondment from the School of Modern Asian Studies, Griffith University, Brisbane). He obtained his Ph.D. in modern Chinese history from the University of Colorado at Boulder, where his studies also included Soviet and Southeast Asian history and politics and American diplomatic history. He has taught at the University of Colorado (Boulder and Denver), and the Maryland University (Far East Division, Taibei, Taiwan). He has been a Visiting Scholar at the Universities Service Centre (Hong Kong), the Institute of International Studies (Beijing, China) and the Institute for International Relations (Taibei, Taiwan). Dr McMillen is the author of *Chinese Communist Power and Policy in Xinjiang, 1949–77* (1979) and has written numerous articles and chapters on Chinese affairs in such journals as *Asian Survey, Australian Journal of Chinese Affairs, World Review, Asian Studies Professional Review* (US), *Asian Pacific Community* (Japan), *International Journal* (Canada), and *China Quarterly*.

Dr T. B. Millar has been a Professorial Fellow in International Relations, Australian National University, since 1968. He joined this Department in 1962, was the first Head of the Strategic and Defence Studies Centre, 1966–70, and was reappointed in 1982. He was also Director of the Australian Institute of International Affairs, 1969–76. His publications include: *Australia's Defence* (Melbourne, 1965); *The Commonwealth and the United Nations* (Sydney, 1967); *Australia's Foreign Policy* (Sydney, 1968); *The Indian and Pacific Oceans: Some Strategic Considerations* (London, 1969); *Foreign Policy: Some Australian Reflections* (Melbourne, 1972); *Australian Foreign Minister: The Diaries of R. G. Casey, 1951–60*, (ed.) (London, 1972); *Australia in Peace and War: External Relations 1788–1977* (Canberra, 1978); *The East West Strategic Balance* (London, 1981); *International Security in the Southeast Asian and Southwest Pacific Region*, (ed.) (Brisbane, 1983); and *Current International Treaties*, (ed.) (London, forthcoming).

Dr Sang-woo Rhee is Professor of Political Science and Chairman of the Department of Politics and Diplomacy at Sogang University, Seoul. He served as Assistant Director of the Dimensionality of Nations Project at the University of Hawaii, 1971–3. He has been Chairman of the Research Committee of the Korean Association of International Relations, 1978–9, Chairman of the Publication Committee of the Korean Political Science Association, 1981–2, and Secretary-General of the Korean Association for Future Studies from 1975–8. Professor Rhee is at present Vice-President of the Korean Association for Communist Studies, and Editor of *Korea and World Affairs*. He has authored *The Security Environment of Korea* (2 vols, Seoul, 1977 and 1980), *Contemporary Theories in International Relations* (Seoul, 1978), and *Korean Security and Unification* (Seoul, 1983).

Dr Robert Springborg is Senior Lecturer in the School of History, Philosophy and Politics at Macquarie University, North Ryde, New South Wales, Australia. He obtained his Ph.D. in Middle Eastern politics from Stanford University, and subsequently held teaching and research appointments at the University of Pennsylvania. He authored *Family, Power and Politics in Egypt: Sayed Bey Marei – His Clan, Clients, and Cohorts* (University of Pennsylvania Press, 1982) and many articles in *Middle East Journal, World Review, Politics, Australian Outlook, Comparative Political Studies*, and *International Journal of Middle East Studies*.

Notes on the Contributors

Mr K. Subrahmanyam is Director of the Institute for Defence Studies and Analyses, New Delhi. He has been Secretary (Defence Production), Ministry of Defence, Government of India; Chairman, Joint Intelligence Committee, Cabinet Secretariat, Government of India; and Home Secretary, Tamil Nadu State. He was a Rockefeller Fellow in Strategic Studies in the Department of International Relations, London School of Economics (1966–7) and has been associated with the Institute for Defence Studies and Analyses from 1968–75 and again, since April 1980. He has been a member of the UN Secretary General's Expert Panel on the Indian Ocean (1974); a Member of the UN Intergovernmental Experts' Group on the Relationship between Disarmament and Development (1980–1); and Member of the Indian delegation to the Second UN Special Session on Disarmament and Seventh Non-Aligned Summit. His publications include: *The Liberation War*, with Dr Mohammed Ayoob (New Delhi, 1972); *Bangladesh and India's Security* (New Delhi, 1972); *Perspectives in Defence Planning* (New Delhi, 1972); *Defence and Development* (Calcutta, 1973); *Self Reliance and National Resilience*, (ed.) (New Delhi, 1975); *Nuclear Myths and Realities: India's Dilemma*, (ed.) (New Delhi, 1982); and *Indian Security Perspectives* (New Delhi, 1982).

Dr Carlyle A. Thayer is Lecturer in Southeast Asian Politics in the Faculty of Military Studies, University of New South Wales, Royal Military College, Duntroon. Dr Thayer received his Ph.D. from The Australian National University. He visited Vietnam and Kampuchea in August–September 1981 as a guest of the Vietnam Social Science Committee's Institute of Economics. His recent publications include a chapter on Vietnam-Lao relations in Stuart-Fox, (ed.) *Contemporary Laos* (Brisbane, 1982) and articles on Vietnam's foreign policy, economy and leadership in *Southeast Asian Affairs 1983*, *Current Affairs Bulletin* (March 1983) and *Current History* (April 1983). In 1983, Dr Thayer will be a Visiting Fellow and consultant at the Political Science Department and the Southeast Asian Refugee Project, Yale University.

Mr Jusuf Wanandi graduated from the School of Law, University of Indonesia, and subsequently lectured at that university and at the Atma Jaya Catholic University. Currently he is Executive Director of the Centre for Strategic and International Studies, Jakarta. Mr Wanandi is also Deputy Treasurer of the Central Board of Golkar, a member of the People's Consultative Assembly (MPR), and a member of the editorial boards of *Asian Survey* and *Indonesian Quarterly*. He edited, with Robert A. Scalapino, *Economic, Political, and Security Issues in Southeast Asia in the 1980s* (Berkeley, 1982).

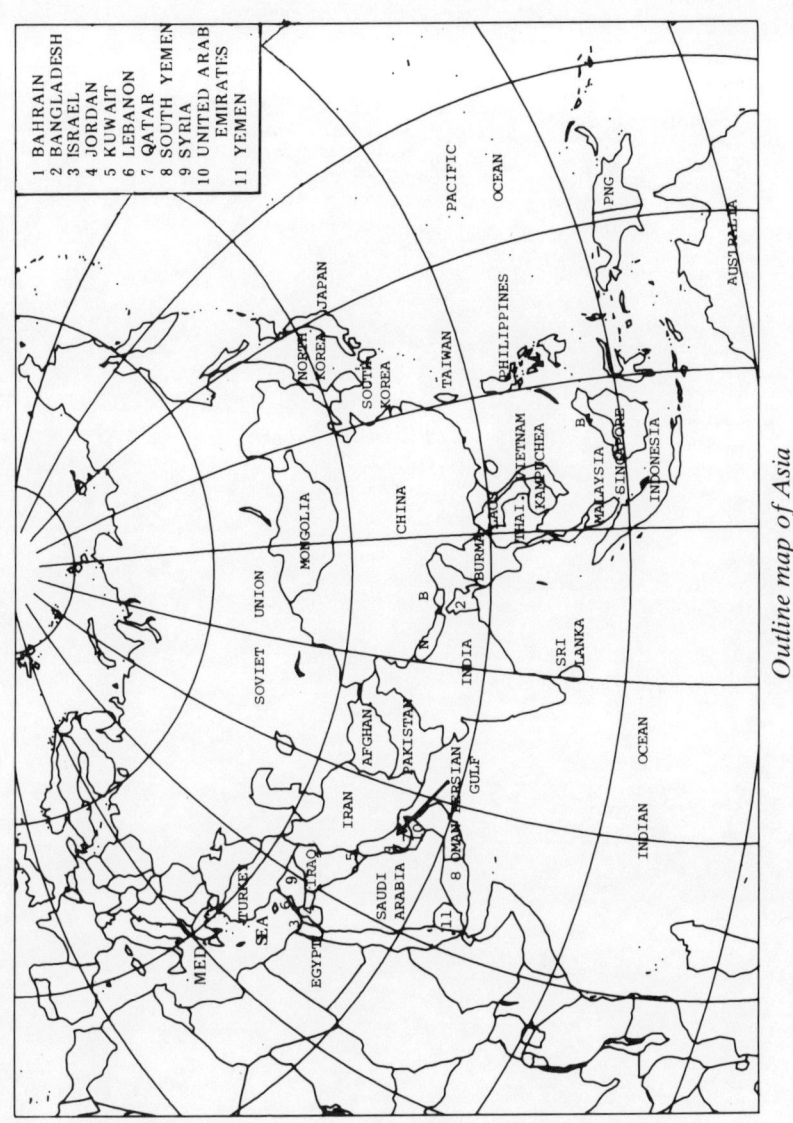

Outline map of Asia

Introduction: Asia in the Global Balance

T. B. MILLAR

The global balance of power – such as it is – operates at three main levels: in the rough equivalence of strategic nuclear power as between the United States and the Soviet Union; in the rough equivalence again, nuclear and conventional, between NATO and the Warsaw Pact; and, in the rest of the world, in largely stable if marginally frictional regional patterns of force, where the competing superpowers are either irrelevant or act within accepted spheres of influence, or operate across blurred boundaries to keep conflict regionally contained.

In 1904 the English political geographer Halford Mackinder read a paper to the Royal Geographical Society in London entitled 'The Geographical Pivot of History'.[1] In this paper he used just once a word that was to pass into the language of strategic thought, the word 'heartland'. It referred to the vast inner areas of the European-Asian continents. He saw these as the pivot around which the world of political power was roughly balanced. His thesis was effectively if not intentionally a response to, and in some respects complementary to, the ideas of the American Admiral Alfred Thayer Mahan, who saw seapower as the main factor of international political power. Mackinder, who developed his ideas over the ensuing two decades, believed that the role of seapower was declining and the role of land power – large ground forces backed up by large industries – was increasing. He had a vision throughout history of armies of horsemen (Tatars, Cossacks and many others) galloping back and forth across the vast plains of Euro-Asia creating great empires. He observed the development of industrial power at the extremities, in Siberia, Japan and Western Europe. The heartland thus became the strategic centre, or pivot, of what he called the 'world island'. The major powers contending, as in the 'Great War', for the control of the world island's heartland were contending in fact for the control of the world. In a book published in 1919, *Democratic Ideals and Reality*, Mackinder developed his heartland thesis further, encapsulating it in his famous lines:

> Who rules East Europe commands the Heartland:
> Who rules the Heartland commands the World-Island:
> Who rules the World-Island commands the World.²

This has never been true, but throughout this century it has been portentous.

Mackinder foresaw and indeed advocated the eventual combination of the West European states and the USA against the Eurasian heartland as a way of containing its power and establishing a stable balance. Late in life, during World War II, he wrote in *Foreign Affairs*:

> All things considered, the conclusion is unavoidable that if the Soviet Union emerges from this war as conqueror of Germany, she must rank as the greatest land Power on the globe. Moreover, she will be the Power in the strategically strongest defensive position. The Heartland is the greatest natural fortress on earth. For the first time in history it is manned by a garrison sufficient both in numbers and in quality.³

Note that Mackinder saw the USSR as a defensive rather than an offensive power.

Mackinder's theories were not wholly appropriate to his time; neither are they to ours. Perhaps because he based his maps on Mercator's projection, he overestimated the separateness of the United States. The US was the predominant world power for more than twenty years after World War II without dominating the Euro-Asian heartland. It did not control but did have considerable influence over parts of the periphery – in Western Europe, some of Southeast Asia, Taiwan, South Korea and Japan. It did not control China, or the Indian subcontinent, or Southwest Asia, and had only selective influence there. The Soviet Union's present world-wide capacity to exercise conventional military power springs partly from the heartland and its industries, but equally from the navy with its numerous submarines and steadily growing fleet of helicopter and fixed-wing aircraft carriers, from a long-range air lift capacity, and from access to foreign strategic facilities in Vietnam, Angola, Ethiopia and South Yemen. As with the US, there is thus something of a marriage, and a fairly formidable one, of Mahan and Mackinder, although the US constituted its own heartland away from Europe and from there dominated the new world through Mackinder and much of the old through Mahan. The British Empire provided the basic evidence for Mahan, but established its heartland, such as it was, in the Indian sub-continent where wealth, bases, manpower and military experience provided substance for the exercise of empire. When India left the Empire, the Empire disintegrated.

The key long-term strategic factor about Asia in the global balance is that the USSR lives there and the US does not, and that to be the eventual predominant power of Euro-Asia Moscow doesn't have to do anything more than it has done for several centuries: press outwards from the pivot (set at about the Ural mountains) operating from internal lines of communication, and acting out the imperatives of power and the corruption of opportunity. For the US to exercise constraints on Soviet power *in Asia*, it cannot be other than a political, cultural and geographical intruder operating over long distances on external lines of communication at the margins of an essentially alien continent. This applies to US use of nuclear as well as conventional forces.

The major differences between the Asian situation of today and that of the turn of the century when Mahan and Mackinder wrote are: the disappearance of the European empires in Asia; the military emasculation of Japan by the continuing impact of Hiroshima; the development of China and India as major powers (so long as they stay at home); and the Sino-American global confrontation and the advent of nuclear weapons. The Imperial Russia of yesterday is the Soviet Union of today, more able because of its tighter political control, modern military technology, and its World War II territorial acquisitions to exercise power, but by that fact running into greater resistance from neighbours whose independence is threatened. To be a global power, the USSR must operate out of its extremities. Hence, the development and fortification of Siberia and Sakhalin, the fortification of the Japanese northern islands, the invasion of Afghanistan, the interest in Iran, and the pressures on Scandinavia. Hence also, the acquisition of new, hired and therefore vulnerable 'extremities' in Vietnam and elsewhere. Because the USSR is still inherently an imperial power and the United States (outside its own hemisphere) a post-imperial power, countries on the periphery of the heartland still look to America to help contain the local superpower – thus, American support of South Korea, Japan, the Philippines, Thailand, Egypt and Western Europe. In the event that there were no such support, one can only speculate about the effect of the outward pressures stemming from the imperatives of power, the corruption and seduction of opportunity, constrained as they may be by a range of internal problems.

Mackinder's thesis was taken up by his German disciple, General Karl Haushofer, translated to the German situation and further transposed to East Asia where he served as a military attaché and developed an attachment to Japan. He advocated that Japan develop good relations with the USSR, and that it expand not into China but into the Pacific. The invasion of China – the triumph in effect of the generals over the admirals – was the triumph also of Mackinder's theories, with Japan seeking on the continent the heartland it did not have among its tiny group of islands. In destroying the European empires in East and Southeast Asia, Japan imposed an empire of its own which was not more acceptable and which still remains in the memories of contemporary regional leaders. In trying to acquire a heartland for an empire, Japan devastated itself.

Japan in the 1980s bears little relationship to Japan in the 1930s. As one Japanese professor has suggested, World War II taught Japan that to pursue economic ends by military means is a very uneconomic proposition. Economically, Japan is interdependent with the United States and Australia and almost totally dependent on Middle East oil transported by sea. What is Japan's part in today's global balance? It is essentially to serve as the principal US forward base for the containment of Soviet power in the Northwest Pacific. Without that US presence, without the one-sided US-Japan security treaty, Japan would presumably do one of two things: become non-aligned, or engage in massive rearmament. The traumas of World War II and its devastating climax, plus the extraordinary economic achievements of the people, have turned Japan away from war as an instrument of policy, as the Constitution declares with misleading accuracy. But Japan's unresolved dilemmas are how to reconcile economic strength with political weakness and how to make those sufficient preparations for war which are the only convincing assurance of peace without arousing either the old nationalist chauvinisms or the apprehensions of its neighbours. Japan sits astride several of the ice-free maritime exits from Soviet Siberia and North Korea. On its own, it could not block those exits in war without risking nuclear annihilation.

Japan is placed politically at the weakest corner of the Asian quadrilateral (China, Japan, USSR, US). She has no 'cards' to play, no lever except to offer technology in return for raw materials. She has to fit in as best she can with the policies of her three disparate associates. The danger for Japan is less physical than psychological: the humility of continuing dependence, and the possibility of a severe check (through trade barriers) to the rising standard of living. Either or both of these could conceivably one day turn Japan in upon itself, with incalculable consequences. Japan can compensate for the implications of its geography, as it is now doing, but it cannot eliminate them. If some future Japanese government were to be tempted again to empire, it would inevitably again destroy all that its people had built up through their energy and intelligence. For Japan in the nuclear age, *there is no alternative to peace*.

China is a heartland of itself, even if it was marginal in Mackinder's thesis. Because of the communist revolution it has become the eastern counterweight to the USSR, the giant at the back gate. A Sino-Soviet combination would dominate all of Asia east of the Urals, but this would require a community of interest and outlook that has never existed, even during the 1950s. The galloping horsemen from the east still strike fear into the Russian consciousness, hence those fifty-two Soviet divisions in Siberia. Contained by Soviet forces on the north and west and by the sea on the east, China has been determined to exercise hegemony in the south, only to find itself also running into the extensions of Soviet power there which, in China's present state, can only be countered by limited and surreptitious operations.

Both Russians and Americans are aliens to the Chinese, who see them as members of less respectable cultures even though having access to superior technology. China has no permanent regional affinities. It does not want to be anyone's 'card'. Its problems are overwhelmingly internal. It is vulnerable to Soviet attack; it is invulnerable to Soviet occupation. To make the progress it desires it must have Western capital and technology, preferably in conjunction with a balanced and sophisticated diplomacy. The clumsy approach of the Reagan administration, as this writer sees it, is a legacy of the never valid assumption that China and Russia were a joint heartland bent on world domination.

Northeast Asia is an area of dangers to world peace because it provides the nexus between four great powers with competing ambitions: the Soviet Union, determined to develop the resources of Siberia and to have unimpeded access to the Pacific for mercantile shipping and the projection of naval power; China, determined to be influential over its continental sphere; Japan, a maritime power, lying across the Soviet exits and dependent on the US for protection against Soviet hegemony; and the US, dependent on Japan for its Western Pacific strategic presence. The Korean peninsula lies at the nexus, manifesting by its division the competing ambitions, pulled and pressed within and without, a self-propelled pawn in a complex power game.

Southeast Asia is strategically relevant to the global balance mainly because it includes the nexus between two great oceans. Neither superpower, nor China, could afford to see the whole region dominated by a single power. With the Europeans departed, there is a rough balance of power between Indochina supported by the Soviet Union, rebel movements supported by China, and the ASEAN group supported by the US and Australia.

The continuing struggle of India is not to come to terms with the world but to come to terms with itself. The world is but a continuation, or externalisation, of the problems of India, which is slowly and jerkily *being* a nation, discovering and developing a sense of the unity of what one might call the 'soul' of India, still torn by the passions of its long history but overall coping with enormous poverty and disparities of wealth, education, culture, class and caste to become one of the world's major industrial and military powers. The English-educated elite, the 'brown *sahibs*' who guided India to independence and beyond, are passing, but their children are still there at the top, having inherited a national polity they did not make and struggling to give substance to an economic, political and strategic independence they know to be continuingly precarious. Having called in the Soviet Union to redress the global balance with the West and the regional balance with first Pakistan and then China, Indians now find their powerful friend looming too heavily, too closely, even a little threateningly, in Afghanistan. It is not that the USSR is actually threatening India directly or indirectly; it is not. But its presence and posture in Afghanistan arouse Indian apprehensions that have lain latent since the days of Kim O'Hara. Despite some tentative moves towards reconciliation between India and Pakistan, the sub-continent has yet to evolve that necessary strategic unity which the British thrust upon it and about which Kipling wrote. And if Pakistan, for whatever motive, were to explode a nuclear device, it would simultaneously explode whatever hope for sub-continental strategic unity is conceivable in this century. The Gulf-Middle East region is an area of strategic danger and contention for two main reasons: because of its supply and stocks of petroleum which the USSR does not yet need but which the US, Japan and most of Western Europe find essential; and because of the American *de facto* guarantee of the security of Israel. For the first of these, President Carter said the US would go to war, and set up the Rapid Deployment Force, or forces. President Reagan has continued this policy. For the second, for domestic political considerations, the US would go to war if all else failed. The USSR has taken note of American priorities and appears to be respecting them. The region also provides the contended junctions between the Christian, Muslim and Jewish worlds; and between the Mediterranean and Black Seas and the Indian Ocean; and between Europe, Africa and Asia. It provides areas of dispute between Muslim sects and between fundamentalist and modernist elements. It is thus a region of continuing upheaval. If, in the long term, the USSR finds it must have Gulf oil for economic survival, then it is hard to see how the United States operating at such a distance can effectively compete. Afghanistan, if it remains under Soviet control, would be a factor *for* the Russians in that equation.

This has all been a very broad-brush, large-sweep analysis, and the trouble with large sweeps by broad brushes is that they tend to raise some dust while leaving a lot more under the carpet. This essay has not done more than touch on the implications of the fact that the USSR and China have strategic nuclear weapons, India has a demonstrated capacity to produce at least simple nuclear bombs, Israel is believed to have them, Taiwan and South Korea are 'threshold' nuclear weapons powers, while Iraq has moved towards such a threshold. One cannot see any part of Asia where the use of nuclear weapons is at all likely in the near future, or where *if* used, it could lead to anything except disaster for both user and victim.

It is said of Europe that it is both a geographical expression and a state of mind, whereas Asia is only a geographical expression. There is a lot of truth in that, even though the word 'Asian' is more than a geographical adjective. Because it is the world's largest single land mass, Euro-Asia has a unity which the Soviet Union, by spanning it, demonstrates, and to which by the widespread deployment of military power it gives strategic significance. We cannot talk about the security problems of any segment of Asia without bringing in the Soviet Union, without realising that just 'up there' or 'across there' lies this complex empire with so many of the problems of an imperial power approaching the stage of decline.

This is not say that the USSR is about to disintegrate (it is not) nor that it dominates Euro-Asia or Asia, or will inevitably do so. Neither Mackinder nor Haushofer (who saw Germany-Russia as an invincible combination) gives all the answers. The vastness of the continent of which the USSR is the northern half allows for the existence of powerful and almost inevitably unsympathetic nations around the Soviet periphery, with influences of race, religion or nationality reaching across the border in both directions. The global balance of power impinges on Asia in many ways, but Asia also impinges on the global balance, placing constraints on both superpowers while additionally offering occasional opportunities for intervention in varying degrees. Pervading the whole continent is the influence of nationalism, whose power both for defence and offence is inflated by modern military technology. Herein, it seems to this writer, rather than in the basic East–West confrontation, lie the principal immediate dangers to international peace and security. If these dangers can be contained, whatever the grand strategists may say, then perhaps the longer term will be more able to look after itself.

NOTES

1. Reproduced in the *Geographical Journal*, 23, 1904, pp. 421–37.
2. Republished by W. W. Norton, New York, 1962, p. 150.
3. Sir Halford J. Mackinder, 'The Round World and the Winning of the Peace', *Foreign Affairs*, XXI: 4, July 1943, pp. 595–605.

1 A South Korean Perspective: Implications of the Eroding Superpower Balance in East Asia

SANG-WOO RHEE

INTRODUCTION

Those whose lives are under threat usually perceive situations far more pessimistically than those whose lives are not. South Koreans experienced a most devastating war just three decades ago. Their homeland is located where the four most powerful nations – the United States, the Soviet Union, the People's Republic of China (PRC), and Japan – are all competing for influence.

One's threat perception is shaped by the interrelations between one's own and others' interests, will and capabilities. And one's understanding of these relationships is formulated on the basis of facts as well as philosophical or ideological orientations. If fed distorted factual information, one may misjudge or misperceive a situation. If one believes that human beings are by nature good and rational enough to share common ideals, one tends to interpret other's intentions positively. On the other hand, if one believes men are greedy, egoistic and not trustworthy, then one is always suspicious about others' words and deeds.

The Republic of Korea (ROK) promotes an independent, libertarian society in which civil rights and private property are protected and the freedom of individuals to enhance the quality of their lives is guaranteed. As in other pluralistic societies, there are diverse opinions about what kind of society South Korea should have. Some may prefer a planned economy to a free market one, or a stronger government to a weaker one. In general South Koreans value even more the preservation of liberal democracy than such important goals as national reunification, which they eagerly pursue, of course, but not at the cost of the former. Incessant student demonstrations against past authoritarian Korean regimes clearly reveal this value orientation.

By nature South Koreans are not a hawkish people. They want to avoid war by every available means, since war will devastate human lives and property. Nevertheless, South Koreans would prefer war to losing liberal democracy. The South Korean interest in preserving liberal democracy directly conflicts with the revolutionary goals of communist countries. For this reason communist expansionism is the primary source of South Korean threat perception. As a derivative of this, ideology becomes the most important singular criterion to identify friends and foes. Accordingly, despite great cultural differences, the US and other Western European nations are regarded as friends, and the Soviet Union and the PRC as foes. South Koreans even transcend their historical animosity to accept Japan as a friend in international politics, while they perceive their own brethren, North Korea, as an enemy. Thus, the preservation of a preferred politico-economic system far exceeds all other interests.

Regarding the intensity of interest in communising South Korea, North Korea is at the top of the scale among the three East Asian communist nations. While it is simply one of the strategic targets of world-wide communist revolution, South Korea is the target of North Korea's supreme goal of national unification. As long as North Korea insists that the ROK should be integrated under its communist system, there will be confrontation. Considering the intensity of will, South Koreans rank North Korea, the USSR, and the PRC in descending order along the danger scale. South Koreans believe that the North Korean communists are determined to expand their communist rule to South Korea at any cost. The Soviet Union, however, would not provoke the US before it is fully prepared to decisively challenge the American presence in East Asia. It will refrain, at least for the time being, from threatening South Korea. The PRC presently seems to emphasise its own domestic development rather than the export of revolution, and thus ranks as the least dangerous among the East Asian communist countries.

Considering the capabilities of these potential enemies, South

Korea again ranks them in the same order. Though far weaker than those of the two giant communist neighbours, the entire North Korean military strength is aimed at South Korea, while the strength of the Soviet Union and the PRC are directed at various targets. Also, South Korea is physically separated from their territories by North Korea, in this case an important buffer. And more importantly, any military move by the Soviet Union and the PRC against South Korea would be likely to invite US military involvement, which is much less likely in the case of a purely North Korean military attack on South Korea.

Threat perception is also affected by the perceiver's judgement of the international power structure, through which nations exert power through complex mutual interactions. Thus, without knowing a nation's perception of the state of the international political system, we can hardly understand its feeling of threat. The most critical element in evaluating a nation's threat perception is how it perceives the balance among the powers working in its security environment. In terms of military capability, the ROK cannot match the surrounding big powers, especially the Soviet Union, the PRC, and the US. Naturally, South Koreans correlate the imminent threat of North Korea with the superpower balance in East Asia. For example, they believe that they can cope with the North Korean threat if Soviet support to North Korea is deterred by the US. For the PRC, so long as the United States maintains detente with it, the South Koreans believe they need not worry about China. And a direct threat by the USSR is deemed unlikely while the US shows strong interest and will by retaining military forces in Korea. In sum, South Korea's anxiety rests basically on its fear and suspicion of an erosion of the superpower balance in East Asia.

This chapter will focus, then, on the South Korean perception of the changing power balance between the US and the USSR in East Asia and the anticipated effects of such changes on the region in general, and on inter-Korean relations in particular. Above all, it will illustrate and explain the distinct features of South Korea's security perceptions.

THE CHANGING PEACE SYSTEM IN EAST ASIA

For the first twenty years after World War II, peace had been maintained in East Asia by a firm and stable power balance between the Soviet Union and the United States who both accepted a clear demarcation of their spheres of influence and control. East Asia and other parts of the world were divided into two ideologically opposed realms, the communist and democratic worlds. Japan, the ROK and the Republic of China belonged to the latter, while the PRC and the Democratic People's Republic of Korea (DPRK) belonged to the former. The Sea of Okhotsk, the Sea of Japan, the 38th parallel on the Korean peninsula, the Yellow Sea and the Taiwan Strait served to divide these regions. In each bloc, the polar state exercised unchallenged leadership in controlling inter-bloc relations, and inter-bloc hostility resulting from ideological differences reinforced the intra-bloc cohesion. Overall peace was thus sustained by this genuine bipolar international system.[1]

During the Cold War period, especially after the Korean War, non-communist nations in East Asia felt little threat to their national security, despite the incessant militant advocacy of communist revolution by the Soviet Union and the PRC, because the US firmly endorsed the security of its client nations and maintained military forces sufficient to deter communist military adventure there. At that time the national security of each nation was inseparable from that of the bloc, and the overall responsibility of protecting bloc members rested on its leader. Thereafter, a stable peace system was sustained in East Asia because the US was not only the dominant power in the region, but also supported the status quo. This was the *Pax Americana* era.

The peace system sustained by the superpower balance, however, did not last long. By the first half of the 1970s two important changes had precipitated the erosion of the bipolar system: the Sino-Soviet conflict and the stalemate resulting from a rapid increase in Soviet nuclear capability. These two changes combined to reduce inter-bloc hostility and open a new door to increased multilateral interactions across the blocs, loosening the tight bipolar system and nullifying many of the principles underlying the Cold War era.

The PRC broke away from Soviet control in the early 1960s and had established detente with the US and Japan by 1972–3. The Soviet Union, too, improved its relations with Japan and the US. As a consequence, in East Asia the old stable bipolar peace system faded out, and a new complicated Bismarckian balance of power system emerged.[2] This new system consisted of two partially overlapping pseudo-alliance systems of the US–Japan–PRC and the US–Japan–USSR. Theoretically, peace was to be secured by the US acting according to the following rules: when the Soviet Union is stronger than the PRC, the US with the help of Japan will strengthen the US–Japan–PRC alliance in order to counterbalance the Soviets; and if the PRC becomes aggressive, then the US simply would move its weight toward the US–Japan–USSR alliance. In this way, the US with relatively reduced power would still remain at the helm of the operation of the system and could maintain peace in East Asia at its own discretion.³ After a series of successive diplomatic manoeuvres, including Kissinger's secret visit to Beijing in 1971 and Nixon's official visit in 1972, the US persuaded China to join a new US–Japan–PRC alignment and finally brought the system into orbit. Released from tensions of the Cold War by detente and this new diplomatic arrangement, the US even reduced by half the size of its ground forces in South Korea in 1973. This transition from the old Cold War system to a new one was in fact not designed intentionally by the US, but was an outgrowth of the changed power balance between the US and the USSR. In other words, the US was forced into this new peace system because of its lost power supremacy. In the 1950s, with a unilateral nuclear strike capability, the US could adopt a strategy of massive retaliation to deter Soviet military adventure. But in the late 1960s, it could no longer rely on this strategy, since the USSR had developed an effective nuclear strike capability. Reflecting on this new situation, the US retreated one step backward in its counter-Soviet strategy, moving from massive retaliation to mutual assured destruction (MAD). The core of this new strategy was a mutual deterrence or a planned nuclear stalemate in which neither side would attempt a nuclear attack for fear of retaliation by the other. In the 1970s, when the nuclear balance began to tilt toward Soviet superiority, the US again had to make a further strategic retreat toward a policy of appeasement. It tried to harness superior Soviet nuclear capability through negotiations, and the Strategic Arms Limitation Talks (SALT) resulted.⁴

This strategic retreat had great policy implications, since it meant that the US discarded its military response to Soviet challenges. Therefore, the US had to look to its allies to supplement its deficient power, and had to resort to diplomatic arrangements to live with superior Soviet military power. The Nixon Doctrine formalised the US policy of detente with the USSR in July 1969. This policy stated that while keeping treaty commitments and providing a nuclear shield for allies or nations vital to US security who are threatened by a nuclear power, and furnishing military and economic assistance against other types of aggression in accordance with treaty commitments, the US would otherwise look to the nations directly threatened to assume the primary responsibility of providing manpower for its defence. The open-ended promise to defend nations threatened by communism envisioned by the Truman Doctrine of 1947 was finally scrapped.

Detente involved a tacit agreement between the US and the USSR to change the game from direct confrontation to indirect competition. This meant that they would shift the life of confrontation to the Third World and use means other than an all-out nuclear war. Detente was a short-term diplomatic success for the US, in the sense that it lessened considerably the risk of a Soviet nuclear attack on its homeland. Nevertheless, detente hardly resolved the Soviet-American conflict. Instead, it created new dimensions for their conflict elsewhere. Detente was an obvious strategic defeat for the US, since it guaranteed that Soviet activities would be unchecked in the Third World.[5] It is hard to believe that detente and its related strategic schemes were the result of thoughtful strategic considerations.

The new peace system based on the two-pronged power balance to be manipulated by the US in East Asia began, however, to visibly erode in the late 1970s. The Soviet Union's power dominated the stagnating PRC defences, and even exceeded the entire military capability of the US; and the US simply became unable to provide the necessary minimum power to sustain the peace system. Thus, the system degenerated into a new bipolar system as the PRC was at first secretly and then openly invited to join the US camp. The US was looking towards a new balance to be maintained between the Soviet Union on the one side, and the US, Japan, and the PRC on the other. This balance is now, at least implicitly, in place.

The new balance of power system contains, among others, two critical structural deficiencies. First, it is based on the premise of a continuing rivalry between the PRC and the USSR. The stability of the system therefore rests, not on US intentions, but on the will of the PRC and the Soviet Union. So far as the PRC supports the current status quo, the system will be sustained; but if the PRC restores amicable relations with the USSR, the system must collapse.

Another structural deficiency is in the relationship between the regional balance system in East Asia and that in the Korean peninsula. On the regional level, the PRC is supposed to side with the US and Japan against the Soviet Union; but on the local level in the Korean peninsula, it is to be on the opposite side of the US alliance. Within the Korean peninsula, a balance has been maintained for the past thirty years between a South Korea strongly supported by the United States, and a North Korea still retaining defence treaties with both the Soviet

Union and the PRC. Therefore, the PRC is formally obliged to fight against the US.

The stability of this new peace system is thus dubious as the onus for stability rests not with the US, supposedly the major operator of the system, but with the PRC who has the dual role of helping the US check Soviet expansionism in the region while supporting North Korea against South Korea and American forces at the local level. This is why South Koreans cannot comfortably accept the PRC as a partner in the American East Asian entente.

The Japanese role in keeping peace in Asia is also very complicated. Japan has become an indispensable element in globally checking the Soviet Union, for it is one of the very few US allies that has the ability to really supplement American power deficiencies. But, it is reluctant to be an American lieutenant. For the past few years, the US has increased its pressure on Japan to assume a greater share of the burden for the defence of East Asia against the Soviet threat. Japan's response, however, has been very ambivalent. It has cautiously moved to comply with the US demand, but with visible reluctance. So far as the Soviet Union refrains from directly threatening it, Japan will not assume an active role in pressing the Soviet Union to discard any designs in East Asia.

How long will this precarious peace system last? There are two opposite prognoses. If the US recovers sufficient military power in this region to cope with the Soviets without relying on the PRC, and keeps the PRC out of the Soviet camp, then the current peace should last. On the other hand, if the US remains militarily inferior to the Soviets, or the PRC returns to the Soviet side, then peace in East Asia is in Soviet hands.

South Koreans are quite pessimistic about peace in East Asia. They strongly wish to see the resurrection of a *Pax Americana*, but realise that this is very unlikely. At the global level, they believe that the superpower balance is tilting towards Soviet superiority. South Koreans once thought that the US would remain the predominant world power, keeping a peaceful global order. That notion of a *Pax Americana* has gradually faded. Now the US is just one of several competing great powers, only able to influence world politics to a limited extent. The defeat of the US in the Vietnamese War in 1975 was a threshold for the South Korean perception of the superpower balance. Subsequent events, such as the Iranian Revolution, the Teheran hostage crisis, the Kampuchean War, and the invasion of Afghanistan, were understood as undeniable evidence of American impotence and the end of *Pax Americana*.

In the nuclear strategic balance, the US position has changed from dominance to a rough numerical parity with the Soviet Union. As of 1982, the US possessed about 2,000 nuclear delivery vehicles and 9268 warheads, while the Soviet Union deployed about 2600 vehicles with 7300 warheads.[6] If we consider the Physical vulnerability of the US in an all-out nuclear war, the balance has already moved to Soviet superiority. For example, in the US most people and industries are concentrated in the east and west coast areas, while in the USSR, the targets are widely scattered, and this difference increases US vulnerability to the same number of warheads.[7] The US position in the current Strategic Arms Reduction Treaty (START) negotiations is not to recover the balance, but to forestall a greater imbalance. This implies that the US has already accepted the fact that it can no longer recover superiority over the USSR.

Rough nuclear parity between the US and the USSR significantly changes the global superpower balance. Nuclear strategic forces are virtually the only means the US has employed to check Soviet expansion, while it has been only an auxiliary means for the USSR in the pursuit of its global strategy. Its main tool has been conventional forces, and nuclear strategic forces have been developed only to intimidate the US and its important allies. What really matters is not the nuclear imbalance, but the disparity in conventional forces. In conventional military forces, the US cannot match the Soviet Union. As of 1982, the US maintained nineteen division equivalent forces (DEF), composed of sixteen army and three marine divisions, and about ten independent brigades, including nine army and one marine, on active duty. These troops totalled 790 800 in the Army and 192 000 in the Marine Corps. The Soviet Union, on the other hand, operated 180 divisions and eight brigades totalling 1 825 000 men. The imbalance in naval forces, too, is obvious. In the 1950s and 1960s, the oceans were virtually American lakes, but the situation now is quite different. Now the US dominance on the high seas is seriously challenged by the Soviet Navy. In 1982, the US Navy operated 96 attack submarines and 211 major surface combat ships on the seas, while the USSR had 377 attack submarines and 274 major surface combat ships on duty.[8] In the same year, the US had 3650 combat aircraft and the Soviet Union had 4480. Thus, in the air the US also can no longer claim unilateral dominance. If a military confrontation should occur on the rim of the Asian continent, the forces the US can utilise in the area would be seriously limited due to insufficient airlift capability.[9] The US has only one Rapid Deployment Joint Task Force (RDJTF) consisting of one army corps (three divisions and one brigade), three carrier battle groups, one and a half marine divisions, two B-52 H squadrons, and six fighter wings.

On the basis of the present global strategic military balance, how far can the US go in facing the Soviet challenge? If its homeland is attacked by the Soviets, the US may retaliate with its nuclear strategic forces. In case of a small contingency provoked by a Soviet surrogate, the US may take military countermeasures by sending RDJTF units to the troubled spot. But if the USSR launches large-scale military actions, the US would probably not dare to counter the Soviet's superior war capability. After all, the Soviet invasion of Afghanistan in 1979 was left seriously unpunished, and Kampuchea is left unaided in fighting the Soviet-instigated Vietnamese invasion.

Then why has the US, with a more prosperous economy and stronger allies, become so helpless against a weaker challenger? It may be that, among other reasons, the ill-conceived American strategic plan is responsible for the present humiliating situation. It seems that the strategic planners of the Soviet Union learned from Sun Zi (Sun Tzu), while the American strategists stuck to a Clausewitzian way of thinking. Sun Zi, among others, emphasised that the best strategy in dealing with a strong enemy is to make him kneel down without fighting. He suggested that the enemy's strategic design should be destroyed first, the alliance system next, and lastly the enemy forces. The Soviet strategists, too, seem to put their priorities in that order. From the beginning, the Soviet Union did not attempt a direct military engagement with the US. It has carefully avoided confrontation with American troops. In the Korean and Vietnamese Wars, in which the US was directly engaged, the Soviets sent no troops. In Afghanistan, however, it did send troops because no risk of American intervention was envisaged. Following Sun Zi's dictum, confrontation with the United States, the principal enemy, should be avoided, since directly fighting a strong enemy will incur tremendous damage. Attacks on American allies also should be avoided in the initial stage, because this would provoke retaliation by the principal enemy. They instead are only to be intimidated so that they do not take any serious anti-Soviet actions. In the first phase, all effort should be concentrated on Third World nations who are beyond the reach of effective American control and easily victimised. Once most of these nations are within its sphere of influence, the Soviet Union then would move on to neutralise American allies. The US, having been isolated in a sea of hostile or neutral nations, would not be able to resist the Soviet Union and would eventually succumb, probably without fighting.

Recently the Soviet Union has deployed new SS-20 IRBMs against Western Europe, and in East Asia as well.[10] While the range of the SS-20 from these sites covers all of Western Europe and Japan, the US is clearly out of its reach. This is very significant as it seems to be a prelude to the Soviet's second phase in which, without giving a direct threat to the US that may arouse it to take counteraction, the USSR is increasing pressure on the nations allied with the US.

What has been the US strategy against the Soviet Union? The core concept has been 'deterrence'. Clausewitz suggested that to win the war, one should first identify the heart of enemy forces, concentrate on destroying it, and not scatter one's strength around the enemy's periphery. The US seemed to follow this Clausewitzian dictum faithfully and developed a formidable nuclear striking force, aimed directly at the heart of the Soviet Union. The US has not built up its ground forces, nor has it focused on naval power.

In the 1950s and 1960s, this strategy seemed to work well. Now, however, the situation has changed. With its nuclear strategic forces cancelled out by the Soviet Union's, all of a sudden the US lacks the military tools to cope with Soviet conventional forces required if it does not want to see its allies fall one by one. But rebuilding conventional armed forces takes a long time and tremendous resources. The only alternative for the moment is to get help from its allies, thus explaining the current US pressure on its European allies and Japan to share this burden. According to the South Korean prognosis, under the Reagan administration, the US has begun to improve its military preparedness. In the next ten years, however, it will be difficult for the US to regain the military supremacy it once enjoyed.

For the US, Asia is not the core of its global strategic plan; Europe is. The US seems determined to protect Europe at any cost, with East Asia secondary and important only for tying down a portion of Soviet forces. The US keeps only two DEF in East Asia to symbolically show that it is still an Asian power. And in East-Northeast Asia, only about half of the US Seventh Fleet, about sixty major combatants, operate.[11] Previously when the US was militarily superior, a two and one-half war concept provided strategic guidance: one major war in Europe, another in Asia, and a minor one elsewhere simultaneously.[12] Now, the US has had to revise this downward into a one and one-half war concept, that is, preparation for only a Soviet attack in Europe and a minor conventional war in the Middle East simultaneously. In Asia, the US seems to plan on stopping a Soviet attack or invasion only with the help of the PRC and Japan. This means that in East Asia the Soviet-American power gap will be even more drastic in the 1980s. For the Soviet Union, East Asia is a strategically important gate into the Pacific and South Asia. Asia is also a better place to initiate its second-phase strategy of world revolution, since US interests are much less here than in Europe. The USSR keeps about one-third of its conventional forces in East Asia.

Table 1.1 shows a general picture of the conventional military balance between the US and the USSR in East Asia. Notable vulnerabilities of the US forces in East Asia include its far inferior ground combat capability and weakened capacity to protect the vital sea lines of communication (SLOC) in the Western Pacific. With such limited ground forces, the US cannot conduct any significant combat in

TABLE 1.1 *The US–USSR military balance in Northeast Asia (to end 1981)*

	USA	USSR
Ground Forces	2 DEFs (55 900 men) 1 infantry div. 1 marine div.	47 divisions (460 000 men) 6 tank div. 40 motorised rifle 1 marine
Naval Forces	60 major combatants (650 000 tons) 2 carriers 5 cruisers 9 destroyers 7 frigates 4 submarines 220 naval aircraft	176 major combatants (1 580 000 tons) 1 carrier 9 cruisers 28 destroyers 38 frigates 100 submarines 330 naval aircraft
Air Forces	192 combat aircraft 3 fighter-bomber wings 72 F-15 C/D, 48 F-16 36 F-4E, 18 RF-4C, 18 A-10 (a bomber wing, B-52)	2 210 combat aircraft 450 bombers (TU-16/22) 1600 fighters (MiG-23/27, SU-24) 160 patrol aircraft

SOURCES: *The Military Balance, 1982–83*; The Joint Chief of Staff, US, *United States Military Posture For FY 1983*; and Self-Defense Agency, Japan, *Defense of Japan, 1981* (Japanese edition).

East Asia without allied help. Now, East Asia is the most heavily armed area in the world. Beside the Soviet forces, the PRC maintains about 340 DEFs (220 as main forces and 130 as local forces),[13] and North Korea has 40 divisions and 47 brigades on active duty. Against these communist forces, South Korea maintains 22 divisions (including marines) and 13 brigades. Japan has only 155,000 ground self-defence personnel, which are difficult to employ outside of Japanese territory due to various internal political factors. Unless the ground forces of the PRC can be augmented by US allied forces in a war against the USSR, the US can mobilise for combat only 30 DEFs.

SLOC protection is a crucial issue for US security interests in East Asia. The US alliance system there simply cannot operate without maintaining SLOC. If the North Pacific sea lanes are disrupted, the US cannot provide the necessary logistical support to its allies in war; if the oil routes that link US allies and Arab nations are under Soviet control, they have to give up resistance against the Soviet Union. Until the end of the 1970s, the Soviet Navy did not possess an effective operational capability in the open ocean due to the lack of air support and overseas tendering bases. The situation has changed drastically in the past few years. Now the USSR operates one VTOL carrier in the region and has extended land-based air cover for its fleet as far as Guam and the Bashi channel with her Siberian based TU-26s.[14] The USSR now also uses the Cam Rahn Bay and Danang bases in Vietnam and the newly expanded Petropavlovsk base in Kamchatka to reduce the effects of the US blockade at the four traditional choke points.[15] Considering the PRC's naval power, the issue becomes more complicated. The PRC navy is believed to have a remarkable SLOC interdiction capability in the waters adjacent to its territory (out of the 146 major combatants, 105 are submarines). The PRC navy, however, has no efficient SLOC protection capability. The navy can mobilise only 15 destroyers and 26 frigates for ASW work. Therefore, whether or not the PRC joins the US allies makes no difference to the SLOC protection capability of the US. On the other hand, if the PRC turns out to be an adversary, the Northeast Asian SLOC will be further endangered.

Can the US regain a superior military position in East Asia? Chances are slim. The existing power gap is already so great that even in ten years it will not be possible to alter the present imbalance. Will the PRC provide the necessary help to the US were it engaged in a war outside its territory? It is very doubtful. Will Tokyo offer its forces to the US when Japan's territory is not under direct attack? Again it is unlikely. It may provide bases for US airplanes and ships and probably some logistical support, but hardly more than that. Therefore, at least in the 1980s the present great power imbalance in East Asia will remain uncorrected.

THE INTER-KOREAN HOSTILITY SCENARIO

The greatest concern of South Koreans is to prevent another inter-Korean war. Those who remember the enormous devastation of the Korean War of 1950–3 are hypersensitive about this. One survey conducted in 1982 revealed that 39·2 per cent of Korean leaders responded that such a war is highly possible in the 1980s.[16] Most South Koreans believe that North Korea under Kim Il-Song will not give up the goal of national liberation nor hesitate to use military means to achieve it. And, South Koreans also believe that North Korea is well prepared for such a war. North Korea began a military build-up in the early 1960s, while the ROK followed suit in the mid-1970s. Until the US revealed its intention to withdraw American ground forces from South Korea in 1976, Seoul had not felt an urgent need to build up its forces. But President Carter's blunt announcement of his troop withdrawal plan jolted South Korea and ended its belief in security under American protection. With a more prosperous economy, South Korea is now outpacing North Korea in military investment[17] and is gradually narrowing the existing military gap. Still, however, North Korea is dangerously superior.

North Korea's present ground forces are formidable. According to a South Korean Government research institute, in 1981 the size of the North Korean army reached 700 000 active personnel. North Korean reserves comprise some 260 000 troops, plus 2·3 million second-reserve forces. By comparison, South Korea's ground forces are still much smaller. The army has about 520 000 men on active duty, one marine division and two marine brigades. Its reserves consist of eight divisions, which retain only basic functional elements. Thus, overall, North Korea has a two-to-one ground superiority over South Korea. More importantly, North Korean troops are better equipped. North Korea operates about 2800 battle tanks and 1100 BMP/APCs, while South Korea has only 1100 tanks and 600 APCs. North Korea also boasts stronger firepower. It has 6300 guns and howitzers and 36 FROG SSMs, while South Korea has only 2700 guns/howitzers and 12 Honest John SSMs. Again North Korea maintains more than a two-to-one superiority over South Korea in armoured vehicles and guns.

The really menacing fact about the North Korean military forces is their composition and deployment. They are trimmed and deployed for the offensive, being heavily equipped with highly mobile weapons. The number of light infantry and special combat units whose primary function is to fight and disrupt C3 (command, control and communication) structures in rear areas, comprises an unusually large ratio of its forces, which are deployed very close to the DMZ for a surprise attack.

North Korea's naval forces also consist of ships that are suitable for coastal attack and blockade of South Korean harbours. North Korea has very few destroyers or other surface combatants which can protect its sea lanes or be used for anti-submarine warfare (ASW). But it does have twenty submarines and about 100 landing craft for small-scale amphibious operations and the mining of harbours. North Korea has a larger air force than South Korea, operating about 700 combat airplanes, 90 of which are bombers (IL-28s). The South Korean Air Force has better planes, but the number remains at 400.

With North Korea's superior forces deployed only 40 kilometres north of the capital city of Seoul, South Koreans cannot but be anxious. In this situation it is quite natural for South Koreans to strongly desire the presence of US forces in Korea to strengthen their capability to deter North Korea. But the US presence aside, South Korea urgently needs to supplement its forces if it is to defend itself adequately against North Korea. First, it needs about 100 modern fighters to maintain air superiority. Second, in order to stop an invasion by North Korea's heavily armoured units, at least 1000 modern tanks, and more than 100 attack helicopters that can launch TOW missiles are needed in addition to present anti-armour capabilities. Third, some highly mobile combat units with infantry fighting vehicles and large helicopters are required to cope with North Korea's airborne troops and special combat forces. Presently, North Korea is believed to have more than 100 000 special combat troops trained for irregular wars beyond the front line. Fourth, long-range howitzers or SSMs are needed to match North Korea's surface-to-surface missiles. Fifth, to keep the sea lanes open to allies and discourage any amphibious attack, ASW capabilities should be augmented. South Korea's ASW forces are not now sufficient in size and quality to fight off North Korean submarines. Sixth, and most urgent of all, equipment is needed to run an early warning system capable of detecting North Korea's war preparations at least a few hours before an invasion. South Korea has no sophisticated equipment for this purpose, as US Forces now provide such surveillance.

The scenario that worries South Korea the most is that of fighting a war with a North Korea fully supported by the Soviet Union. Considering the size of Soviet forces in the Far East, it is obvious that South Korea stands no chance alone. It thus strongly hopes that the US will keep sufficient military force in this part of the world to deter Soviet intervention in Korea. In the last three decades the Soviet Union has not threatened South Korea while the US has kept its armed forces on and around the Korean peninsula. Were the US to give any hint that South Korea is excluded from its 'concerned areas', or that its military forces in this region are much weaker than those of the Soviets, then the possibility of a Soviet proxy war in Korea would have to be considered as realistic and likely.

How long and to what extent will South Korea need American military support? Although this is hard to predict, one thing is very clear. Considering that South Korea is outpacing North Korea in their current arms race, the necessity of an American direct military involvement to deter an invasion should rapidly diminish. Almost certainly, by the end of the 1980s South Korea should have acquired an adequate capability to stand alone.[18] A US military presence still will be needed to deter Soviet intervention, however.

In contrast to these South Korean views, most Americans do not believe that North Korea will launch an all-out war. First, Americans will not believe that North Korea can attack South Korea alone. They underestimate North Korean war capabilities as well as its will. Second, Americans expect the PRC and the USSR to restrain the North Koreans under the assumption that both do not want to disturb the present status quo in East Asia. And third, Americans believe that they could stop any North Korean invasion with their air and naval striking power alone. This 'perception gap' has produced distrust between the two allies for the past fifteen years,[19] and created numerous policy conflicts between them. For example, South Korea is concerned with developing a self-defence capability of its own, while the US has been trying to restrain an independent ROK fighting capability. The basic policy of US military assistance toward South Korea is to maintain the above 'complex balance' of mutual deterrence in the Korean peninsula.

While the US has helped South Korea to improve its ground forces, Washington has refused to provide more modern air and naval weapons. Given its present unbalanced composition of land, sea, and air forces, South Korea cannot defend itself without direct American help. It thus remains dependent on the US for its security. In this way, the US seems to be deterring not only a North Korean invasion, but also a South Korean pre-emptive war against North Korea. This situation increases South Korean anxiety. The ROK must rely on American forces to supplement its inferior defences, but American support is deemed untrustworthy, despite recent reassurances from Washington.[20]

CONCLUSIONS

As discussed above, South Korea has a different perception of its security environment than the US, the only nation with which South Korea has a Mutual Defence Treaty. On the following three points this gap is especially significant. First, South Korea believes that North Korea will invade it if the US withdraws its defence commitment. The US, however, believes the chance of another inter-Korean war would be very low. Second, South Korea perceives East Asia as very important for sustaining the global balance between the US and the USSR, and that therefore the US should give more weight to the defence of Asia. The US, however, thinks that Asia is of secondary importance to European defence and is reluctant to strengthen its military presence in the region. Third, South Korea does not believe that it will initiate war, but the US does not trust South Korea in this regard. The US has not properly recognised the value of South Korean military forces in its strategy for maintaining a regional power balance.

These gaps in mutual perception have led the US to pursue policies that South Korea will not willingly accept. First, the US still does not consider South Korea a partner in an anti-Soviet alliance, and instead is trying to keep it as an auxiliary dependent on the US. The South Koreans demand that they be accepted as a coequal partner to Japan in the US alliance system in Asia. Second, the US will not allow South Korea to develop an independent self-defence capability. In exchange for its defence commitment, the US retains operational control over the entire South Korean armed forces in order to prevent Seoul from initiating war against North Korea. This simply is not acceptable to South Koreans, who do not feel secure leaving deterrence in the hands of a US that has not been so reliable elsewhere (e.g. Southeast Asia, Angola, Iran, Nicaragua).

For South Koreans, the future peace of East Asia is questionable, and the chance of war is increasing rather than decreasing. In order to reverse this unhappy trend, what can and should be done? To begin with, South Korea hopes that the US will develop a more realistic assessment of the security situation in East Asia within the global context, and formulate a sound long-term strategy to cope with Soviet expansionism. Without such a broad American strategic scheme, no American ally will fully trust its policies. The US should realise that Soviet activities around the isolated periphery of US interests are just a prelude to a critical attack on Western Europe, Japan, and other important allies. Presently, the most urgent military preparations the US should make do not involve nuclear weapons. Instead, the US should concentrate on improving its conventional war fighting capabilities, especially by strengthening its naval forces to secure the SLOCs linking its allies and by developing a much larger Rapid Deployment Joint Task Force to cope with diverse Soviet Third World challenges. The US should also work towards a true collective defence system with its allies. In Asia, the US should consider a NATO-type treaty organisation, in which all members share the common defence.

What can South Korea do to improve its security environment? Its options are quite limited due to its small size and capabilities. Of course, it will try to build up its own deterrence measures at any cost. Being a small nation, it will not be able to have threatening military forces, but it may develop a sufficient denial capability to discourage potential invaders. A porcupine cannot overwhelm a lion, but it does have enough bristles to discourage the latter's attack. South Korea considers herself to be a porcupine in a lion's cage.[21]

NOTES

1. For definitions of a bipolar international system, see John Spanier, *Games Nations Play*, 2nd edn, Praeger, New York, 1975, p. 61; and Morton A. Kaplan, *System and Process in International Politics*, John Wiley, New York, 1967, pp. 38–9.
2. This is defined in Frederick H. Hartmann, *The Relations of Nations*, 4th edn, Macmillan, New York, 1973, p. 361. Zbigniew Brzezinski pointed out that Nixon's policy was Bismarckian balance of power. See his 'US foreign policy: The search for focus', *Foreign Affairs*, LI: 4, July 1973, pp. 708–27.
3. For a detailed discussion of the system, see Yi Sang-U (Sang-Woo Rhee), 'Mi-So tetangt-eui Chaebunseok (Re-analysis of the US-Soviet detente)', *Kukmin Hoei Bo*, XII, 1976.
4. The history of US nuclear strategy toward the Soviet Union is well documented and analysed in R. J. Rummel, 'Current Strategic Reality', in *Defending A Free Society*, to be published in 1983; and Aaron L.

Friedberg, 'A History of the U.S. Strategic "Doctrine" – 1945–80', *Journal of Strategic Studies*, III:3, December 1980, pp. 37–72.
5. Many people warned of the adverse consequences of the agreement. For example, see Joseph Fromm, *U.S. News and World Report*, 26 January 1976, pp. 22–6; Donald H. Rumsfield, *Annual Department of Defense Report FY 1977*, pp. 7–8; and R. J. Rummel, 'Detente and the Russian Threat', *Honolulu Star-Bulletin*, 6 January 1976, and his book, *Peace Endangered: The Reality of Detente*, SAGE, Beverley Hills, p. 7. In my opinion, it is only a matter of time before the PRC and Soviet Union establish a new detente. See Sang-Woo Rhee, 'Possibility of the Sino-Soviet Detente: Prognosis for the 1980s', in my *Security and Unification of Korea*, Sogang Press, Seoul, 1983.
6. These figures are from *The Military Balance 1982–83*, Institute of International Strategic Studies, London, 1983. Hereafter, unless otherwise cited, all the figures are from this source.
7. In an all-out war, the hardness or softness of targets, or their separation, would be irrelevant – all will be hit, and both sides have the redundant capacity to do so. In a limited nuclear war, however, these would be relevant distinctions.
8. Including all the minor combatants and auxiliary ships in their active fleets, the US had 514 and the USSR 2016. In 1969 the US had 926, the USSR 1670. This means that in 12 years the number of US naval ships was reduced by 412, while the USSR added 346. See Office of the Chief of Naval Operations, Department of the Navy, USA, *Understanding Soviet Naval Developments*, fourth edition, 1981, p. 72; and Casper W. Weinberger, *Report of Secretary of Defense, FY 1983*, 1982, Appendix, 'Soviet Military Power', p. 40.
9. In 1981, the US air fleet for wartime airlift consisted of 70 C-5s, 234 C-141s, 218 C-130s (294 reserved C-130s), and 324 Civil Reserve Air Fleet (CRAF).
10. It is reported in *The Cbosum Ilbo*, February 1983, that now 108 SS-20s are deployed in eastern Siberia.
11. See Joint Chiefs of Staff, US, *United States Military Posture for FY 1983*, and Self-Defense Agency, Japan, *Defense of Japan, 1981* (Japanese edition), 1981.
12. The concept is clearly explained in James Schlesinger, *Annual Defense Department Report FY 1976, and FY 1977*, pp. 9–10.
13. Estimates by the Research Institute for International Affairs (RIIA), Seoul, in *Force Mobilization Plans of the U.S.A., USSR, PRC, and Japan: An Assessment of Major Powers' Military Intervention Capabilities in the Future Korean Conflict*, mimeo, 1979.
14. The normal operational radius of the TU-27 (Backfire) is 6000 km. If it is refuelled in the air, its operational range is extended to the Hawaiian Islands and New Zealand.
15. Namely, the Soya, Tsugaru, Tsushima and Korean straits.
16. See Kwan-Shik Min, *International Relations of the 1980s and the Korean Peninsula*, Asian Institute for Public Policy, Seoul, 1982, Table 11, p. 45. See also my article, 'Public Opinion on Unification and Nuclear Armament Issues: Security Concerns of the College Students', published

(in Korean) in my book, *Hankuk-eui Anbo Hwankyong* (The Security Environment of Korea), II, Goshiyongu, Seoul, 1980, pp. 425–51.
17. According to a South Korean government source, in 1981 the ROK spent US$3300 million (22.5 per cent of the GNP). The GNP of South Korea for the year was $74 200 million, while the estimated GNP of North Korea was $15 000 million.
18. Based on basic data supplied by the Board for National Unification, Republic of Korea, and assuming that current trends will continue for the next decade and that cumulative military investment (expenditure spent for hardware procurement) indicates military capability, the author has projected that by the end of the 1980s, South Korea will be able to obtain military parity with the North.
19. Americans are astonishingly ignorant of international affairs in general and of Korea in particular. One survey conducted in 1979 by Potomac Associates showed that only 28 per cent of the respondents knew that South Korea was more economically prosperous than North Korea; only 16 per cent were aware that South Korea is one of the top fifteen trade partners of the US. The survey also revealed that 56 per cent of American citizens disagreed that the US should come to the defence of South Korea if it is attacked by the North. The problem is that such people have significant influence on US foreign policies. For a detailed discussion on this see Richard Sneider and William Watts, *The United States and Korea: New Directions for the '80s*, Potomac Associates, Washington, DC, 1980.
20. By its words and deeds, the Reagan administration has greatly enhanced the credibility of the US commitment. See, for example, *Far Eastern Economic Review*, CX:47, 14 November 1980, p. 12; and *Washington Post*, 1 April 1982. Also, starting from 1981, the US government has strengthened the US forces in South Korea by improving their weapon systems.
21. This theme is developed in my article, 'Yaksoguk Bangwui-wa Gosumdochi Iron' (Defence Capability of the Weak Nations and the Porcupine Theory), *Kukje Chongchi Nongchong* (Korean Journal of International Relations), XVI, 1976, pp. 131–9.

2 Japan's Security and the International Environment in the 1980s

FUJI KAMIYA

EAST ASIA'S REGIONAL SECURITY

Fortunately, it can be said today that the stability of East Asia's regional security surpasses that of the Middle East, Southwest Asia, Africa, and even Europe. Although Japan, like other developed countries, has experienced various difficulties in the past decade beginning with the first oil crisis, it has continued to show relatively better achievements than Western countries. On the political scene, six consecutive changes of the Cabinet during this period made Japan appear unstable, but this was not actually so. The Liberal Democratic Party (LDP) dominates the Upper and the Lower Houses of the Diet with a stable majority and maintains a single-party Cabinet. The possibility that this situation will fundamentally change in the foreseeable future is close to nil.

Under these circumstances, Japan should contribute to the development and stability of East Asia more than it has been doing to date. In fact, there has been a tendency in some quarters in Asia in the past few years to worry about the possibility of Japan becoming a great military power. However, as will be explained later in this essay, Japan, in the framework of the 'Peace Constitution' and the US-Japan Security Pact promulgated since the Pacific War, only intends to make necessary adjustments to its defence forces within the context of self-defence. There exists a public consensus that Japan will strictly avoid maintaining military strength which might seem threatening to its neighbouring countries in the Asia-Pacific Region.

China, after experiencing great domestic turmoil during the Cultural Revolution, has since regained stability. Beijing continues to insist on its reunification with Taiwan and has recently stressed its sovereignty over Hong Kong. There are, however, no signs that it will attempt to realise these aims by taking extreme measures which might also endanger the stability of East Asia. The economic and political achievements of the ASEAN countries, on the other hand, have demonstrated that this 'loose form of regional integration' has been one of the most effective regionalisms in the world over the past few years. Oceania and Australia and New Zealand remain stable as well.

There are, however, three factors which might lead to instability and conflict in the Asian region. First is the situation in the Korean peninsula. This peninsula has been left far behind the tide of change in the world situation since the 1950s, with the relationship between the North and the South continuing to be governed by Cold War logic. Nor has South Korea's attitude of referring to 'the threat from the North' for the purpose of obtaining aid and cooperation from the US and Japan changed over the past decade. While the situation in the Korean peninsula will be characterised by tension and instability, none the less 'unstable stability' or 'stabilised instability' can be found there. During the period after the assassination of President Park in October 1979, Korea suffered serious domestic confusion and turmoil. If the North–South relationship was truly so unstable and critical, this confusion in South Korea would have provided a great opportunity for North Korea to make a move against Seoul. Yet no such outbreak of hostilities occurred between the North and the South, and the South's internal difficulties were solved by its own efforts. These events show that the instability of the peninsula is in reality only a part of the unexpectedly 'stabilised instability'.

The second factor promoting instability in Asia is Indochina. Here, the international civil war between the Heng Samrin administration, which is backed up by Vietnamese military power, and Democratic Kampuchea, which consists of the remnants of the Pol Pot administration, already has been going on for a few years. Many people publicly say that the armed conflict in Kampuchea must be ended soon, but in actuality, most probably do not desire the termination of the conflict. The ASEAN countries, including Thailand which borders Kampuchea, are generally anxious about Vietnamese moves. Therefore, the situation in which Vietnam is caught up in the morass of Kampuchea is exactly what Bangkok wishes, just as China wishes it. On the other hand, even though Kampuchea is still recognised as the legitimate government by the UN, there is hardly any possibility that Democratic Kampuchea will regain its power in Phnom Penh. In Japan, there is an old saying: 'one illness will ensure health'. From time to time, a person who has no illness and who is too confident of his health may die suddenly due to negligence. In comparison, a person with a chronic disease will always be more prudent than others in maintaining his good health. The conflict in Kampuchea, from an objective point of view, may just be the 'one illness' for the health of Southeast Asia and nothing more.

The third factor of instability in Asia is the Sino-Soviet conflict. But, the degree of danger from this factor has decreased tremendously in the past few years. Today, people's interests concentrate on how far the Sino-Soviet reconciliation can go. The improvement (or normalisation) of Sino-Soviet relations will move ahead, but it is inconceivable at the present that this trend could possibly result in the return to their alliance of the 1950s. The first objective for the Soviet Union in the sphere of foreign policy is the restoration of its relations with the US, especially the search for compromise and agreement in the European INF and START talks. The most important objectives for Chinese foreign policy also are the enhancement of friendship and cooperation with Japan and the improvement in its relationship with the US. Sino-Soviet relations are not the number one goal for China, nor for the Soviet Union. It is only a supplementary goal, in that they must strictly avoid adversely influencing their relations with the US and Japan by placing too much emphasis on their Soviet connections.

A PERSPECTIVE ON THE SOVIET UNION

In decades past, Japanese-Soviet relations have never been smooth, nor have public feelings in Japan ever been warm toward Moscow. Like a 'thief at a fire', the Soviets broke the Soviet-Japan Neutrality Treaty and went to war against Japan immediately before its surrender in August 1945. They trampled on international law and humanism by hauling numerous Japanese who had lived in Manchuria and Siberia away to long-term forced labour in terrible conditions after the war. These actions, in addition to those in the pre-war period, made the anti-Soviet emotions of the Japanese people definite. Moreover, the continuation of the illegitimate occupation of the Northern Territories, especially when compared with the return of Okinawa by the US, and Moscow's ruthless militaristic oppression of the satellite countries as reflected by the Hungarian Uprising (1956) and the Czechoslovakian intervention (1968), have made even the Japan Socialist Party and the Japan Communist Party (JCP) revise their original pro-Soviet stance.

In the 1970s, the Soviet Union achieved 'parity' with the US in general nuclear forces and even surpassed the US in some sectors of nuclear and conventional forces. In East Asia, the Soviet Union has notably pursued a military build-up in the past few years, including approximately 100 SS-20 missiles, 25 Backfire bombers, the aircraft carrier *Minsk*, and even deployed a division of ground forces in three of the four islands in the Northern Territories. The Soviet Union not only acquired the right to use naval and air facilities in Vietnam by helping Hanoi's invasion of Kampuchea, but also invaded Afghanistan at the end of 1979.

These factors all contribute to the consistent showing in all public opinion polls that the Soviet Union is the least liked foreign country. Only 2 per cent reply that they like the USSR and this situation is unlikely to change in the foreseeable future. Nevertheless, these attitudes are not translated into bellicose feelings toward Moscow. After the war, passivist sentiments ran extremely deep in Japan, with a consequence being a certain public idealism that seeks the avoidance of foreign entanglements. For the Japanese whose attitudes toward military power in the post-war period reflect a curious mixture of antipathy and indifference, the Soviet threat is only an indirect psychological threat rather than a direct military threat.

Also, there is in Japan more of a tendency to balance Soviet military power against its economic and political weaknesses in the overall assessment of how Japan should respond to it. The Japanese basically think about security in terms of 'comprehensive security', balancing both military and non-military aspects. If the USSR is judged 'comprehensively', the vulnerability of its national power is evident in the non-military domain where Japan excels. Because of this, no matter how powerful the Soviet Union is militarily, the Japanese tend to discount overall Soviet power and are even contemptuous of it. And, Japan tends to put a low evaluation on the efforts of the US to counter Soviet power simply by military means. Thus, American calls for a common or joint strategy *vis-à-vis* the USSR do not receive positive reaction from the Japanese in general.

On the other hand, there has been a shift in Japanese attitudes toward the Soviet Union in recent years. The Japanese are paying greater attention to the fact that Soviet military expenditure has been some fifteen times greater than that of Japan for many years while the GNPs of the two countries are almost equal. There is also increased awareness of the USSR's accelerated expansion of its sphere of influence, as evidenced in Vietnam, Angola, Ethiopia and Afghanistan.

Since the late 1970s there has been a steady, though gradual, strengthening of Japan–US relations and a greater willingness on the part of Japanese governments to emphasise Japan's political solidarity with the Western world as part of its larger burden-sharing of international responsibilities. At the same time, since 1982, Japan has set 7 February as the 'Day of the Northern Territories', and representatives of all political parties from the LDP to the JCP attended a national convention on that day, demanding the reversion of the territories.

Prime Minister Nakasone, who came to power in November 1982, tried to establish, through his meeting with President Reagan in January 1983, the basic policies of strengthening the Japan-US alliance and stepping up Japan's defence efforts. This was warmly welcomed in Washington. Also, initially, on the Japanese domestic scene, there was sympathy with his efforts to speak in a straightforward manner about defence issues and to solidify the Japan-US security system.

Scenarios for Japanese policy toward the Soviet Union

This leads to one possible scenario for future Japanese policy, that is, reinforced solidarity with the US and confrontationist attitude toward the Soviet Union. This policy does have overall advantages in terms of Tokyo's relations with the US, which is the most important political and economic partner of Japan. It does, however, also have serious liabilities. The biggest of these is that it would not be supported by a broad enough base of Japanese public opinion. This is evident from the media and public reaction to Mr Nakasone's emphasis on the Soviet threat after his return from Washington. When Nakasone had likened Japan to an 'unsinkable aircraft carrier' in the strategy toward the Soviet Union and also emphasised the operational concept of the 'blockade of the three straits' which are the exits from the Sea of Japan to the outer ocean, the media and the Diet in Japan expressed anxiety and criticism, thus affecting public opinion.

As a result, three public opinion polls, released by the NHK (Japan Broadcasting Corporation) on 16 February, the *Asahi Shinbun* on

19 February, and the *Yomiuri Shinbun* on 23 February, showed fairly strong public dissatisfaction with his foreign policy stance and demonstrated that non-support considerably exceeded support for the Nakasone administration. Even within the LDP, it was reported that more moderation was called for in the Prime Minister's statements on defence issues because there were planned or probable elections at the local levels in April 1983, for the House of Councillors that June, and for the House of Representatives. There also were some elements within the LDP who were blaming its defeat in the Hokkaido gubernatorial election in early April 1983 partly on public dissatisfaction with the Nakasone defence statements. In other words, a confrontationist attitude could invite a public backlash and jeopardise the political position of those in Japan most concerned about the Soviet threat.

A second possible option for Japanese policy would be a stronger effort to separate political and economic relations. Tokyo upheld the principle of the separation of politics and economics *vis-à-vis* Beijing in the normalisation of relations in 1972, but the territorial question between Japan and the USSR remains. Tokyo has refused to expand Japan-Soviet economic cooperation, including Siberian development, unless Moscow yields on such matters. Japan cannot compromise on the territorial question with the Soviet Union, and in this regard, politics has priority over economics. This governmental position is and will continue to be supported by the majority of the nation, even though it is true that the separation of politics and economics remains popular with some Japanese business groups. Recently, in fact, there seems to be another upsurge in business interest in Siberia, partly stimulated by the world recession and the fear of protectionism in major Japanese markets. Some Japanese businessmen have also been resentful of the trade opportunities lost because of Japan's acceptance of US sanctions against Moscow which saw much business diverted to European countries. The problem with this option is that it can be damaging in terms of Japanese alliance relationships. It can also encourage political adventurism on the part of the USSR because it would appear to have no economic costs. More fundamentally, perhaps, Japan has simply grown too large to separate economics from politics. A major world economic power, Japan's economic relations with other countries do have political implications.

Maintaining some economic and other ties with the Soviet Union, that is, keeping channels of communication and exchange open, could be useful in a time of increased political tensions – if done in a prudent way. This suggests a middle course that is a balanced response recognising the Soviet threat, with due cognisance of alliance relationships, but which does not attempt to needlessly isolate or provoke the Soviet Union.

There is general acceptance within informed government and private circles that the Soviet threat has increased. This suggests a strong need to reinforce coordination in strategies among the Western countries. Open disagreements among allies and friends on trade sanctions and arms control policies do undermine our position. Thus, Japan would like to find some appropriate means and forum for discussing trade and political questions relating to the Soviet Union with its allies and friends (not just the US, but also European and Asian-Pacific countries).

There is more interest in Japan, although still confined to relatively specialised circles, in current developments in nuclear arms control negotiations between the US and the Soviet Union. Japan realises that it does have a stake in the INF discussion; it does not want missiles now directed toward Europe simply to be redirected toward Asian targets. At the same time, there is a certain unhappiness with what appears to be too inflexible a position by the United States. Therefore, there is a need for broader-based discussions of these issues as well.

To summarise, Japan does not regard itself as a major target of current Soviet interest or threat, but it is increasingly concerned about the Soviet forces in East Asia, about current developments in US-Soviet and Sino-Soviet relations, and about appropriate Western responses. While a strongly confrontationist policy is not likely for domestic political reasons to be pursued, Japan will probably continue to emphasise its solidarity with allies and friends. Japan's relations with the USSR cannot be divorced from its relations with the US, nor can its economic ties with Moscow stand apart from current political tensions.

RECENT DEVELOPMENTS IN JAPANESE POLICY

Japanese defence policy has recently become the target of discussion in various spheres inside and outside the country. From the one extreme, it is criticised as being an inadequate one in which the remnants of 'a free ride' have still not disappeared; while from the other extreme, it is attacked as pointing to the direction of becoming 'a great military power'. Where does the truth lie? Perhaps a partial answer can be gleaned from Tables 2.1 and 2.2 which show the increases in Japan's

TABLE 2.1 Changes in Japan's defence-related expenditures (after 1965)

FY	Defence-related expenditure (first stage budget)[a] (Unit 100 m yen)	(Unit 1 m dollars)	Rate of increase over previous year (%)	Proportion to GNP[b] (%)	Proportion to expenditure in gen. account (%)
1965	3,014	837	9.6	1.07	8.24
1966	3,407	946	11.8	1.10	7.90
1967	3,809	1,058	11.8	0.93	7.69
1968	4,221	1,173	10.8	0.88	7.25
1969	4,888	1,344	14.6	0.84	7.18
1970	5,695	1,582	17.7	0.79	7.16
1971	6,709	1,864	17.8	0.80	7.13
1972	8,002	2,598	19.3	0.88	6.98
1973	9,355	3,037	16.9	0.85	6.55
1974	10,930	3,549	16.8	0.83	6.39
1975	13,273	4,309	21.4	0.84	6.23
1976	15,124	4,910	13.9	0.905	6.22
1977	16,966	5,489	11.8	0.88	5.93
1978	19,010	7,256	12.4	0.90	5.54
1979	20,945	10,741	10.2	0.90	9.43
1982	25,861	11,293	7.754	0.93	5.21
1983[c]	27,542	11,150	6.50	0.97	5.47

NOTES: [a] Dollar exchange rate until FY 1971: $1 = 360 yen, FY 1972–7: 308 yen, FY 1978: 262 yen, FY 1979: 195 yen, FY 1980: 225 yen, FY 1981: 217 yen, FY 1982: 229 yen, FY 1983: 247 yen. Moreover, if we convert the defence expenditure of FY 1982 and 1983 into US dollars by the average exchange rate of January (for FY 1983, the rate of 1/4), respective expenditure will be 11 465 million dollars and 11 944 million dollars.
[b] The proportion to GNP is the proportion to the anticipated GNP.
[c] FY 1983 shows the government proposal.

TABLE 2.2. World's ten biggest defence spenders (defence expenditures in US$ million; per capita expenditures in US$)

Country	FY 1980					FY 1981			
	Defence expenditures[a]	Share of total budget expenditures %	Ratio to GNP %	Per capita expenditures	Ranking (estimated)	Defence expenditures	Share of total budget expenditures %	Ratio to GNP %	Per capita expenditures	Ranking (estimated)
USSR	—	—	—	—	1	—	—	15	—	1
United States	142,000	23.6	—	644	2	176,100	23.5	6.1	782	2
China	—	—	—	—	3	—	—	—	—	3
Germany, FR	33,611	28.3	—	548	4	29,047	28.2	4.3	471	4
Saudi Arabia	20,766	28.1	—	2,525	7	24,417	27.7	20.5	3,014	5
UK	25,921	10.7	—	463	6	24,223	12.1	5.4	433	6
France	26,067	19.5	—	483	5	23,524	20.7	4.1	437	7
Japan[b]	12,637	5.8	(0.9)	108	8	10,453	4.8	0.9	89	8
Argentina	3,060	9.7	—	113	—	10,084	15.1	8.1	360	9
Italy	9,579	5.4	—	168	9	8,769	5.6	2.5	153	10

SOURCE: *The Military Balance 1982–1983*, International Institute for Strategic Studies, London.

NOTES: To facilitate comparison, each country's defence expenditures are converted into U.S. dollars computed according to the average exchange rate for the fiscal year. (In the case of Japan, the ¥ rate per dollar was ¥ 176.48 for 1980 and ¥ 229.59 for 1981).

Although *The Military Balance* places Japan's defence spending in 1980 and 1982 at 5.8% and 4.8% of budget expenditures, respectively, defence spending was actually 5.2% and 5.1%.

defence-related expenditures since 1965 and place it as the eighth largest in the world at present.

If the 'comprehensive security' concept is followed in Japan's security thinking, efforts in both the military and non-military domains should be well-balanced. These efforts in the two domains are complementary, but not mutually exchangeable, so it does not mean that increased efforts in one domain will reduce the need for efforts in the other. The plan for comprehensive security does not negate the fact that the basis of security lies first in the military-defence realms. The two pillars of Japan's military security posture are the maintenance of the US-Japan security system and the build-up of Japan's own defence capabilities. It is nearly impossible for Japan to rely on itself alone for security, even in economic terms. But even if it were possible and even if Japan was to possess a large-scale defence force of its own, its relations with the US and Asian countries would deteriorate.

Japan has consistently adhered to three basic national endeavours since the Pacific War. First, in the political realm, Japan has been setting liberal democracy as the most important basic value. Second, in the military realm, Japan has been a pacifist country concentrating on self-defence and an exclusively defensive posture which avoids the course of becoming a great military power. Third, in the economic realm, Japan has been aiming at prosperity and stability in a free and open international economic trade system. These options mean that Japan's national interest is closely linked to that of the Western nations as a whole, including the US, Europe and Oceania, and that in circumstances relating to the security of the entire Western society Japan should act in solidarity and cooperation with them. Therefore, Japan must make further contributions to the formulation of policies of the entire Western world and pay its fair share of the overall costs. Cooperation and burden-sharing with the US is particularly important.

Defence Efforts in Fiscal 1983

Finally, let us turn to a discussion of Japan's defence efforts in fiscal 1983. Responding to Prime Minister Nakasone's basic policy of stressing the importance of defence and close cooperation with the US, Japan's ultra-austere budget for the current fiscal year gives top priority to expanded defence spending, with rigorous curbs on outlays for social security and other domestic spending. There is no increase in the government's general expenditure over the previous fiscal year, so the increase in defence spending is met by decreasing other items.

Defence spending in the new budget will rise by 6.5 per cent over the previous year. This appears to be less than the 7.8 per cent increase for fiscal 1982, but is misleading since the last budget included pay rises for the Self-Defence Agency, whereas the fiscal 1983 amount does not. Without these pay increases, the 1982 budget would have shown an increase of 5.4 per cent, contrasted with the current year's increase of 6.5 per cent. The new budget is notable for a substantial increase of 21.2 per cent in outlays for frontline equipment such as F-15 and P-3C aircraft, tanks, warships, helicopters, artillery, and so on. This is nearly twice the rate of increase of the previous year. In addition, Japan's contributions to improving facilities used by US Forces in Japan will be raised by 24.8 per cent.

At Japan's low level of inflation, a 6.5 per cent increase in defence spending will amount to a real growth of 4.3 per cent, substantially higher than the 3 per cent rise targeted by the NATO countries for defence spending. Moreover, the share of defence spending in the government's general expenditures has risen from 7.3 per cent in 1980 to 7.9 per cent in 1982 to 8.4 per cent for this fiscal year. As a percentage of GNP, the new budget ratio of defence spending will be 0.98 per cent. Comparison of defence spending with other major items in the new budget is thus striking. Total government expenditure will show a zero increase, while that for social security will rise 0.6 per cent, public works will register a zero increase, and education spending will decline by 0.9 per cent. Foreign economic assistance, on the other hand, which Japan considers an important element in its comprehensive security, will rise 7 per cent with Official Development Assistance up by 8.9 per cent.

CONCLUSIONS

Japan is thus making efforts today to build up its defence forces which, up to this point, have been far too inadequate. Nevertheless, it should be repeated that Tokyo does not intend to mold Japan into a big military power. Japan's defence plan, persistently based on the Security Pact with the US, is to counter: (1) limited and small-scale aggression with Japan's self-defence forces; (2) large-scale conventional invasion with its self-defence forces plus US cooperation under the Japan-US security system; and (3) nuclear threats under the nuclear umbrella provided by the US.

Japan's basic defence policy is to stick to the concept of nonoffensive defence under its 'Peace Constitution', without becoming a big military power, and to follow the 'three non-nuclear principles' as guidelines. Its aim is to continue efforts by adhering to a long-term perspective while searching for a national consensus. For the time being, it is an urgent necessity to achieve the goals set in the National Defence Programme Outline decided in 1976 for the five fiscal years, 1983–7. But, the actual situation is that while the US is demanding its attainment ahead of schedule, Japan's present budgetary size makes the attainment of the goals within the schedule rather difficult. Therefore, the 'defence friction' between Japan and the US is not likely to dissolve easily in the short term. In fact, it can be said that Japan's defence policy problem lies in the fear of not being able to accomplish enough to satisfy Washington rather than in the fear of making superfluous defence efforts.

Japan's defence capability in the 1980s will continuously show gradual increase according to the 'middle-road framework' that has been described here. In contrast to this majority-supported policy, there are those who believe in a more self-assertive, nationalist posture that would have Japan revise its constitution and the Japan-US Security Treaty and thereby become more autonomous militarily. There are also a few Japanese who worry about the Reagan administration's priority on a military build-up to meet the Soviet challenge. They oppose the Japanese government's move to follow it, and would like to follow the 'carrot-and-stick approach' in countering the Soviet Union. But, they fear that Reagan's policy lacks the 'carrot'. These people, for example, do not support the notion of defending the sea lanes to the extent of 1000 nautical miles south of Japan on the grounds that it signifies a commitment to a 'regional defence' beyond the framework of 'self-defence'. Despite the criticisms from both sides, the middle-road framework will not relinquish its dominant position in the foreseeable future, unless there should occur a collapse of the free trade system in the world and the rise to dominance of international protectionism.

3 ASEAN Perspectives on International Security: an Indonesian View

JUSUF WANANDI

INTRODUCTION

Any discussion of Association of Southeast Asian Nations (ASEAN) views on international security must be based on a recognition that the varying historical experiences, socio-political systems and economic development of the individual ASEAN countries result in different nuances and emphases in the formation of their perceptions. In addition, while all ASEAN countries are located within the Southeast Asian region, their geographic position does affect their perceptions as well.

Fortunately, although ASEAN had been set up as a regional association to promote cooperation in the economic, social and cultural fields, changes in the latter half of the 1960s did provide a strong impetus for consultations among ASEAN members on security and international political issues affecting the region. Indeed, the practice of consultation and cooperation amongst them gradually led to a greater convergence of perceptions and views on a number of important regional political issues and problems. The Kuala Lumpur Declaration of 1971, known as the ZOPFAN (Zone of Peace, Freedom and Neutrality) idea for Southeast Asia, was the first manifestation of the growing convergence in the individual countries' perception of Southeast Asia's regional security. It took another five years for the ASEAN countries to enter into a Treaty of Amity and Cooperation.

This chapter will discuss the ZOPFAN concept as a reflection of the

ASEAN states' desire to work for a 'regional order'. It will treat the nuances and the different emphases of the individual ASEAN members in realising that idea, particularly in overcoming its main obstacle, the Kampuchean conflict. It will assess ASEAN's relations with the great powers, and the relations among the great powers – notably between the US and the USSR – that have an influence upon developments in the region. It will conclude with a summary of Southeast Asia's security problems and how they could be dealt with by the states of the region.

ZOPFAN AND A REGIONAL ORDER FOR SOUTHEAST ASIA

Created on 8 August 1967, ASEAN manifested the serious and conscious efforts of the five Southeast Asian states of Malaysia, Singapore, Thailand, Philippines and Indonesia to establish a firm ground for regional cooperation and the promotion of peace, progress and prosperity. Embodied in the Bangkok Declaration was the ASEAN aim of accelerating economic growth, social progress, and cultural and scientific development in the region. Although ASEAN was set up primarily to bring about greater cooperation in the economic, cultural and scientific fields, the changing politico-strategic situation also contributed to its creation, especially the anxieties that accompanied the outcome of the war in Indochina. Therefore, the defence and security dimension was not neglected by the ASEAN states, although there was no desire to create either a military pact or a multilateral military bloc.

There are two reasons why the ASEAN states have rejected the idea of a military pact. First, they do not perceive the existence of a major external threat. Rather, they are concerned with the threats from within their national borders which could invite outside forces to create instabilities through subversion and infiltration. A military pact is not an effective way to deal with such threats. Second, a military pact would only arouse unnecessary fears on the part of the Vietnamese and create the impression that ASEAN is a grouping aimed at confronting them militarily.

Instead, ASEAN has adopted the concept of national and regional resilience. The core of this concept is that if each of the member nations can accomplish an overall national development and overcome internal threats, regional resilience will automatically result much in the same way as a chain derives its overall strength from that of the individual links. It is in accordance with this idea that the ASEAN states carry out bilateral cooperation on a number of matters, including defence and security. This is done mainly in the form of an exchange of experiences in dealing with internal threats, which in many cases are similar. It also includes an exchange of information and intelligence, the holding of joint land, sea and air exercises and joint patrols or operations in border areas, exchanges of officer training, as well as the standardisation of military equipment and logistic support for the sake of efficiency and economy.

Since its inception, significant results have been achieved by ASEAN in the political field, namely in overcoming inter-ASEAN problems which previously created political tensions and caused security lapses in the region. Among these problems were the border dispute between Malaysia and Thailand; quarrels between Singapore and Malaysia arising out of the history of Malaysia's creation and Singapore's secession from the Malaysian federation; problems between Singapore and Indonesia over the conduct of contraband trade; the dispute over Sabah between Malaysia and the Philippines (which remains unresolved, but has been prevented from escalating into a confrontation that would weaken ASEAN cooperation in other spheres); the border problem between Indonesia and Malaysia which led to a confrontation in the mid-1960s but was resolved successfully to the extent that Indonesian–Malaysian border cooperation today could serve as a model of ASEAN cooperation; problems involving Indonesia's Archipelago Concept which have been settled with Malaysia; and the question of the Malacca Straits which has been settled with the conclusion of an agreement between Singapore, Malaysia and Indonesia.

The ZOPFAN idea came out of the special ASEAN ministerial meeting at Kuala Lumpur in November 1971. It was based on an assessment by the ASEAN countries of international developments affecting the Southeast Asian region. The foreign ministers decided then that a Treaty of Amity and Cooperation should constitute the first operational step since the ZOPFAN idea would be self-contradictory unless the ASEAN states could first put their own houses in order. This Treaty of Amity and Cooperation was signed in Bali by the ASEAN heads of state in February 1976.

The ZOPFAN concept aims at the realisation of an overall national development and increased well-being in each of the ASEAN countries and the promotion of regional cooperation and solidarity in accordance with the purposes and principles of the United Nations Charter and free from any form or manner of interference by outside powers. The hope that this concept could gradually be realised is based on a favourable external environment, which should include some degree of certainty in the Indochinese sub-region as well as on the steady developments in each of the ASEAN countries and in intra-ASEAN relations.

The ZOPFAN idea is to create a regional order in which different ideologies, political, social and economic systems adopted by the Southeast Asian countries can coexist. Through a regional order the multiplicity and plurality of relations among Southeast Asian countries and the great powers in the region are recognised, but their presence must be in a balanced and controlled fashion so that no one of them could obtain a dominating position.

ZOPFAN is based upon the concept of national and regional resilience, implying that the member states' goal achievement will largely be determined by their own capabilities and by their own rules. ASEAN's Treaty of Amity and Cooperation not only suggests the foundation for cooperation but also defines the means by which differences amongst member states should be resolved. Whether a regional order for Southeast Asia would be agreed upon by both ASEAN and the Indochina states depends to a large extent upon the resolution of the Kampuchea conflict. In fact, the Kampuchean problem provides a test for the feasibility of creating a regional order based upon the ZOPFAN idea. The ZOPFAN concept has been accepted in principle by Vietnam, albeit with minor differences. It is of prime importance that greater cooperation and consultation be promoted between the ASEAN and the Indochina states. Both groupings seem to share a common vision of Southeast Asia's future, although it still is unclear as to the role that each grouping will play in this region. It may well be that Vietnam's consent to the ZOPFAN idea is only a medium-term tactic in the realisation of its long-term goal of dominating the region by way of a continuous support for the 'progressive-revolutionary' forces in the ASEAN countries. It seems unlikely, however, that Vietnam could dominate the Southeast Asian region in view of her limited capabilities in the political, economic and military fields. Meanwhile, the ASEAN countries themselves have achieved a higher degree of national and regional resilience.

The search for a regional order in Southeast Asia based on the ZOPFAN idea entails several objectives. The first is to structure relations among the ASEAN states in accordance with the Treaty of

Amity and Cooperation which was adopted in 1976. In this regard, ASEAN achievements have been most encouraging. The second entails structuring relations between ASEAN and the Indochina states of Vietnam, Laos and Kampuchea. The third involves structuring relations between the countries of the Southeast Asian region and the great powers (the US, USSR, PRC and Japan) so that their balanced presence in the region would be guaranteed. The Kampuchean conflict also constitutes an obstacle in this regard. If the conflict becomes a prolonged one, the PRC may step up its support of the Khmer Rouge. There also looms the danger of Thailand becoming too dependent upon the PRC in dealing with pressures from Vietnam. Likewise, the Vietnamese, in spite of their firm national aspirations, may become hostage to Soviet pressures.

Nuances in the ASEAN states' perceptions of external threat pose another obstacle to the realisation of the ZOPFAN idea. To countries such as Thailand and Singapore, the PRC does not pose an immediate threat in view of its limited military and economic capabilities. They consider the threat from the USSR as more urgent and argue that the Soviets not only have become a global military power but have established a permanent presence in Southeast Asia underscored by their access to facilities in Cam Ranh and Danang. Indonesia and Malaysia view the PRC threat as being more urgent because Beijing continues its solidarity with the communist parties of the region and displays uncertainty in its attitude and policies towards overseas Chinese in the region. From the historical and geopolitical points of view, there always has been the tendency of the Chinese to view Southeast Asia as their sphere of influence. While Indonesia and Malaysia do recognise the growth of Soviet military power since 1975, they also take note of the fact that the Soviet military presence in the region is not accompanied by an economic presence and an ability to influence the ASEAN countries politically. Moreover, the USSR's military capability in the region remains neutralised by the US military presence. It can be argued that a prolonged conflict in Indochina would tend to create greater divergence in the threat perception of the ASEAN states.

THE KAMPUCHEAN CONFLICT AND ITS SOLUTION

The Treaty of Amity and Cooperation was not meant for ASEAN alone since a regional order in Southeast Asia requires the participation of the three Indochina states. The Kampuchean conflict, however, has created severe hostilities between ASEAN and Vietnam. It also provides greater opportunities for the great powers to involve themselves in the affairs of the region so as to further their own interests. In fact, the conflict has brought Southeast Asia further away from a regional order based on the ZOPFAN idea. Therefore, it is in the interest of the ASEAN countries to find a political solution to the conflict. But, while the urgency of reaching a satisfactory solution is clearly recognised by ASEAN, the process by which the solution should be achieved is considered to be of equal importance.

The ASEAN countries have clearly stated their position on the conflict in the International Conference on Kampuchea in New York. Since Vietnam's invasion of Kampuchea was a violation of Kampuchea's sovereignty and integrity, as well as a violation of one of the main principles of international relations and the UN Charter, a solution to the conflict must be based on the following three principles: the withdrawal of Vietnamese forces from Kampuchea; the act of self-determination by the Kampuchean people under international supervision; and the adoption of a non-aligned foreign policy by Kampuchea so as not to create a threat to its neighbouring countries. In the view of ASEAN, negotiations for a solution to the conflict must be accomplished through an international conference. The involvement of the great powers in the conflict clearly suggests the inadequacy of a regional conference as proposed by the Vietnamese.

The Vietnamese continue to claim that their involvement in Kampuchea has been at the request of the Kampuchean people to save them from the extreme harassment by the Khmer Rouge. The Vietnamese argue, therefore, that so long as the threat from the Khmer Rouge exists they will maintain their forces in Kampuchea. Moreover, on historical grounds, Kampuchea will always be seen by the Vietnamese as posing a problem for its own survival, especially in view of Hanoi's failures so far to absorb its own southern territories. Therefore, it is in Vietnam's interest to help establish a government in Kampuchea which in one way or another can be influenced by the Vietnamese.

Vietnam recognises the Kampuchean conflict as basically a conflict between Vietnam and the PRC that has implicated Thailand. However, the suggested Vietnamese solution of the conflict through a regional conference by which it was hoped that all views could converge held that the conference could be attended by the Secretary-General and members of the UN Security Council and India as observers. The question is whether or not the two parties could come to some form of compromise. The ASEAN states feel that a compromise could be produced by continuing to exert diplomatic pressures on Vietnam and to isolate it economically. Vietnam, on its side, is determined to maintain its control over Kampuchea even at a high cost to its own development. Indeed, thus far each side feels that a status quo in their positions can be maintained. Moreover, the great powers, which are directly or indirectly involved in the conflict, do not see the necessity of changing the situation. The PRC still aims at bleeding Vietnam and continues to support the Khmer Rouge to the extent necessary to frustrate the Vietnamese occupation of Kampuchea. The Soviets continue to provide economic aid and armaments to the Vietnamese in return for use of the military facilities in Cam Ranh and Danang. The US is too preoccupied with security issues in other regions to be able to give the necessary attention to the Kampuchean conflict. Apart from this, the US remains unwilling to compromise with the Vietnamese because the effects of the Vietnam war have not been forgotten.

The prospect for a settlement of the conflict remains dim, although there are some recent indications that the stalemate may be disappearing slowly. First, the new round of Sino-Soviet negotiations could affect a political settlement of the Kampuchean conflict if, for the sake of their relations with the Chinese, the Soviets are prepared to force the Vietnamese to compromise. The PRC has offered the Soviets a gradual approach towards normalising its relations with the Vietnamese that is contingent upon Vietnam's agreement to withdraw from Kampuchea. The PRC is prepared to respect the outcome of a general election in Kampuchea held subsequent to the total withdrawal of Vietnamese forces. The Summit Meeting of the Indochinese states in Vientiane in early 1983 indicates some readiness on the part of Vietnam to entertain the possibility of an orderly and unilateral withdrawal from Kampuchea, when the security conditions in Kampuchea have improved. But it remains unclear whether the Soviets are prepared to or capable of pressuring the Vietnamese to compromise. Furthermore, the Soviets may be more interested in the settlement of their border conflict with the PRC rather than in the resolution of the Kampuchean conflict. Second, the recent secret negotiations between Vietnam and the PRC in Romania could lead to encouraging developments. Third, Vietnam's proposal to directly negotiate with the ASEAN states without insisting on the participation of the Heng Samrin regime could become the first step leading to an international conference. The Vietnamese failed to indicate, however, whether they are genuinely prepared to discuss the Kampuchean issue in their proposed regional meeting.

The above examination of the problem suggests how increasingly complicated the issues have become as the stalemate continues. This is clearly recognised by Indonesia as a member of ASEAN. On the one hand, a viable Vietnam is seen by Indonesia as a prerequisite for the creation and maintenance of a regional order in Southeast Asia. Thus, some accommodation of Vietnam's security concerns is considered warranted. On the other hand, being a front-line state, Thailand's security concerns are legitimate as well, and are the subject of concern by all ASEAN states – including Indonesia. Therefore, in full support of the Thai position, ASEAN as a group continues with remarkable success to apply diplomatic pressures on Vietnam in international fora. There exist some apprehensions over whether these pressures would lead to a severe weakening of Vietnam. Moreover, some worries have been raised that an ever greater Thai reliance on the PRC could lead to a dangerous polarisation within ASEAN which could weaken its solidarity. It is generally believed that in order to keep ASEAN's unity intact there needs to be a greater willingness on the part of Thailand to seek new approaches with the Vietnamese. On the other hand, it goes without saying that Vietnam on its part must show a greater willingness to compromise and change its attitude towards Thailand. While Vietnam's and Thailand's policies, positions and attitudes are crucial, the views from the other ASEAN countries cannot be ignored. In broad terms, there is general consensus in Indonesia on the need to find a proper balance between the regional interest of strengthening ASEAN's unity in supporting the principles of non-intervention and self-determination of the Kampuchean people and the regional interest of realising a regional order based on the ZOPFAN idea with a viable Vietnam taking part in it.

ASEAN AND THE SUPERPOWERS

The adoption of the ZOPFAN idea by ASEAN implies the desire to make the Southeast Asian region free from the conflict between the US and the USSR, or between other great powers. The ZOPFAN idea clearly recognises the presence of the superpowers in the region, but it argues for a balanced presence of these powers with neither gaining a dominant position. This superpower presence should not be limited to a low-level military presence alone but should encompass other activities as well in order to minimise the likelihood of armed conflict in the region.

Meanwhile, the global trend of increasing tension and arms competition between the US and the USSR could lead to a new Cold War situation, with quite alarming implications for the Southeast Asian region. This could increase the likelihood of conflicts in the Third World, including Southeast Asia, largely because no clearly defined sphere of influence of either superpower has been established. Increased Soviet-American tensions have resulted from mutual charges that the other party does not abide by the rules of detente. The US charges the USSR with continuing its strategic and conventional arms build-up and as having a greater propensity to intervene in Third World areas to upset the global balance. The Soviet Union charges the US with not fulfilling its promises in the area of trade and finance and with failing to ratify the SALT II agreements. Moscow believes that the erratic policies of Washington are responsible for continuing misperceptions. Given the mood of the Reagan administration and the Soviet Union's reaction to it, a new round of the arms race seems far from a remote possibility.

The majority of Third World countries formally adopt a neutral or 'equidistant' attitude with regard to East–West competition. In practice, however, most of them basically retain more intensive and extensive relations with Western countries. In the political field, the relationship is somewhat ambivalent in nature because many are ex-colonies of the West. In the immediate post-colonial period they strove for complete political independence, implying an anti-Western attitude, and thus were attracted initially to the Soviet Union. But the second generation of leaders in many Third World countries, having been through the various revolutionary stages of national development, are now more pragmatic and politically more neutral. This was shown in the Non-Aligned Summit Meeting in New Delhi in March 1983. Relations will become even easier if the Western countries make more effort to understand (and take a less *a priori* attitude with regard to) social systems, systems of government, societal values and the dynamism of change in the Third World.

Relations in the economic field are already quite extensive. The West possesses great leverage with the Third World in this respect. The need to restructure economic relations, as stipulated in the Report of the Brandt Commission, is an important task for both sides. Although the Soviet Union has itself almost nothing to offer in this field, dissatisfaction on the part of Third World States with their economic relations with the West can easily be exploited by Moscow for its own political gain. The West is also a major source of science and technology for the Third World. Yet the transfer of science and technology is a delicate matter, for it touches upon the socio-cultural values of the receiving society. This calls for close cooperation and great understanding between the Third World and the Western countries.

As stated earlier, relations in the military field are not likely to be the dominant factor. From the Third World perspective, it is expected that the US and its allies will try to maintain a level of military presence which balances that of the Soviet Union. It is hoped that the West could become a 'consistent' source of military arms, but the old pattern of military relations, whether in the form of military pacts or in the form of overseas bases, has become outmoded from the Third World perspective. Thus, there is a need to find new forms of military cooperation which are more flexible and respect the sovereignty of Third World countries. The cases of Egypt and Oman have shown this to be possible.

The relationship between the Third World and the West needs broader foundations. This implies, first, that Western countries (and especially the US) should formulate more comprehensive, consistent, credible and long-term policies towards the USSR because the relationship between the US and the Soviet Union remains the most important factor in maintaining world peace and security. It is a relationship that must be handled with great care and sensitivity since a host of contradictions are embedded in it. The need to cooperate must coexist with inevitable competition. Specifically, the conclusion of START is an urgent task, because these talks touch upon the main issue in the superpower relationship. There also need to be arrangements to ensure a balance in conventional weapons and to regulate arms sales to the Third World. Relations in the economic field should also be promoted with a view to lessening the tensions between the two countries. Lastly, there is a need to seek arrangements through which both sides could support the creation of regional order in the Third World. These would limit the rights of outside powers to intervene and might aim to prevent either superpower achieving dominance.

At the same time the US and its allies in Western Europe and Japan must restructure their relationships to conform to the new realities. The US is no longer the dominant power that it was, either in political or economic terms, and must share the responsibility with its allies.

This implies a relationship on a more equal footing. Structuring this relationship may not be easy because, at least in the area of defence, both Western Europe and Japan are still dependent upon the US. This, however, can be circumvented if new mechanisms of consultation are developed between the US, Western Europe and Japan. The issues affecting the relationship between these countries have expanded beyond their traditional concerns. For example, the security of the Persian Gulf can no longer be separated from the security of Western Europe and Japan. The EEC and NATO cannot cope with new areas of interest outside Europe. The Summit Meeting in Venice in June 1980, in which political and security matters were both discussed, perhaps indicates a desire to reshape the Western (and Japanese) relationship.

It is equally encouraging to see the emergence of a division of responsibilities between the US, Western Europe and Japan. France is taking care of the security of French Africa and maintains a fleet in Djibouti. West Germany is providing greater economic assistance to Turkey and Pakistan. Japan is increasing its political role and has supported ASEAN in its efforts to stabilise Southeast Asia.

Overall it can be said that the capabilities of the Western countries *in toto* are still very credible, provided they can cooperate constructively and can formulate workable policies regarding the division of responsibilities between them in the political and economic fields, in the transfer of science and technology, and in the military field. Because the division of labour includes an increased defence commitment by Western Europe and Japan, the resources of the US can more readily be diverted to maintain a power balance in the Persian Gulf.

Lastly, relations between the Third World and the Western world in various fields must involve more concrete cooperative programmes. To ensure long-lasting cooperation, mechanisms of dialogue and fora for consultation must be permanently established. ASEAN, for instance, can be most useful in this respect for the Southeast Asian region. Also, the division of labour amongst the Western countries and Japan must be extended to their relations with the Third World. The US cannot alone take care of all the areas of the world. Furthermore the too obvious presence of the US might be disadvantageous in some circumstances.

All this will depend to a large extent upon initiatives originating in the US. It is there that adjustments are taking place which will affect the processes of decision-making and the American political dynamic. To cope with these adjustments, the US needs a more consistent leadership, and a better relationship between the executive and the legislative branches. Equally important is the performance of the US economy. In all these respects the friends of the US must give support. It should not be forgotten that the US has contributed massively to the maintenance of an international order which has brought relative stability to the world for the last thirty-five years. In the years to come the US will face great challenges, and it is in the interest of all that it can cope with them.

The Soviet Union on the other hand does not have the potential to assist the Third World's search for prosperity. The Soviet Union is respected only for its military might. Newly-independent countries may initially be attracted to the Soviet Union because of the anti-colonialist flavour of its political propaganda, but most Third World states see the USSR only as a balancing power when such a balance is considered necessary, or as a source of military hardware.

It is likely that a decrease of US presence and credibility in a particular area could create a situation in which the countries of that area feel the pressure of the Soviet Union directly. Such is the case after the Soviet invasion of Afghanistan. This was seen by most Third World countries as a violation of the sovereignty of an independent, non-aligned, developing country. Whatever the reasons behind this action, most Third World countries reacted strongly against it. Nevertheless, this does not mean that the Third World does not admit the legitimate presence of the Soviet Union. It may even be necessary to invite the Soviet Union to join international efforts directed at maintaining some form of regional order in parts of the Third World. On the other hand, concern is expressed in the Third World regarding the future direction of Soviet global policies. This arises from the fact that Soviet military power could be used to obtain distinct advantages, especially in the last half of the 1980s when the Soviet Union is expected to undergo many difficult internal changes that might involve radical adjustments in policy due to changes in leadership, economic stagnation, resource scarcity, or demographic shifts which create imbalances in the ethnic composition of its population.

Therefore, the Third World argues that all must have the courage to continue to work towards the creation of an environment where detente could work. In such an environment, the Third World could find the opportunity both to develop and to participate in international affairs. The development of national resilience helps to guarantee world stability for it can prevent the East–West conflict escalating through the exploitation of the national vulnerabilities that exist in many parts of the Third World. Consequently, the Third World could become a stabilising factor for the world as a whole.

To the ASEAN countries, increased tension between the US and the USSR would not be conducive to stability and security in the Southeast Asian region. The Soviet military build-up in the Pacific, accompanied by the access to the facilities in Cam Ranh and Danang, definitely creates anxieties in the ASEAN countries, especially since it is still considered a threat on ideological grounds. But, Soviet ideology has lost its appeal in many developing countries. Subversion and infiltration by the Soviets will find no support in ASEAN countries. Ideology alone no longer constitutes a real threat to Indonesia where internal conditions have been consolidated politically and ideologically and significant progress has been made in the economic field.

The overall superpower balance during the last ten years, even with the increase of Soviet military might, still is a comfortable one for the US and its allies. Occasionally, doubt has been raised, but it has been influenced more by America's own perception of its power rather than by careful analysis and calculation. While growing Soviet military power definitely is a major security issue for the region in the 1980s, the US remains an important factor there, and its policies towards the states of the region can greatly affect the security and stability of Southeast Asia. Gross errors, which by themselves can become a threat, can be avoided if the US can structure its relations with its allies and friends in the region on the basis of a recognition of the great diversities there, as well as on the foundations of mutual policy consultations and coordination.

There are, however, three issues which have a direct bearing on the US military role in the region. First, how far has the credibility of the American military presence and defence umbrella been restored? Earlier problems in this area were indicative of the lack of the necessary mechanism for consultation between the US and its allies (and friends). Second, how far has the US Seventh Fleet kept up with the growing Soviet navy in the Pacific and Indian Oceans? Should the US response be insufficient, how could others cooperate with the US to share this burden? In view of the necessity to mobilise public support in the US, it is widely recognised that a 'fair' burden-sharing formula would enhance US security commitments in the Pacific region. Third, how far could the US harmonise its global interests with its regional interests, as well as with regional complexities, sensitivities, and nuances? The two interests are not necessarily parallel with one another.

If it is accepted that the US military role is of major importance to the maintenance of regional security and stability, its political and economic relations are equally important instruments for strengthening cooperation in the region. Since the US still is a major source of capital and technology as well as a major trading partner, greater US economic cooperation with the developing countries in the region could contribute to the alleviation of the major source of internal stability there.

Japan as the most important US partner in the region must accept a greater share of the regional defence burden. This has been recognised by many in Japan itself, and there is little doubt that Japan will increase its self-defence capabilities both at home and in its surrounding waters. Other countries in the region must and will gradually accept this development. A regional role for Japan, because of the sensitivities involved, needs to be formulated in concert with the US and other friends of Japan in the region. There is still no clarity as to how far away from its homeland Japan would play a military-security role. The re-militarisation of Japan will remain a major regional concern.

An increased regional security role for Japan would have serious implications. First, it may encourage the US to greatly reduce its Seventh Fleet. Objectively speaking, Japan can only complement, but cannot become a substitute for, the US naval presence in the Pacific in the immediate future. Second, as a response, the USSR may be encouraged to further increase its military presence in the region. Thus, a burden-sharing scheme for Japan, short of a greater regional military role, should be encouraged. It would involve two major tasks: to increase the self-defence of its homeland and surrounding waters by developing air and naval capabilities, especially in anti-submarine warfare; to assist the ASEAN countries' efforts to enhance their capability to protect vital sea lanes through the transfer of defence-related technologies and other forms of cooperation.

Japan has greatly improved its relations with ASEAN states, especially in the economic field. Increased Japanese cooperation in economic development could further enhance regional stability and security. This has been recognised in the formulation of Japan's comprehensive security policy. In order for this policy to be effective, Japan should emphasise areas which would result in a more horizontal economic relationship. Political consultation has enhanced the understanding between Japan and ASEAN, as reflected by Japan's full support for the ASEAN position on the Kampuchean conflict as well as by its intermediary role in the North–South dialogue.

Recently, it has become more obvious that the US cannot expect too much from the PRC. It was made clear at the Twelfth Congress of the Communist Party of China in 1982 that although the PRC was in great need of Western capital and technology, it would only act in its national interest. A strategic alliance between the US and the PRC cannot be effective in facing the Soviet menace. Apart from the still uncertain developments internally, the PRC does not have a credible military capability. Its defence modernisation programme is given only fourth priority, suggesting that even in the next five to ten years the PRC will not acquire the necessary capability to confront the Soviet Union militarily. It is known that Southeast Asia in general has great apprehensions about the PRC, despite the latter's still weak military capabilities. These uneasy feelings towards the PRC have deep historical roots, when China exercised its sphere of influence over them. Thus, analogous to fears in Western Europe of a 'Finlandisation' by the USSR, the Southeast Asian nations cannot accept a 'Burmanisation' by the PRC.

The PRC's policy towards Vietnam today only shows that it is willing to destroy its Southeast Asian neighbour. In addition, the PRC has remained ambiguous on the problem of the overseas Chinese, despite the explicit demands by Southeast Asian countries for a final clarification of this problem for reasons of internal security. In the broader regional context, it is recognised by ASEAN that the PRC needs to be encouraged to participate in some regional or international structure so that it can play a stabilising, rather than a destabilising, role in the Pacific region. Normalisation of US–PRC relations is consistent with this proposition. However, there are American tendencies, less so today than in the recent past, to overestimate the value of this relationship and to seek security cooperation, including the sale of arms, with the PRC. This has created great uncertainties in other parts of the region, and it is logical that ASEAN cannot accept the kind of US policies towards the PRC which might endanger or nullify the stability of the region. More important, if viewed from the regional perspective, is the consistency in US policies towards the PRC. The US should recognise that the PRC's policies towards the West are based on considerations of national interest in support of its economic development and modernisation programme. In the same vein, the PRC's initiatives to seek normalised relations with the USSR should be viewed as a natural development which is not necessarily detrimental to US interest, since normalisation in Sino-Soviet relations could enhance stability in the region.

Another disturbing international factor affecting the region relates to uncertainties in world economic development caused by a prolonged and deep recession. The Third World has been hardest hit by it as countries can find only limited markets for their exports as their debt problems become more problematic, and their economies grow much more slowly. Political instabilities may arise with slower economic growth, which frustrates efforts to increase per capita income levels, general employment, and the provision of basic needs. Most Third World governments have gained legitimacy by their successes in developing the economy. While the ASEAN economies are in a relatively better position than other Third World states, a prolonged recession could have severe effects on them, since adjustments to economic stagnation could arouse political dissatisfaction within the growing middle class which constitutes the effective political power base of the ASEAN governments.

CONCLUSIONS

For the 1980s, there do not seem to be new major sources of threat on the horizons of Pacific region security. For the ASEAN countries, the major threat to security still is perceived to originate from within. Therefore, of major importance to the maintenance of security and stability in the ASEAN states is the ability of the respective governments to rigorously pursue their own national development efforts. This is not an easy task in view of the changing aspirations of the people and the changing global environment

This does not mean that external threats are non-existent. External sources of threat are perceived to be of a secondary nature. They could reinforce internal sources of threat or create additional complications in the realisation of national development objectives. Both the USSR and the PRC pose a potential threat to the Southeast Asian region, partly because of ideological considerations and partly because of the potential military threat. Psychological and historical reasons are also important in this regard. While the Soviet Union is recognised as a dangerous power in view of its acquisition of global military might, the PRC is perceived as a more immediate threat. It is geographically closer to Southeast Asia and its policies towards the region still bear great ambiguities. Therefore, it is important to Indonesia that its friends in the region understand the subtleties of Indonesia's perception of threat and take them into consideration in the formulation of regional security policy.

The above proposition also suggests that while the military balance is an important factor, other factors – social, economic, political and cultural – have an equally important bearing on the security and stability of the Pacific region. The strategy adopted by the ASEAN countries to develop their national and regional resilience has contributed to regional stability, and has also enabled ASEAN to play a constructive role in many international fora, especially among the developing countries. It is to be recognised that global conflict is likely to originate from local and internal conflicts in the Third World rather than as a result of direct confrontation between the superpowers. Japan's so-called comprehensive security policy is consistent with this proposition. Such a policy, if properly worked out, would provide a valuable basis for cooperation between Japan and ASEAN.

Despite the fact that the various countries in the Pacific region (Japan, South Korea, the ASEAN countries) have undertaken serious efforts to increase their defence capabilities and have contributed to the stability of the region, the US is the only military power which can counterbalance the Soviet Union. US security commitments in the region as well as the credibility of its military presence will depend upon the willingness of other countries, especially Japan, to share a fair burden. Burden-sharing, however, should be interpreted comprehensively and not narrowly. The US and Japan, being important sources of technology, should be prepared to transfer military technologies to the ASEAN countries or South Korea. The US needs to manage its relations with its allies and friends in the region within a structure which is comprehensive and based on mutuality, without leading to an alliance system. ASEAN's idea of a ZOPFAN for Southeast Asia complements such a regional order for peace and stability. The idea of Pacific economic cooperation also offers an alternative venue through which dialogue and consultation on a regional basis can be practised.

4 Vietnamese Perspectives on International Security: Three Revolutionary Currents

CARLYLE A. THAYER*

After decades of Western involvement in Vietnam, the nature of its decision-making system and the personalities of its top leadership still remain a neglected area of research. Vietnam today is a closed and secretive one-party state which carefully regulates contact between outsiders and its citizens. The press and electronic media are carefully controlled to reflect the official party line. In the absence of legal pressure groups, opposition spokesmen and a free press, it is all but impossible to discern the international security perspective of informed Vietnamese opinion.

In light of these serious constraints, this chapter approaches the question of Vietnamese security perspectives by limiting itself to a decision-making level of analysis[1] and by considering the official – or publicly stated – views of the Vietnamese leadership as they appear in the regime-controlled media. This chapter has been divided into four parts for convenience of analysis. Part one reviews the three main contending approaches to the study of the decision-making process in Vietnam. Part two discusses the declaratory views of the Vietnamese leadership. Part three reviews current regional security perspectives, while part four considers Vietnam's future probable orientations on security issues.

* The author would like to thank Frank Frost of the Australian Parliament's Legislative Research Service and Lew Stern of the University of Pittsburgh for their comments on an early draft of this chapter.

CONTENDING APPROACHES TO VIETNAMESE SECURITY PERSPECTIVES

Since the partition of Vietnam in 1954, the nature of foreign policy formulation has changed very little. The key personalities involved have remained basically the same. The decision-making system, although now more complex and structurally differentiated, has altered only slightly. There is agreement among analysts that the key decision-making structure is the Political Bureau of the Vietnamese Communist Party (VCP) and its substructures,[2] including the Secretariat and the Central Military Party Committee. The Central Committee is too large a body to effectively manage national security policy.

Three basic paradigms dominate the study of Vietnamese foreign policy formulation at the decision-making level: the factional model, the nepotistic-dictatorial model, and the collegial model. With the exception of one analyst employing quantitative techniques,[3] all other Hanoi-watchers have constructed their models on the basis of the methodology known as Kremlinology.[4]

The Factional Model

The proponents of the factional model of decision-making view the Vietnamese Political Bureau as being divided into two, perhaps three, factions that continually engage in a struggle for personal power. Contemporary analysts have been heavily influenced by the writings of P. J. Honey in the early 1960s.[5] At the time, Honey asserted that the Political Bureau elected at the 1960 Third National Party Congress was divided into two contending camps based on the deep personal animosity and rivalry between Vo Nguyen Giap and Truong Chinh as well as between Le Duan and Le Duc Tho. This inherently unstable state of affairs was kept in balance by Ho Chi Minh until his death in 1969. Honey has written, for example:

> For many years past it has been clear that rival factions exist within the Lao Dong Party, and it has even appeared probable that Ho Chi Minh encourages them, for he imposes his wishes upon the Party by lending his weight to the faction which happens to advocate the policy he considers the most appropriate at any given time. Ho's backing ensures that the views of this faction prevail and, in this way,

he continues to exercise the powers of a dictator while appearing to act in the most democratic fashion.⁶

Generally, these rival factions were said to be split along pro-Soviet and pro-Chinese lines. However, with the advent of the Cultural Revolution in China, and as a result of other developments, these categories became so vague as to be meaningless. In their place, Honey⁷ coined the terms pragmatists and ideologues to refer, respectively, to the factions led by Le Duan – Vo Nguyen Giap and Truong Chinh – Le Duc Tho. Other analysts, such as Zorza⁸ and Zagoria⁹ have applied such labels as 'builders vs. fighters' and 'economist faction vs. southern-orientated faction' to describe these rival groupings. Nguyen Tien Hung, ¹⁰ has posited the existence of a third or neutral faction led by Pham Van Dong.

Douglas Pike has summarised the literature on factionalism in this way:

> In recent years it was fashionable among scholars to divide the Politburo members into hard–soft factions: the dogmatists or pro-Chinese faction versus the moderate or pro-Soviet faction, with a smaller faction called the semi-opportunists or nationalists-*cum*-Communists standing in between. In somewhat simplified terms, Hanoi was seen as a debating forum for arguing the merits of furthering communism by means of wars of liberation versus the method of peaceful coexistence. Onto this was grafted the local debate of how best to achieve unification of North and South Vietnam. The Politburo then could be divided into the pro-Soviet or dove camp and the pro-Chinese or hawk camp.¹¹

The implications for national security policy were relatively straightforward as long as Ho Chi Minh (or a third faction) held the balance of power: Vietnam could be expected to follow a non-aligned posture in the Sino-Soviet dispute. Honey has argued, in fact, that the zig-zag course pursued by Vietnam up until 1963 could be attributed to the momentary ascendancy of one faction over the other.¹² With the escalation of the war in Vietnam from 1965 onwards, each of the three Political Bureau factions advocated a different strategy towards ending the war: regular force strategy (Ho Chi Minh – Le Duan, Vo Nguyen Giap, Van Tien Dung); neo-revolutionary guerrilla warfare strategy (Truong Chinh, Le Duc Tho, Pham Hung, Le Thanh Nghi); and negotiated settlement strategy (Nguyen Duy Trinh, Hoang Van Hoan, Tran Quoc Hoan).¹³

A decisive change in Vietnamese military strategy only became possible, according to this view, with the deaths of neo-revolutionary warfare advocates Nguyen Chi Thanh in 1967 and Ho Chi Minh in 1969. The on-going stalemate between the conventional warfare advocates and those favouring a negotiated settlement was not broken until August-September 1972 when the two Political Bureau vacancies were filled. Both new members favoured a negotiated settlement strategy and their appointment tipped the scales against the advocates of conventional warfare.

In the present period, factional model advocates still stress the notion that personal enmity between Le Duan and Truong Chinh (and between Giap and Chinh as well as between Duan and Tho) remains the main axis dividing the Political Bureau. Such labels as 'pro-Soviet' and 'pro-China' have been dropped in favour of pragmatists versus ideologues.

There are several fundamental weaknesses of the factional model, the most important of which is its failure to account for the stability of the leadership in the fourteen years since Ho Chi Minh's death. Secondly, Vietnam's 1978 pro-Soviet foreign policy line has not been accompanied by the fall from power of those individuals who were identified in the past as being pro-Chinese (e.g. Truong Chinh, an alias which means literally 'Long March'). Thirdly, it would appear that attempts to classify individuals into one of two categories oversimplifies the complexities involved. An important and authoritative 1969 US study concluded that

> There is general agreement that knowledge of the existence and significance of possible factions within the Hanoi leadership is imprecise. There are differences of opinion within the leadership on tactics as opposed to ultimate objectives but there are not stable 'Moscow' and 'Peking' factions. The Hanoi leadership will form different alignments on different issues.[14]

A final weakness of the factional model is the imprecision with which members of the Politburo are classified. Often information is lacking about the views of particular members (especially less senior members) on a variety of issues. Even in the case of well-known figures such as General Giap or Truong Chinh, there is disagreement among specialists. The US study cited above also stated:

> The attempts by the agencies to ascertain the position of various

North [sic] Vietnamese leaders on specific issues shows the imprecision of our information and analysis. For example, different agencies set forth sharply conflicting identifications of the position of individual leaders such as (Vo Nguyen) Giap on particular questions.[15]

Nepotistic–Dictatorial Model

Proponents of the nepotistic-dictatorial model argue that since the death of Ho Chi Minh, and more especially since the VCP's Fourth National Congress in 1976, Vietnam has come under the domination of a small clique consisting of Le Duan and Le Duc Tho, their family members and other Vietnamese who owe their positions to the clique leaders. According to former Political Bureau member Hoang Van Hoan,[16] Le Duan engineered the dismissal of one third of the Central Committee in 1976 and replaced them with his supporters. Among the notable victims of this alleged purge were Hoan himself who was dropped from the Political Bureau and a group of Party officials who held 'pro-Chinese' views: Ngo Minh Loan, Ngo Thuyen, Nguyen Trong Vinh and Ly Ban (all alternate members). Hoan's dismissal marked only the third occasion since 1956 when a person had been dropped from the Political Bureau for policy reasons.[17] Hoan, a former ambassador to Beijing, was allegedly strongly pro-Chinese in his views and was dropped for this reason.

Based on the accounts of Hoang Van Hoan, Truong Nhu Tang[18] and other defectors, the Le Duan–Le Duc Tho clique exercises control of the political system through family members.[19] Le Hong, Le Duan's elder son, reportedly runs the regime's secret police. Le Anh, the other son, heads Vietnam's missile defence system. A brother-in-law, Tran Lam, a colonel in the intelligence service, is said to control the entire television, radio and propaganda services. Lam's brother, Tran Quynh, directs the Nguyen Ai Quoc Institute of Marxist-Leninist Studies. Le Duan's son-in-law, Dao Dinh Luyen, is commander of the Air Force, while his second wife is secretary of the Ben Tre province VCP committee. Reportedly, Le Duc Tho has three brothers, all of whom hold powerful posts. Mai Chi Tho is a dominant figure in the VCP's apparatus in the Ho Chi Minh City where he heads the security service. Dinh Duc Thien, a general and former division commander, was appointed in February 1980 as Minister of Transport and Communications. He previously served in the Prime Minister's Office with the rank of Minister. Tho's third brother, Nguyen Duc Thuan, is secretary-general of the Vietnam Confederation of Trade Unions. Le Duc Tho's sister is Ambassador to Romania, while a cousin, Nguyen Duc Tam, has replaced Tho as head of the Organisation Department of the VCP Central Committee. In 1982 Tam was given full status on the Political Bureau.

Advocates of the dictatorial model assert a direct correspondence between the views of the clique leaders and Vietnamese foreign policy. Vietnam's pro-Soviet line arises from Le Duan's personal proclivities, while Vietnam's 'hegemonist and expansionist' policies towards neighbouring Cambodia are allegedly fashioned by Le Duc Tho.

As with the case of the factional model, it would appear that the nepotistic-dictatorial model likewise contains several fundamental deficiencies. First, the continued presence of Truong Chinh as number two in the Political Bureau is not satisfactorily accounted for. Since the 1976 Party Congress, Vietnam promulgated its third state Constitution which created a new powerful position, Chairman of the State Council. There were then persistent rumours that Le Duan would fill this position, becoming the second leader after Ho Chi Minh to hold the top party and state positions. Yet in 1980 when the State Council chairmanship was announced, it went to Truong Chinh and not Le Duan. A second shortcoming of this model is that it does not account for how two such seemingly intractable rivals could team up. Such a combination would be a very powerful one. Yet Le Duc Tho's brother, Dinh Duc Thien, was recently dismissed as Minister of Transport and Communications and dropped from the Central Committee. Prior to the Fifth Party Congress in March 1982 Le Duc Tho himself was removed as head of the Central Committee's Organisation Department (while, on the other hand, he was replaced by a cousin). Further, Vo Nguyen Giap, an alleged supporter of Le Duan, opponent of Truong Chinh and perhaps pro-Soviet in his views, has been progressively demoted. In 1980 he lost the Defence portfolio and in 1982 he was dropped from the Political Bureau. In all three of these cases, if one accepts the conventional wisdom of Hanoi-watchers, the victims were members of the Le Duan or 'pro-Soviet' faction. Finally, the nepotistic-dictatorial model proponents have not provided sufficient detail on the Le Duan–Le Duc Tho loyalists appointed to the Central Committee in 1976. This is important, for 43 per cent of that Central Committee was dropped at the Fifth Party Congress in 1982.

Both of the above decision-making models, contain flaws which seriously limit their usefulness in predicting future Vietnamese policies. The factional model exaggerates the alleged personal antagonism between leaders and overstates their personal ambition to attain unbridled power. The nepotistic-dictatorial model entirely ignores the influence of other leaders on the policy-making process.

Collegial Model

In attempting to reconstruct an alternate model at the decision-making level, two features of the Vietnamese system become readily apparent: the continuity of leadership and the cohesiveness of the leadership elite. Vietnam's leaders, in the period 1954–82 now under consideration, are all from the same generation. They were radicalised by the political environment of the late 1920s and 1930s. They became founding members or early associates of the VCP. Many served prolonged periods of time together in French prisons. For over five decades they have directed the course of Vietnam's revolution in the face of incredible hardship and adversity. Remarkably, there have been no purges or executions. Two members have died (Nguyen Chi Thanh in 1967 and Ho Chi Minh in 1969).

The nature of this leadership elite was succinctly captured by Hoan Tung, then editor of the Party's newspaper *Nhan Dan*, in response to a question by a Western journalist in 1973 as to how the Political Bureau functioned:

> In the inner activities of our officials some differences of views are normal. When they once deliberate each has his own view on a specific issue (but there is no disagreement on fundamental principles). If necessary, we take a vote, if necessary, we work on the basis of a majority. The leaders have been working together over 30 years already and they have carried out their liberation struggle for 40 years, they are all comrades who know each other well.[20]

The decision-making system which has evolved over the past decades may best be described as a collegial system. Its key features have been aptly stated by Paul Kattenburg:

> The number of key decision-makers is small; that security and secrecy pertain; that decisions are reached collectively by a process in which personality, political, affiliational, and other individual traits of decision-makers blur in favor of a common outlook; that

this outlook conforms to what the elite consensually determines to be the 'mass' or 'national' interest on the basis of a prudent cost-benefit calculation; and that the official pronouncements and commentaries are designed to communicate the elite's consensual view.[21]

In brief, the collegial model allows for the identification of individual and even factional disagreements. However, the system is not one of contention for power by competing rivals, but one in which there is basic agreement over ultimate ends and disagreement over the means to achieve these ends. The system has evolved and remained stable because the ultimate ends have remained relatively constant for so long: national reunification and national survival in the face of a more powerful adversary (France, USA, China).

While today very little is known about the views of the newer members of the Political Bureau, evidence has accumulated over the years about the perceptions of the top four leaders who have served continually since 1960.[22] These men and their colleagues may be described as Vietnamese nationalists as well as Marxist-Leninists. As nationalists, they are ardently committed to maintaining the independence and unity of Vietnam.

Despite individual policy differences, the VCP decision-making system has remained a collegial one. For example, Douglas Pike in a study of the VCP Political Bureau, has analysed the impact of such factors as the political *milieu* and the structure of the *apparat* on the decision-making process. He concluded that as a result of the prolonged interaction of these variables an operational code has been developed through which doctrinal disputes were settled collectively.[23] Although it was possible for Pike to discern opposing points of view on different issues (e.g. hardliners vs. softliners or ideologues vs. pragmatists), the operational code prevented these differences from becoming the basis of permanent factional divisions among the VCP leadership.

Another study attempted to measure the doctrinal orientations of four key Political Bureau members and to determine what impact doctrinal differences had on the policy-making process. On the basis of quantitative content analysis, Rogers classified Truong Chinh and Vo Nguyen Giap as ideologues (more concerned with doctrine) and Pham Van Dong and Le Duan as pragmatists (less concerned with doctrine). However, when analysing the content of their doctrinal orientations, he discovered somewhat to his surprise that 'all four leaders in their public statements are decidedly pro-Soviet and conservative doctrinally, and all manifest a strong nationalistic tendency . . . [and] there is enough evidence to state that a clear pro-Soviet versus a pro-Chinese dichotomy in the Hanoi Politburo is not manifested in public statements, even indirectly'.[24] Rogers concluded:

> Doctrine for the North [sic] Vietnamese leaders thus appears to be (a) a modifier of perceptions of events; and (b) a rationalizing or legitimizing element for policy decisions rather than a prescriptive component of policy formulation. It appears, however, that it is not just Marxist-Leninist perception of events which most clearly sets the basis of North [sic] Vietnamese attitudes. . . . The qualitative analysis also indicates that . . . events tended to be interpreted by the Hanoi leadership through strong nationalistic perceptions. . . . Hence it would seem reasonable to infer that nationalistic interpretations of events . . . may be as significant as a doctrinal aspect.[25]

In summary, given the closed nature of the Vietnamese decision-making process, the lack of specific information on all full members of the VCP Political Bureau, and the weaknesses and flaws of the factional and nepotistic-dictatorial models, the collegial model would appear to offer the best framework for determining Vietnamese perspectives on national security and foreign policies. The explanatory power of the collegial model, however, is limited. This is particularly so since the changes which occurred at the Fifth National Party Congress in March 1982 when six long-serving members of the Political Bureau were dropped and four new members were added.

THREE REVOLUTIONARY CURRENTS

From at least 1970 to the present, Vietnam's communist leaders have stated their belief that the present and future direction of world politics is determined by the interplay of three revolutionary currents (or streams): the strength of the socialist camp since World War II, the upsurge of the national liberation movement in the Third World and the struggle waged by workers and toiling people in capitalist countries. Given this framework, Le Duan advocated in 1970 the following approach to maintaining Vietnam's national security:

> [i]t is necessary to set up a united front of the world's peoples against American imperialism. The core of this front should be constituted

by the socialist countries, the international communist and workers' movement, and the national liberation movement; at the same time the front should attract all peace and justice loving forces and mobilize all potentialities of the world's peoples for this common aim: to isolate the American imperialists and their allies.[26]

Six years later, at the Fourth National Party Congress, Le Duan asserted in his Political Report that:

> the strength of our era is the combined strength of the three revolutionary currents which are the forces deciding the main content, the main direction and the main characteristics of the history of the development of human society and are accelerating the transition of the world from capitalism to socialism.[27]

In March 1982, at the Fifth National Party Congress, Le Duan once again invoked the three revolutionary currents in his analysis of world politics:

> Dear Comrades, during the 1970s, especially after the U.S. imperialists' debacle in Vietnam, the world situation entered a new era of development. The three revolutionary currents of the epoch grew tremendously, creating a tremendous consolidated strength.[28]

The 'three revolutionary currents' formulation represents in abbreviated form the framework through which Vietnamese leaders view changes in the global political system. This perspective arises from the generational experience of the present leadership group. They were born in the first decade and a half of this century and experienced the intellectual ferment of the 1920s when Marxism-Leninism was introduced into Vietnam following the 1917 Bolshevik Revolution. From that moment onward, elements of traditional Vietnamese political culture (e.g. patriotism as distinct from nationalism) combined with an ideology which not only explained how colonialism had come about, but which offered prospects for change.

One historian[29] has argued that the most important Marxist text to influence the Vietnamese revolution was Lenin's *Thesis on the National and Colonial Questions* which so moved Ho Chi Minh.[30] Be that as it may, Lenin's *Imperialism: The Highest Stage of Capitalism*, with its economic framework, had an important impact on Ho's lieutenants. They mastered Marxism-Leninism through membership in Ho's Canton-based Revolutionary Youth League and, more particularly, as a result of clandestine small group discussions held in French prisons – which they termed 'universities' – in the 1930s and 1940s. Quite clearly the perspectives of today's Political Bureau members were forged during this period. Their cohesion as a group was moulded as a result of their political socialisation experiences as young revolutionaries.

As a result of the role played by Ho Chi Minh in the Communist International (Comintern), today's Vietnamese leaders have always accepted the proposition that their revolution is part of the world-wide socialist revolution led by the Soviet Union. Vietnam's membership in this 'Socialist Commonwealth' entails reciprocal obligations under the banner of proletarian internationalism. It is also important to note that the Leninist framework not only offered the strategy and tactics (a vanguard party, the role of the united front, and the use of revolutionary violence) to overcome domestic injustices caused by the colonial/capitalist system, but also offered membership in an alternate international system. In other words, without the internationalist aspects of the Marxist–Leninist framework, Vietnamese revolutionaries faced the prospect of struggling against the inequities of capitalism on the domestic level, only to find at the moment of independence that a newly freed Vietnam was locked into an international system dominated by powerful capitalist states.

The three revolutionary currents framework provides an important insight into how the VCP Political Bureau members view the central balance of power. The central balance is never measured in military terms – whether conventional or nuclear. As Soviet military might is judged to have reached parity with that of the United States, the central balance is measured in terms of economic and political forces. The perspective is a long-term one with current problems and set-backs seen as temporary.

A major insight into Vietnamese perspectives may be gained by reviewing an authoritative article which appeared in the VCP's monthly theoretical journal, *Tap Chi Cong San* in May 1982. According to its author, the world socialist revolution, despite difficulties caused by the 'counter-revolutionary assault force' headed by the 'Beijing reactionary clique', is on the strategic offensive. 'Nevertheless', he writes, 'the "who will triumph over whom" struggle in the world is still going on in a difficult and violent manner.' His argument is presented in two parts: an assessment of the world revolution and an analysis of the factors contributing to the (continued) overall decline of capitalism.

Concerning the 'offensive stance of the world revolution', the author declares:

> Mankind is now at a stage where no force can prevent the uprising of nations. A genuine revolution is apt to be successful and stand firm even if it occurs on a small island. Over the past years, *the national liberation and independence movement has developed with a new strength and a new dimension and with increasingly profound social changes*. The last positions of colonialism are being wiped out, while neocolonialism has been dealt heavy blows. The formation of a block of socialist countries in the Indochinese peninsula is of utmost importance. It is a solid southern vanguard post of the socialist system and a factor for ensuring peace and stability in Southeast Asia.[31]

Among the examples cited in the article are Afghanistan, Iran (which is termed a 'special phenomenon'), the independence of Angola, Mozambique and Zimbabwe, and the likelihood of success of revolution in Namibia and the development of revolution in South Africa, El Salvador and Nicaragua. The author specifically underlines the role of the Non-Aligned Movement and, in particular, India's new enhanced role. On this point, he concludes that

> *national independence linked to socialism is an outstanding and ever growing trend in the present era*. The developing countries, especially the non-aligned, play an increasingly important role in international relations and in the struggle for peace, security and disarmament against colonialism and neocolonialism, racism and Zionism. The developing countries represent more than two thirds of the UN members and have an important voice in solving world issues.

He then discusses the 'struggle movement of the working class and labouring people' in the capitalist countries by highlighting the following 'new characteristics' of this revolutionary current:

> The struggle is no longer limited to economic problems as in the past, but has switched its focus to conflicts with the monopolistic capitalist states; the scope of struggle is no longer within an enterprise or a corporation, but now covers each production sector, each economic field or an entire country; and the social forces participating in the struggle are becoming even larger.

The author's second major contention is that capitalism has been in overall decline since 1945. He cites as evidence various cyclic crises of the capitalist system which have led to higher inflation, rising unemployment and a decline in the rate of economic growth and labour productivity. In addition, he underscores the emergence of non-cyclic contradictions in the capitalist system:

> Most important of all are the rapid surge of inflation and sectoral and structural crises (concerning energy, raw materials, finance and money, grain and so forth), the rising struggle movement for economic independence of peoples of liberated countries (directed against the rear base of capitalism), and the growing competition among imperialist countries for old and new sources of raw material and for investment areas. All these factors are closely related to the cyclic development of capitalist production.

As a result of these economic difficulties, political differences have emerged among the capitalist states, especially between the US and Western Europe and the US and Japan. In the former case, he cites Reagan's economic sanctions against the USSR and US attempts to expand NATO's scope into the Persian Gulf (e.g. to cooperate with the US Rapid Deployment Force). In the latter case, he mentions US pressures on Japan to increase defence spending and problems arising from the imbalance of trade between the two countries. The author ends this section by citing US-Western European differences over how to best meet the challenge of liberation movements: 'the US is inclined toward using military force . . . while US allies want to use political, economic and diplomatic pressure.'

As a result of the development of the three revolutionary currents, the author argues, the US has redesigned its global strategy in the following manner:

> U.S. imperialists are launching a *global counter-offensive in order to materialize their ambition to regain military superiority and lost positions, to check the world's liberation movement, and to re-establish U.S. control over the imperialist system*. In collusion with Beijing, the U.S. imperialists have readjusted their global counter-revolutionary strategy by directing the spearhead toward the Soviet Union and other socialist countries. . . .
> *The adventurous military policy of the U.S. imperialists and reactionaries is an extremely serious threat to world peace*. However,

the present balance of forces does not permit them to implement this policy easily. The integrated strength of the socialist system, of which the Soviet Union is the mainstay, is superior to the imperialist system. Socialism, which is a little inferior to imperialism from the economic viewpoint, possesses not only political superiority but also a military force equivalent to that of imperialism. Considering the strength of the three revolutionary currents, we can say that this is the great strength capable of frustrating all of the imperialists and reactionary plots.

Dissenting Views

In the absence of an open political system which would permit the free expression of dissenting views, it is extremely difficult to assess alternate Vietnamese perspectives – either originating within the VCP or outside the one-party framework by intellectuals or others concerned with national security and foreign policy questions. There are no organised foreign policy interest groups in Vietnam other than regime-sponsored and controlled bodies.

Quite clearly the defection of former Political Bureau member Hoang Van Hoan to China is evidence that at the highest levels of decision-making there was disagreement over the course of Sino-Vietnamese relations. This has been followed by the purging of party members considered to be Maoist. It is highly unlikely that a substantial pro-China lobby exists in Vietnam today or that any of its members exercise any influence on the policy-making process.

In 1981, in the lead-up to the Fifth National Party Congress, one glimpse into dissenting views was obtained by the publication overseas of a letter written by a prominent regime propagandist, Nguyen Khac Vien, to members of the National Assembly. According to accounts of this letter, Vien stated that there were still 'people' (high officials?) with a 'narrow nationalist outlook' who 'want to play two, even three sides, and who harbor the illusion that the imperialists can help us if we move away from the Soviet Union'.[32]

REGIONAL SECURITY ISSUES

In his address to the Fifth National Party Congress, Le Duan picked up the theme that the US acting in collusion with China was conducting a global counter-offensive against the socialist camp. He revealed that at the Fourth Plenum of the Central Committee in 1978 the VCP had concluded China would attack Vietnam and from that time China replaced the US as the 'direct and most dangerous enemy of the Vietnamese people'. Turning to regional issues, Le Duan declared:

> In Southeast Asia, the Chinese reactionaries and imperialist forces spearhead their attacks at Vietnam, Laos and Kampuchea. At present, the Chinese reactionaries, aided and abetted by the United States, are waging a kind of sabotage war against Vietnam on the military political, economic and cultural front, using various forces and resorting to very wicked tricks. . . . [The enemy] attempts by every means to tarnish the image of Vietnam in a bid to isolate our country in the international arena. Along with these anti-Vietnam schemes and acts, China also colludes with the United States, gathers together reactionary stooge forces, and entices ASEAN countries to oppose the revolution in Kampuchea and Laos.[33]

In the face of these security threats, Le Duan declared that all Vietnamese – the people, army and party – must unite and carry out two strategic tasks domestically: 'first, to build socialism successfully; secondly, to stand combat-ready to defend the socialist Vietnamese fatherland effectively. These two strategic tasks are closely interrelated.'

On the international level, Le Duan set forth two major strategic propositions which guided Vietnamese national security policy:

1. Solidarity and all-round cooperation with the Soviet Union has always been the cornerstone of our party's and state's foreign policy.
2. The special Vietnam–Laos–Kampuchea relationship is an evolutionary law of the revolution in the three countries. It is a matter of survival for the destiny of the three nations.

In addition, Le Duan also stressed as a lesser but none the less important set of priorities, the development of Vietnam's relations with other socialist countries within the framework of the Council for Mutual Economic Assistance (CMEA/COMECON) and the development of Vietnam's role as a member of the Non-Aligned Movement. Quite clearly Vietnam sees itself as part of two of the three revolutionary currents.

The major national security concerns of Vietnam's present leadership are to successfully weather Chinese pressures and to consolidate all the nations of Indochina into an alliance structure. The former preoccupation is a complex one as the following extract from Le Duan's Political Report indicates. Internally, Vietnam must design policies to cope with China's multifaceted war of sabotage:

> The enemy positions troops close to our northern borders, provokes partial armed conflicts, wages a war of encroachment aimed at gnawing away our border lands; at the same time, active preparations are made for a large-scale war of aggression. Through psychological and espionage warfare, he tries to undermine us politically, ideologically and organisationally, to sow division among the various ethnic groups, to drive a wedge between the people and the party; he covertly rallies the reactionary forces, organises opposition activities in an attempt to foment disturbances and subversion. He engages in economic sabotage, tries to undermine production, connives with the imperialists in pursuing an embargo policy, and sows the venom of reactionary, depraved culture.

Clearly, the present threat posed by China is seen as being similar in scope and magnitude to that posed by the French, Japanese and Americans in previous periods. In all four cases, Vietnam was compelled to respond to foreign aggression by waging an Indochina-wide war of resistance using the physical geography, resources and people to best advantage. The importance of this historical legacy is that the contemporary Vietnamese leadership is wedded to the idea of uniting Vietnam, Laos and Kampuchea into a unified confederation. This perspective was forcefully presented by Senior General Hoang Van Thai in an article published in early 1982. According to General Thai, throughout the history of contemporary warfare in Indochina, both the indigenous peoples and foreign aggressors (France, Japan, United States and China) saw Indochina as a strategic theatre of operations. As a result of cooperation between the communist parties and armies of Laos, Kampuchea and Vietnam, dating to the 1930s, special relations had been forged. After 1975, this relationship was transformed into a regional strategic alliance as a result of treaties signed between Vietnam and its neighbours. General Thai then advances the notion that this regional alliance network had become part of an international alliance structure led by the Soviet Union. In his words:

We, the Vietnamese Communists, clearly understand that the Vietnam–Laos–Kampuchea solidarity bloc is a regional alliance that is part of the international alliance of member countries of the socialist community of which the Soviet Union is the pillar. ... Today, the world socialist community, especially the Soviet Union, is the strategic ally and the firmest support of all revolutionary forces in the world, including the revolution of the three Indochinese countries.[34]

CONCLUSIONS: THE FUTURE

In 1980, two American political scientists attempted to explain 'recent Vietnamese behavior' (e.g. the events of 1978–9, sometimes termed the Third Indochinese War) by constructing a list of its fundamental national security goals abstracted from the literature on Vietnamese foreign policy published between 1964–79.[35] The list composed by Dutter and Kania consisted of five fundamental goals: (1) political independence from all non-Vietnamese influences; (2) as far as possible, independence from foreign (non-Indochinese) sources of economic and/or military aid and/or material; (3) territorial integrity and unity – i.e. the gathering of all ethnic Vietnamese into one political territorial unit and the 'ethnic purification' of such a unit; (4) military security from any potential or real threat, attacks or invasions; and (5) the conversion of the SRV into a regional power in Southeast Asia through achievement of the first four fundamental goals *and* domination of the SRV's immediate neighbours to the west.

Kania and Dutter also made a distinction between these long-term fundamental goals and 'instrumental goals' which related directly to the pursuit and/or achievement of one or more fundamental goals. These relatively short-term goals included the expulsion of extra-regional influences from Indochina; obtaining aid from all available sources for reconstruction and economic development, as well as military strength and security; the expulsion of dissidents 'so as not to impede economic, political, and social development'; the acquisition and maintenance of a preponderance of influence over the domestic and foreign policies of Laos and Cambodia; and increased influence in northeast Thailand 'so as to hold that traditional enemy at bay'. The latter point should perhaps be modified to take into account Vietnam's interest in the large ethnic Vietnamese community there. It is reasonable, in this author's view, to accept the above five instrumental goals as a guide to future Vietnamese national security and foreign policies as they relate to the attainment of the above-listed fundamental goals.

In the next five to ten years, Vietnam's present generation of leaders is likely to pass from the scene. This generational transition will have profound consequences on the collegial decision-making system described above. Until such a transition takes place, and it is already under way, it is unlikely that present Vietnamese national security and foreign policies will alter radically. Vietnam will remain the dominant power in an economically underdeveloped Indochina. Vietnam's economic and trading ties with the Soviet Union and other CMEA countries will be further strengthened. Vietnam will also devote much energy to participation in the Non-Aligned Movement, for it is by acceptance in this forum that Vietnam retains some measure of independence in its foreign policies. All other relationships – with ASEAN/China and the West – hinge on a resolution of the Kampuchean situation (either by settlement or acceptance over time of Vietnam's dominant position) or by a change of governments in those countries currently hostile to Vietnam.

NOTES

1. See the discussion in John W. Spanier, *Games Nations Play: Analysing International Politics*, Thomas Nelson, London, 1972, chs 1 and 2.
2. For example, according to communist defectors and Western intelligence sources, the VCP Politburo set up an office in 1966 to handle Cambodian affairs. In 1982 this office was identified under the code name 'B-68'. Le Duc Tho, a VCP Politburo member, has continually headed this office. See Timothy Carney, 'Heng Samrin's Armed Forces and Military balance in Cambodia', paper presented to a conference on Kampuchea, Princeton University, Princeton, New Jersey, 12–14 November 1982, and John McBeth, 'Bureaucrats from B68'. *Far Eastern Economic Review*, cxviii:42, 15 October 1982, pp. 16–17.
3. Robert F. Rogers, *Risk-Taking in Hanoi's War Policy: An Analysis of Military Versus Manipulation in a Communist Party-State's Behaviour in a Conflict Environment*, PhD Thesis, Georgetown University, 1974.
4. For a discussion, see Donald S. Zagoria, *The Sino-Soviet Conflict, 1956–61*, Atheneum, New York, 1964, pp. 24–35.
5. P. J. Honey, 'The Position of the DRV Leadership and the Succession to Ho Chi Minh', in P. J. Honey (ed.), *North Vietnam Today*, Praeger, New York, 1962, pp. 55–9; and Honey, *Communism in North Vietnam*, MIT Press, Cambridge, 1966, ch. 2.
6. P. J. Honey, 'Divided Counsels in the Party', *China News Analysis (CNA)*, 508, 13 March 1964, p. 1.

7. P. J. Honey, 'The Death of Ho Chi Minh and After', *CNA*, 785, 12 December 1969, pp. 6–7.
8. Victor Zorza, 'The end of a war', *Washington Post*, 15 October 1972.
9. Donald S. Zagoria, *Vietnam Triangle: Moscow/Peking/Hanoi*, Pegasus, New York, 1967, p. 103.
10. Nguyen Tien Hung, 'Hanoi: Peace as a Pause', *Washington Post*, 29 October 1972.
11. Douglas Pike, *War, Peace and the Viet Cong*, MIT Press, Cambridge, 1969, pp. 133–4.
12. Honey, 'Divided Counsels in the Party', p. 2.
13. Pike, *War, Peace and the Viet Cong*, pp. 165–6.
14. United States National Security Study Memorandum (NSSM), 1, reprinted in the *Congressional Record*, 10 May 1972, p. E4978.
15. Ibid. NSSM, 1 included both a summary of responses and the replies from various US government departments and agencies contacted.
16. P. J. Honey, 'The Seats of Power', *CNA*, 1179, 25 April 1980, p. 3.
17. The two other members were dropped for their role in the land reform campaign in 1956. Until Hoan's dismissal in 1976, no member of the Politburo had been dropped since the 1960 Third National Party Congress.
18. Truong Nhu Tang, 'The Myth of Liberation', *New York Review of Books*, 21 October 1982, pp. 31–6; Seki Tomoda, 'Doublecrossed: The Vietnamese Revolution', *Sankei Shimbun*, 1981, records the lengthy testimony of Truong Nhu Tang. The 158-page translation from the Japanese of this source is in the author's possession.
19. The family relations detailed here are based on the testimony of communist defectors and may be factually incorrect. For example, there is some doubt that Thuan is in fact Tho's third brother.
20. Cited in Murray Marder, 'Hanoi Politburo Avoids Votes Unless "Necessary"', *Washington Post*, 6 February 1973.
21. Paul M. Kattenburg, 'DRV External Relations in the New Revolutionary Phase', in Joseph J. Zasloff and MacAlister Brown (eds), *Communism in Indochina*, Heath, Lexington, 1975, p. 113.
22. Robert F. Rogers, 'Policy Differences Within the Hanoi Leadership', *Studies in Comparative Communism*, IX:1/2, Spring/Summer 1976, pp. 108–28.
23. Douglas E. Pike, 'Operational Code of the North Vietnamese Politburo', *Asia Quarterly*, 1 pp. 94–5 and 101.
24. Robert F. Rogers, 'Doctrinal Perceptions of the Hanoi Leadership', *South-East Asian Spectrum*, III:1, October 1974, p. 61.
25. Ibid.
26. Le Duan, *The Vietnamese Revolution: Fundamental Problems, Essential Tasks*, Foreign Languages Publishing House, Hanoi, 1970, p. 191.
27. Communist Party of Viet Nam, *Fourth National Congress Documents*, Foreign Languages Publishing House, Hanoi, 1977, p. 247.
28. 'Bao Cao Chinh Tri Cua Ban Chap Hanh Trung Uong Dang Tai Dai Hoi Dai Bieu Toan Quoc Lan Thu Nam' (Political Report of the Party's Central Executive Committee to the Fifth National Congress of Delegates), *Nhan Dan*, 29 March 1982.

29. William J. Duiker, 'Vietnamese Revolutionary Doctrine in Comparative Perspective', in William S. Turley (ed.), *Vietnamese Communism in Comparative Perspective*, Westview Press, Boulder, 1980, p. 45.
30. Ho Chi Minh, 'The Path Which Led Me to Leninism', in Bernard B. Fall (ed.), *Ho Chi Minh on Revolution: Selected Writings, 1920—66*, Praeger, New York, 1967, pp. 5–7.
31. Vu Tien, 'Tinh Hinh The Gioi va Chinh Sach Doi Ngoai cua Dang va Nha Nuoc Ta' (The World Situation and the Foreign Policy of Our Party and State), *Tap Chi Cong San*, 5 May 1982.
32. Paul Quinn-Judge, 'A Vietnamese Cassandra', *Far Eastern Economic Review*, cxv:9, 26 February 1982, pp. 14–16.
33. 'Bao Cao Chinh Tri', *Nhan Dan*, 28 March 1982.
34. Hoang Van Thai, 'Ve Quan He Hop Tac Dac Biet Giua Ba Dan Toc Dong Duong' (On the Special Relations of Cooperation Between the Three Indochinese Peoples), *Tap Chi Cong San*, 1 January 1982.
35. Lee E. Dutter and Raymond S. Kania, 'Explaining Recent Vietnamese Behavior', *Asian Survey*, xx:9, September 1980, pp. 931–42. Two failings of this otherwise excellent study are the authors' omission of several important contemporary studies as well as their neglecting to consult Vietnamese declaratory statements about their objectives and goals. See Carlyle A. Thayer, 'Vietnam in World Affairs', *Dyason House Papers*, III:5 (June 1977), pp. 5–8; Thayer, 'Foreign policy orientations of the Socialist Republic of Vietnam', in Kernial S. Sandhu (ed.), *Southeast Asian Affairs 1977*, Institute of Southeast Asian Studies, Singapore, 1977, pp. 306–24; Thayer, 'Vietnam's External Relations', *Pacific Community*, IX:2, January 1978, pp. 212–31; William J. Duiker, 'The Dynamics of Vietnam's Foreign Policy', in Kernial S. Sandhu (ed.), *Southeast Asian Affairs 1978*, Institute of Southeast Asian Studies, Singapore, 1978, pp. 312–24; and *Vietnam's Foreign Relations, 1975–1978*, Report prepared for the Subcommittee on Asian and Pacific Affairs of the Committee on Foreign Affairs US House of Representatives, US Government Printing Office, Washington, DC, June 1979. This report was written by Douglas Pike.

5 Arab and Israeli Perspectives on International Security

ROBERT SPRINGBORG

Any attempt to analyse Arab and Israeli perceptions of international security begs questions about precisely who those perceivers are, how stable over time those perceptions have been, and upon what evidence the analysis is based. These questions, which are of relevance to the inquiry as a whole, are particularly salient in this essay because of the enormous political diversity of the subjects under study; because of significant shifts over time in basic perceptions; and because of an unusually large discrepancy between public statements and private beliefs among both Arabs and Israelis. Precision requires, then, that the analyst disaggregate the actors into subgroups; that he plot perceptions over time; and that he attempt some form of 'propaganda analysis' whereby the public record can be linked to private beliefs. Unfortunately such an approach is beyond the scope of this paper. Space and other limitations require that observations be made at more general levels. Only very salient internal variations in actors' perceptions over time can be noted, while the data base and linkages between attitudes, expressions of them, and behaviour itself will have to remain largely unspecified. Inferences about perceptions will perforce be based on the author's interpretations, which in turn rest on evidence of various sorts, secondary and primary, and on a mainly implicit, simple model linking attitudes and behaviour. While the sacrifice in precision is regrettable, the more general approach used here may yield some useful insights, as some previous non-specific studies of Arab and Israeli perceptions have already done.[1] It may even be that by operating at a relatively general level the outlines of the forest of

Arab-Israeli perceptions of international security may better be perceived than through close scrutiny of individual trees.

THE MIDDLE EAST: THE SALIENCE OF REGIONALISM

It is appropriate to begin this chapter by specifying the unique in Middle Eastern perspectives of security. What most distinguishes the perceptions of Arabs and Israelis from those of other national political actors is the importance they assign to regional events. This reflects the fundamental underlying reality that the Middle East and the Arab world in particular are comparatively well integrated subsystems of international politics. Cultural, linguistic, religious and other similarities draw together Arab states to a degree that exceeds the bonds which tie together most neighbouring states in Africa, Southeast Asia, and so on. Consequently, the degree of political interaction between Arab states is remarkably high. Indeed, a series of attempts at political unification have punctuated the post-independence period. Even in the wake of impressive nation-building programmes, Arab political systems, with the possible exception of Egypt's, remain vulnerable to penetration by extra-national regional actors. The Lebanese civil war is the most profound recent example of the high degree of interventionism prevalent in the region. For its part, Israel is enmeshed in regional affairs by virtue of the fundamentally antagonistic relationship that exists between it and the Arabs.

Precisely because the Middle East is a political system in which unusually numerous, intense and multiplex interactions occur, it is natural that actors in that system assign to it primary importance. They are cognisant of the dependence of regime and national security on regional factors. Nasserism was but the most dramatic example of an ideological persuasion and political movement which enjoyed regional potency and the capability to destabilise even geographically remote political systems. In the multipolar Arab world of today there exists no equivalent pan-Arab force, although Islamic fundamentalism conceivably could assume such a role. But even with the maturation of the region's states and a fragmentation of power between them, the potential impact of region-wide political trends and events remains critical at the national level. Isolation within the Arab community is as feared by heads of states in the 1980s as it was during the heyday of Nasserism, and for precisely the same reason. Arab publics evaluate their leaders partly by their regional performance, so perceived failure at that level has devastating effects on regime legitimacy. The example of Anwar al Sadat struggling to maintain his authority in the wake of the separate peace with Israel, which sheared him of regional allies, suggests how regional isolation rebounds upon domestic political processes. Similarly, Hafiz al Assad, having manoeuvred Syria into a lonely corner by 1980, sought to salvage his regional and domestic positions through signing in that year a Treaty of Friendship and Cooperation with the Soviet Union. South Yemen's status as regional pariah has contributed significantly to elite instability there. The current president, Ali Nasir Muhamed, rose to power partly because he was identified with a policy of reintegration into inter-Arab affairs.

The impressive intensity and mind-boggling complexity of inter-Arab and Arab-Israeli interactions also has consequences for the Middle East's relations with the global system. External actors, including the superpowers, are precluded from monitoring the area's developments as closely and continuously as those geographically present are able to do. The US, USSR, EEC countries and others simply have too many other concerns to commit themselves full-time to Middle Eastern affairs, but it is not a region whose intricacies can be comprehended adequately on a part-time basis. Not surprising, then, is the fact that the *aficionados* of that game, including Middle Eastern elites and attentive publics, consider Americans, Soviets and other outsiders to be woefully ignorant of the basic motivations, strategies and tactics of regional actors. It is in this dim light in which outsiders are struggling to perceive reality that the Arabs and Israelis manoeuvre to cast themselves in the most advantageous perspective. Bitter enemies on most issues, Arabs and Israelis share common cause in deceiving onlookers over various aspects of their respective political ways and means.

Similarly, they both view the Soviets and Americans as if they were big, tough, but rather stupid hit men whose clumsiness must be endured as the price of their assistance. To ensure that support it is further thought necessary to deceive, flatter, and even bribe the benefactor. So aspects of Soviet and American ideologies and political, social, economic and administrative systems are imported holus-bolus and then displayed as evidence of shared values, heritage, and aspirations. Regional opponents are depicted as lackeys of the contending superpower, and key Soviet and American elites are lobbied energetically. Such duplicity is naturally degrading and irritating to those who are forced to engage in it, but it is a strategy dictated by the structure of inegalitarian relationships.

Another repercussion at the global level of the Middle East's relative integration as a subsystem of international politics is that third-party intervention tends to be indirect. In pursuing their objectives in the area, the superpowers do so through regional allies/clients rather than unilaterally. They do so not out of choice, but out of political necessity. Direct intervention is fraught with greater perils here than elsewhere. While the Philippines can openly host the American Navy at Subic Bay, Arabs talk of 'facilities' and Americans speak of 'over the horizon' capabilities. The Rapid Deployment Force was no sooner conceived than it became bogged down in regional politics. Potential beneficiaries of that deployment assessed the regional political costs as outweighing the military benefits. Nationalisms of the area are extraordinarily sensitive to superpower encroachments, and although that does not preclude Soviet and US involvement, it requires that it be mediated through friendly governments. Moreover, the presence of Soviet and US military equipment and personnel may be legitimated only if directly focused on acceptable regional targets. Soviet bases for the purpose of patrolling the Mediterranean Sea contributed in no small measure to Egyptian hostility toward the Soviets. The use of Egyptian and Omani bases in the Iranian hostage rescue attempt was initially not revealed and subsequently became a regional embarrassment to both Sultan Qaboos and President Sadat. Thus, while Soviet and US forces prowl more or less at will out of military bases in many other parts of the Third World, in the Middle East they are kept on a comparatively short leash.

As a final observation on the salience of regionalism it should be re-emphasised that it is regional politics which are seen by Arabs as the key shield with which to protect their states from international intervention. Nasser's adventurism was inspired at least as much by the desire to build for Egypt a defensive regional coalition as it was by any other incentive. Conversely, a condition of isolation within the region is the key that unlocks the door to direct retribution by a superpower. Thus, Qadhafi's planes could be shot down over the Gulf of Sirte, for the US was fully cognisant of his precarious perch in inter-Arab affairs. Syria likewise has on several occasions made itself a target for intervention by having failed adequately to mend regional fences. In 1970, for example, Henry Kissinger could contemplate putting the Israelis on the road to Damascus, for the radical wing of the Baath, then in its last stand as ruler of Syria, had shorn itself of significant regional support.

Since it is both domestic and global considerations that lead decision-makers in the Arab world to seek salvation in regional affairs, inter-Arab politics are propelled along at a rapid clip whose momentum is only in part self-generated. Disentangling regime, national, regional and global security considerations is thus inordinately difficult, so the resolution of regional problems, not least of which is the Arab-Israeli conflict, is well nigh impossible. Like a large family, the Middle East region is the chief source of support for its members while simultaneously being their main cause of frustration.

ARAB–ISRAELI GLOBAL PERCEPTIONS

Just as Arabs and Israelis both apprehend regional affairs as crucial for national security, so do they hold in common other perceptions of security, although the substance of those perceptions is reversed in mirror image fashion. Malcolm Kerr has correctly observed, for example, that Arabs and Israelis both have a sense of their own unique historical destinies; that they hold caricaturised images of their adversaries; that they believe they must force a fundamental change in their enemy's character and outlook; and that their political attitudes are coloured by religion and quasi-religious symbolism.[2] While Kerr's and other studies have focused on Arab and Israeli self-images and images of one another, structural similarity also characterises their perceptions of international politics, as a review of those dominant perceptions suggests.

Of primary importance is that both parties to this enduring conflict believe themselves and their dispute to be central to the global balances of power, East–West and North–South. Underpinning this belief are several subsidiary assumptions, some based on assessments of geopolitical and/or military-economic factors, and others on less tangible, more psychological considerations. The Arabs, for example, view themselves as natural leaders of the South and as such those most able to mobilise resources in the struggle against the North. In support of this claim they refer to the history of OPEC, to the leading role played by Arab financial institutions in providing funds for Third World development projects, to the prominent role played by Arabs in the emergency 1974 World Food Conference and in other international fora, and so on. Arabs further believe that as a consequence of such activism they have been most exposed to the wrath and retribution of the developed world. The 1967 War is widely viewed as a plot hatched jointly by Israel, the US and Arab 'reactionaries' to destroy Arab nationalism and prevent it from over-running the oil fields of the peninsula. Repeated threats by prominent US spokesmen to seize the oil fields and allegations that oil price rises were solely responsible for world financial dislocations are seen as efforts to deny Arabs the right to use their only precious natural resource as they see fit. By extension this represents in their eyes a broader assault by the industrialised North on the raw material exporting South.

But while the Arabs see themselves as the vanguard of the South, they also perceive themselves, possibly paradoxically, as the primary interlocutor between North and South. The geographical and historical Arab role as middleman between the West and Africa/Asia has blossomed into a new and larger self-image, with Arab acumen, flexibility, and cosmopolitanism, backed up by petrodollars, imagined as being the resources necessary and sufficient for becoming the world's chief mediator. One manifestation of this role is the very structure of the International Fund for Agricultural Development (IFAD), created in 1977 with three voting blocs – OECD countries, non-oil exporting LDCs, and the oil exporting Arab states interposed between the other two. But whether it is as vanguard in a North–South confrontation or as middleman in a North–South dialogue, the Arabs perceive themselves as playing the crucial role, capable of tilting the balance either through economic leverage or skilful persuasion.

A similarly pivotal role is self-cast for the Arabs in the East–West balance of power. From the objective observation that the Middle East has become the key area of the globe for superpower confrontation, the subjective interpretation is that the most numerous inhabitants of that area, Arabs, are able to tilt the balance of power by shifting their weight in an eastward or westward direction. When the Arab masses fell into line behind Nasserism and the leader of that movement aligned his fate with the Soviet Union, not only was the West's role in the Middle East undermined, but the Soviet global position was greatly enhanced. Conversely, Sadat's expulsion of the Soviets from Egypt, his unilateral cancellation of Egyptian debts to the Soviet Union and abrogation of the Friendship Treaty with the USSR, not only reduced to insignificance the Soviet role in Egypt, but it paved the way for similar, although less dramatic measures elsewhere in the Arab world, particularly Iraq. Moreover, the Egyptian example demonstrated globally that the Soviets were paper tigers who could easily be defanged by other 'client' states dissatisfied with their subordinate status.

The Arab shift toward the West has had similar consequences, or at least so the Arabs would have us think. The virtual exclusion of the Soviets from the Gulf and their much reduced presence in the Arab heartland, other than Syria, coupled with increased Western economic and military presence in these areas, has more than compensated the latter for the catastrophe of Vietnam and Southeast Asia more generally. Western gains in the strategic Middle East made possible by Arab cooperation are, because of the strategically vital nature of the area, far more important than alterations in regional balances of power elsewhere in the Third World. Based on this premise the Arabs conclude that the West has been ungrateful for the friendship and assistance it has received. By continuing to support Israel, thereby risking Arab support, the West is in danger of squandering the gains it has made since the period when radical Arab nationalism, aligned with the USSR, had the region's pro-Westerners on the run. Viewed in this light the Arab struggle against Israel assumes heavyweight status in the world balance of power. It is to the consternation of Arabs, most notably the Saudis who have the most to lose, that this apparent fact is not more widely recognised and acted upon.

For their part the Israelis are also convinced of their irreplaceable contribution to the global balance. Were it not for Israel's presence in the area and its implacable resistance to radical Arab nationalism and pan-Islamicism, both stalking horses for international communism, the West would be faced with an impossible dilemma. Either it would have to intervene directly, in which case the fires of Arab nationalism would flare up, or it would be compelled to sit back and watch the Soviets fulfil the Tsarist ambition of gaining access to a warm-water port in the south. Moreover, according to Israeli logic, the Jewish state is not serving Western interests on a tit-for-tat, *quid pro quo* basis. Instead it is acting as a bulwark against anti-Western forces precisely because it is an extension into the Orient of the West and Western civilisation broadly conceived. Unlike any Arab-Western alliance, which could only be based on pragmatism and a transitory coincidence of interest, the Israeli-Western connection rests on the bedrock of shared cultural values. Its long-term durability is not jeopardised by short-term vacillations. For this reason, Israelis (echoing the Arab lament) bemoan the fact that the West fails adequately to recognise their singularly valuable contribution to the strategic balance. That the American public should be grumbling about massive military and civilian aid to Israel reveals how little they appreciate what the Jewish State is actually doing for them.

The argument that Israel serves the West as a vital outpost has to Israelis more than just regional implications. Like the Arabs, they see the Middle East as the vital cockpit of the East–West confrontation. As such it is important not only because of events actually occurring there, but because of what is perceived to be happening. That is, if the West falters in its support of Israel and as a result the Arab–Moslem–Communist forces of darkness triumph, the symbolic importance of that event would reverberate around the globe. In comparison, the American failure to rescue the Shah's regime would pale into insignificance. Enemies of the West and its system of values, newly emboldened, would mount challenges on a global scale. Thus, according to this logic, the West has no choice, culturally, morally or pragmatically, but to continue to support Israel at levels sufficient to guarantee its security and standing as a prosperous, Western enclave.

Although the intensity of Israeli perceptions is much greater on East–West than on North–South issues, it can be gathered from the above observations that the two overlap, particularly in Israeli thinking. According to them countries of the South, being have-nots, tend naturally to ally with anti-Westerners, i.e. the Soviet Union. To prevent this, the West must constantly demonstrate to the South the advantages it offers, chief of which (and most easily transportable) is technology. But Americans and Europeans are handicapped by their very national origins, so the political value of that technology transfer is diminished. But Israelis are not so handicapped. Of the West and South simultaneously, they are uniquely well equipped to be the bearers of Western technology and values to Southern recipients. So while in the Middle East arena Israel's military superiority is crucial to the West, on a global scale her continued ability to conduct development aid programmes is essential to the North.

The self-serving aspects of these perceptions are all too apparent. In aggrandising their regional and global roles, Arabs and Israelis are seeking to lay the groundwork for outside assistance to be used against one another, while simultaneously rationalising the sacrifices made by those rendering that assistance as done out of self-interest, whether perceived or not. The perceptual worlds of both, hence their foreign policy strategies, rest on the unquestioned assumptions that the Middle East region is the swing weight in both the East–West and North–South balances of power and that the Arab (or Israeli) position in the Middle East is the determining one. Basic perceptions of this sort are rarely put to a test, but if one were applied it would presumably reveal inaccuracies in one or the other, or both, of these belief systems.

That prospect does not, however, affect the tenacity and conviction with which they currently are held.

THE AMERICAN ROLE IN THE REGION

Arabs and Israelis also share a belief in American pre-eminence. For Israelis, this view dates back to the immediate post-war period, when it had become clear that the US was emerging as the leader of the Western Alliance. This belief received confirmation in the Middle East setting during and after the 1956 Suez War, when European limitations and US capabilities were abundantly demonstrated. Since then this conviction has not altered, although Israelis frequently bemoan the erratic application of US power. It is American resolve, not capabilities, that is questioned.

For Arabs the situation is more complex. With regard to the dimension of power, most Arab elites came reluctantly to the conclusion of US supremacy in the Middle East only after the 1973 War. Previously, perceptions of global power as projected into the Middle East rested on calculations of a nexus between regional movements and the great powers or superpowers. In the liberal phase of Arab politics, which obtained during the colonial period, faith was placed in Western political oppositions, whose occasional rhetoric in support of Arab independence movements was taken as an indication of intent and capability. In the event, they were neither. Following independence a radical nationalist phase ensued, in which the nexus was seen as an alliance between state-building radical nationalism and global anti-Western forces, which were the non-aligned movement and then the USSR. Again neither external supporter was up to the tasks which the Arabs had assigned to it, as the 1967 War so conclusively demonstrated. In the wake of that disaster a sort of Arab Maoism made its appearance, but it was too weak and unpredictable for even the Great Leader himself to show much interest. So by the early 1970s one conclusion had become inescapable: the US did hold 99 per cent of the cards in the Middle East. While the moderates realised this even before Sadat sent the Soviets packing, the Israeli invasion of Lebanon in 1982 and the failure of radical Arabs and their Soviet ally to provide a meaningful deterrent, brought even the most reluctant and diehard radicals to a similar conclusion. By acclaim America is now seen as having 100 per cent of the cards in that same, interminable Middle Eastern poker game.

But power and intentions are not the same thing. Moderate and radical Arabs agree on US possession of the former, while nevertheless disagreeing as to what determines its use. For the Arabs, as for the Israelis, it is critical to know whether US support for the latter grows out of the neo-Crusader spirit of the Jewish State as an extension of Western civilisation, or whether it is just the result of transitory political factors, chief of which is the pervasiveness of the Zionist lobby. Radical Arabs, whether Marxist or Islamic fundamentalist, know the answer – US support for Israel results from systemic factors. The operative system for Marxists is class struggle and imperialism, in which the materialist dialectic drives the US into an alliance with Israel for the purpose of permanently subordinating Third World polities and economies. For fundamentalists the systemic substructure is religious. The Christian West's current alliance with Jews against Muslims is simply another chapter in the dialectical confrontation of the past fourteen centuries in which Muslims have always been pitted against Western opponents. In the dialectics of both one conclusion emerges – for systemic reasons the US–Israeli alliance is unbreakable. It is folly even to attempt to tamper with it. Because US intentions are immutable, it is only US power that can be altered. The correct strategy must therefore be to confront that power and overwhelm it.

Moderate Arabs tend to interpret US support for Israel as the result of Zionist manipulation rather than the consequence of historical determinism. Given their interpretation, American power need not be confronted for US intentions can be changed. Specifically, the US must be disengaged from Israel, a requirement that demands more rather than fewer connections between Arabs and the US. This viewpoint implies that the chief battlefield is Washington and that the requisite ammunition is public opinion polls, letters to Congressmen, and skilful lobbying in the corridors of power, rather than conventional military ordinance. The latter may prove useful, but ultimately it is the carrot rather than the stick that will bring results. The Soviet connection is likewise useful only to the degree that it can be manipulated to bring pressure to bear on the US, but it must be used very sparingly. It is a dangerous two-edged sword, as Nasser and Arafat learned. When wielded it stirs the passions of anti-communism in the US and renders its users vulnerable to Israeli allegations of being a Soviet lackey. Even King Hussein of Jordan has learned the dangers associated with trips to Moscow, while Sadat felt that his task would be easier if he jettisoned the Soviets altogether.

That moderate Arabs are presently ascendant should not, however, be taken to mean that future Middle Eastern struggles are inevitably going to pit only Arab lobbyists against their Israeli counterparts in Washington. Indeed, the current perception of US hegemony is fraught with peril for all sides. For the Arabs there remains the alternative interpretation of American motives. Witnessing little progress in negotiations over an Israeli withdrawal from Lebanon and virtually no movement on Reagan peace plans, to say absolutely nothing of the Arab plan agreed upon at Fez, initially Arab publics and subsequently Arab elites will fall in behind those who interpret US intentions within a systemic framework. If the US is driven by imperialism and/or anti-Muslim beliefs, then what point is there in hiring Washington law firms to fight Arab battles? Victory in the Middle East can be won only there, not 5000 miles away in North America, or so it will increasingly be argued. So the moderates have but a brief period in which to win their political battles in Washington. If they fail, those who call for a rejection of working within the US dominated regional system in favour of an all-out confrontation will again be back in the saddle.

It should be noted in passing that American perceptions may also play an important role in the unravelling of the current *modus operandi*. Having been told by one and all that the US dominates the Middle East, American decision-makers may make the mistake of actually believing it, overlooking the fact that power is as much a perceptual phenomenon as it is a reality. Given the volatility of Arab perceptions, complacency in Washington is entirely unwarranted, for US hegemony rests on delicate foundations, whose strength many Arabs would already like to test.

The fragility of the current situation is further accentuated when one considers the Israeli perspective. Reference was previously made to Israeli doubts about American intentions – to the belief that the US is powerful but lacks the will to use that power consistently and decisively. Surprisingly the Reagan administration has not dispelled that belief, suggesting to the Israelis it may be a chronic problem rather than just a malady which afflicted Jimmy Carter. This perception is more significant than it might first seem, for it is also bound up in a resentment of US power. Israelis increasingly are persuaded of the view that they are tougher, more adept at the art of war, more 'understanding' of their antagonists, indeed altogether more competent than their superpower patron, who dominates only by virtue of size. In short, American patronage is distrusted, resented and belittled. The argument that Israel can 'go it alone' is heard increasingly and this sentiment has a widening sociological foundation in the Sephardic community. This bellicose attitude chastises the US for not recognising and appreciating gains won through the bombing of the Iraqi reactor, the invasion of Lebanon, the settling of the West Bank, and so on. Neo-Revisionist Zionists who hold to these beliefs are fiercely independent and not inclined to heed cautionary words from US decision-makers, who are seen alternatively as weak, dupes of the oil-rich Arabs, or possibly anti-Semites.

In sum, the situation is reminiscent of the old Palestine mandate, with the US occupying the unenviable role of the former mandatory power. Caught in the middle the US cannot deliver to either the Israelis or the Arabs sufficient for them to be reconciled to the claims of the other party. Unable to resolve the fundamental issues, the best the US can hope for is to continue to be perceived as the only outside force capable of arbitrating the dispute. But if the mandate analogy holds, even that state of affairs will not continue indefinitely. In 1939 the British, after crushing the Arab rebellion and issuing the White Paper that limited Jewish migration, seemed at the height of their powers. Yet less than a decade passed before their inglorious departure. It does not seem far-fetched to imagine that the US 'mandate' over the Arab-Israeli conflict, having been fully assumed only in recent years, will likewise be terminated sooner than most observers now imagine. The perceptual base for the erosion of the mandate already exists among both Arabs and Israelis and seems now to be widening.

THE ROLE OF OTHER ACTORS IN THE REGION

It remains to comment on Arab and Israeli perceptions of other global actors, which like those views discussed above tend to be remarkably similar, although reversed in their evaluative dimensions. Put crudely and simply, but hopefully accurately, Arabs and Israelis perceive global actors other than the US, including the USSR, other OECD countries, and the states of the Third World, as important only in so far as they affect US–Middle Eastern relations. Because individually and collectively none of these actors has demonstrated a consistent capability singlehandedly to influence events in the region, their status is downgraded to that of secondary actors whose chief input is through the US. Even the Soviet Union is cast in this role, although in diametrically opposed ways. For the Israelis the Soviets are important because Moscow's ties to the Arabs, real or putative, are crucial to the argument that the Arab states and the PLO are under Moscow's thumb. This has been the Israeli *deus ex machina* on Capitol Hill since the early 1950s. In its absence it is hard to imagine Israel benefiting so conspicuously and continuously from the American largesse.

For Arabs, the Soviets have been the joker in the pack; a card which they play occasionally in the hope of frightening the US into backing away from Israel. But the US holds too many cards and has been playing the game too long to be bluffed by that Soviet joker, which they know in any case is flawed by Moscow's limited commitment to the Arabs. Since Soviet success in the region has been built on Arab failures, it is hardly credible that Moscow is going to give the game away by underwriting an unqualified Arab victory.

OECD countries other than the US enter Arab and Israeli calculations in much the same way. Arabs try to play the European card in the sense that they work to induce pro-Arab stances by European states for the purpose of pressuring the US. The British, French, Germans, and others are useful to the Arabs not because they can accomplish anything on their own in the region, but because their actions may have favourable repercussions in Washington. So far Arabs have enjoyed only limited success in this manoeuvre, for the hard facts of the matter are that the European states depend psychologically and physically on the US for their security. They are not about to throw that security guarantee away for the sake of the Arabs.

Because of this structural condition, the Israelis have had to play only a marginal role in confronting the Arab challenge in Europe. The Israeli approach has been to depict the Europeans to the crucial American audience as having gone soft, as being effete, frightened of the Soviets and essentially lacking the will to resist outside pressure, be it Soviet or Arab. Pro-Arab stances by Europeans are explained as a result of Eurocommunist machinations, of politicians succumbing to oil blackmail, or to the lure of petrodollar markets. In short, while both the Arabs and Israelis devote considerable diplomatic efforts to OECD countries, and especially European ones, the general impression is that for both sides these activities are a sideshow, a place where young diplomats cut their teeth preparing for the more important game that is played in Washington.

Arab and Israeli perceptions of Europe and the Soviet Union within the context of their relations with the US are paralleled by their perceptions of the Third World. For Israel in particular bilateral relations with the countries of Africa, Asia and Latin America are virtually an extension of US-Israeli relations. Military and development assistance to the countries of Central America, to Zaire and elsewhere in Africa and Asia is for Israel perceived as a means by which it can further ingratiate itself with the US, while simultaneously winning some kudos for itself. Thus, to Israel countries of the Third World provide opportunities for consolidating the US lifeline. In and of themselves, they have to Israel very marginal significance in world politics.

The Arab approach is somewhat different. While Arabs are likewise seeking to gain Third World support to bring to bear on US policy in the Middle East, they attempt to do so not through ingratiation with the US but through mobilising countervailing pressure. But post-1973 Arab successes in Africa in particular have demonstrated the limitations of Third World influence on US policy, to say nothing of having revealed the fickleness of African states. These developments, coupled with the increased salience of the religious bond, have caused Arab states to concentrate greater efforts on fellow Muslim countries, stretching from Pakistan to the Philippines. While some of the most enthusiastic Arab champions of political Islam dream of creating a potent new force in international affairs through the mobilisation of Islamic states, most Arab political elites look upon this as an impossible task. To them Muslim states are politically analogous to European ones in the sense that their support for the Arab cause brings pressure to bear on the US. Being realists, however, they recognise that European support is of considerably greater benefit than that of Third World states, Muslim or non-Muslim.

CONCLUSIONS

In conclusion, it should be emphasised that the Arab and Israeli perceptions discussed above are likely to undergo significant change within a relatively short period. Arab perceptions are the more transient for theirs are less well institutionalised political systems and they have had to suffer the continual frustration of coming out second best in their endless struggle with Israel. As they search continuously for an answer to that problem so does their construction of global political reality constantly evolve.

The Israelis, on the other hand, have benefited from a firmly institutionalised political system and from being the victor in wars against Palestinians and Arab states. Having not to tamper because of success, Israeli perceptions have evolved in a comparatively restricted political space. But there are reasons to believe that Israeli perceptions may be undergoing a profound metamorphosis. A backlash against dependence on American patronage is developing rapidly and coupled with internal demographic changes it could profoundly affect future Israeli perceptions of the global and regional security balances and Israel's roles within them.

It should finally be noted that a great many Arabs and Israelis would take exception to the characterisation here of their dominant belief systems. Indeed, very complex perceptual worlds have been grossly simplified. Moreover, a plethora of viewpoints not only exists, it is commendable. The evolution of political thinking is akin to a Darwinian struggle, with more appropriate adaptations eventually driving out the less appropriate. The presence of a multitude of competitive political perceptions is therefore necessary if reality testing and subsequent adjustment are to prove effective. And of course it is encouraging to believe that incorrect ideas, along with their political manifestations, eventually do end up on the scrap heaps of history, a fate which both Arabs and Israelis fervently hope awaits the other.

NOTES

1. See e.g. Malcolm H. Kerr, 'The Arabs and Israelis: Perceptual Dimensions to their Dilemma', in Willard A. Beling (ed.), *The Middle East: Quest for an American Policy*, Suny Press, Albany, 1973; and Stephen P. Cohen and Edward E. Azar, 'The Psycho-Political Dimensions of the Transition from War to Peace in the Middle East', paper delivered to the International Studies Association Convention at Los Angeles, March 1980. See also, John Edwin Mroz, *Beyond Security: Private Perceptions Among Arabs and Israelis*, Pergamon Press, New York, 1979.
2. Kerr, op. cit.

6 Perspectives from the Gulf: Regime Security or Regional Security?

MOHAMMED AYOOB

INTRODUCTION

In the Western and, one might add, the Soviet perception of international security, the oil-rich Gulf occupies a position of importance second only to that of the central theatre of the original Cold War – Europe. A decade after the Organisation of Arab Petroleum Exporting Countries (OAPEC) oil embargo of 1973 there is no need to belabour the point that, despite the current glut in the oil market, the downward trend in the price of oil, and the display of disunity within Organisation of Petroleum Exporting Countries (OPEC) on questions of production quota and price, continued access to Gulf oil at prices that the market can bear without accelerating recessionary processes in the international capitalist economy remains of paramount importance for developed and developing countries alike. The Iranian Revolution of 1978–9, which reduced oil production drastically and doubled oil prices in 1979, and the continuing war between Iran and Iraq have made consumers of Gulf oil apprehensive about long-term supply trends, particularly in the context of the volatility of the region and the assessment that the problems of the Gulf are inextricably intertwined with larger Middle Eastern issues (primarily the Arab–Israeli conflict) and cannot be tackled in isolation from them. Paradoxically, this nervousness is demonstrated in the barely concealed glee amongst the major consumers of OPEC oil at the current problems being faced by oil producers, particularly the Arab producers.

The three major events which have affected oil supplies and prices in the last decade – the OAPEC embargo, the Islamic Revolution in Iran, and Iraq's invasion of Iran – have also demonstrated that at least the larger countries in the Gulf have the capacity (given the political will) to act autonomously of the dominant powers within the international system, thereby introducing unanticipated complexities into the problem of Gulf (and, therefore, international) security.

In the first case, namely the OAPEC embargo of 1973 imposed in retaliation for the massive US airlift of sophisticated weaponry to Israel during the October War, it was Saudi Arabia which was at least partly responsible for the initiative which led to the embargo despite Riyadh's close links with Washington. The Islamic Revolution and the overthrow of the Shah of Iran was the result primarily of domestic factors, ranging from disgruntlement with the Shah's oppressive regime to opposition to Tehran's international connections, particularly with Washington. Aimed as much against the US as against the Pahlavi monarch, the revolutionary process demonstrated the Iranian political system's capacity to act autonomously even to a degree that changed the entire balance of power in the region. Again, Iraq's decision to invade Iran in September 1980 – whatever the immediate ostensible reason and whatever the external encouragement – was taken for reasons that were primarily determined by calculations regarding the security of Saddam Hussein's Baathist regime and the desire to change the status quo on the Shatt-al-Arab that Iraq had been forced to accept in 1975 as a result of Iran's power superiority in the region under the Shah.

In light of these events, it is logical to analyse Gulf perspectives of international and regional security from the point of view of the three leading powers of the Gulf littoral: Iran, Saudi Arabia and Iraq. However, since more often than not these perspectives are related to, if not the product of, concerns about regime security, the discussion of regional and national security in the Gulf inevitably tends to centre on issues of regime security, particularly as perceived by the respective regimes themselves.

THE FACTORS SHAPING GULF PERSPECTIVES

In order to be able to analyse in greater depth the Gulf regimes' perceptions of their own security as well as their perceptions of national and regional security, it would be useful to distinguish the dominant ideologies, social and economic policies, foreign orientations, and threat perceptions. For only by distinguishing the three actors across this entire spectrum can one begin to appraise realistically their (or their dominant elites') perceptions of problems of regional security and the bases for common or divergent approaches to such problems.

Table 6.1 presents a rough typology based on the categories mentioned above which will provide the reader with a basic appreciation of the nature of politics within Iran, Iraq and Saudi Arabia. These characteristics are, of necessity, defined broadly. Of the five major characteristics mentioned in the table, it seems the first two, dominant ideology and the nature of the regime, largely determine the latter three, socio-economic policies, foreign orientation and threat perception. Moreover, since the dominant ideology in a state is largely a function of the nature of its regime (particularly in the Gulf states where ideological competition is frowned upon), problems of regime security (which are in the dominant elites' perception closely intertwined with, if not indistinguishable from, national and regional security) seem to be the central ones in the security perception of the rulers of these three states. Therefore, we first must turn to the Iranian, Saudi and Iraqi dominant elites' perceptions of regime security in order to determine their approach to larger questions of national and regional (and, therefore, international) security.

In studying these regimes what is most striking is the feeling of insecurity that they share. The Iranian regime, emerging gradually from the throes of a revolution which saw the elimination first of the liberal component of the post-revolutionary dominant order and then of the non-clerical 'Islamic–Marxist' radicals, is still plagued by factionalism within the ruling Islamic Republican Party (IRP), although these factions seem to have more in common than they are given credit for by most analysts.[1] In addition to factionalism within the IRP, the Iranian regime faces enormous problems of economic and social dislocation caused by years of revolutionary upheaval, as well as by the war with Iraq which began in September 1980.

It is, therefore, no wonder that the current leaders of Iran, with this history of struggle behind them, have come to equate the security of the revolutionary regime and the system it has imposed upon Iran with the security of the nation and to work on that assumption. This is why they make no bones about the fact that the revolution's, and Iran's, security depends first upon the elimination of those elements from the power structure whom they consider to be anti- or counter-

Perspectives from the Gulf

TABLE 6.1 *Typology of politics in Gulf States*

Major characteristics	Iran	Saudi Arabia	Iraq
Dominant ideology	Radical Islam	Conservative Islam	Secular; non-Marxist; socialist; Arab nationalist
Nature of regime	Revolutionary; clergy dominated	Conservative; monarchical; familial	Reformist; single-party; narrowly based in terms of region and sect
Socio-economic policies	Radical	Conservative	Reformist
Foreign orientation	Genuinely non-aligned, 'neither East nor West'	Pro-West, linked to the US in security relationship	Nominally non-aligned but with pro-Soviet tilt in matters of arms supply. (Recently adopted a more equidistant policy.)
Threat perception(s) of dominant elite, in order of priority	1. Internal–ideological 2. Iraq 3. USA/USSR 4. Israel 5. Internal – autonomist	1. Iran 2. Israel 3. Soviet Union/ Communism 4. Internal	1. Iran 2. Israel 3. Internal – *Shia* 4. Internal – Kurdish

revolutionary. The war against Iraq and the struggle against superpower hegemony are accorded secondary importance when compared to the struggle against internal opposition. However, in the world view of the Iranian leadership, the three threats – from internal opposition, from Iraq, and from the superpowers (with Israel considered a sidekick of the US) – seen as interlinked have to be met and defeated simultaneously if the revolution is to survive. But they feel that the internal threat (not so much the autonomy-oriented opposition of the ethnic minorities as the ideological one posed by the Islamic left, particularly the Mujahedin) has to be eliminated first, because without success on the domestic front the other battles cannot be waged successfully.[2]

While the initial ideological cleavage in post-revolutionary Iran was between the secular and Islamic liberals on the one hand, and the *ulama* and their lay allies on the other, once the Bazargan government had been ousted in November 1979 and the majority of the liberals had been neutralised politically, the IRP made the radical Mujahedin its foremost target. This appeared almost inevitable given the fact that both the radical *ulama*, who constituted the backbone of the IRP, and the Mujahedin drew their political appeal from the same ideological sources and premises (such as the operationalisation of Islam as the 'refuge of the dispossessed' in the political sphere) and their political support from the same constituency of the *mustazafin* (the oppressed), composed of what Keddie has called the 'sub-proletariat' primarily in the urban ghettoes of Iran – a class which had been produced by the mass migration of the rural poor into the urban areas under the Shah.[3]

It has become increasingly clear over the last two years that, despite major setbacks, such as the assassination of a substantial proportion of its top leadership in June 1981, the IRP has been able to gain the political and the ideological initiative over its opponents in the internal power struggle in Iran.[4] A major reason for the IRP's success at home is its demonstrated ability to ward off the Iraqi and the superpower threats. The Iraqi invasion demonstrated to the average Iranian the truth of the Iranian regime's assertion that the security of Iran and of the Revolution were indistinguishable from the security of the regime. It thereby cemented national unity within Iran and facilitated the mobilisation of the nation's material and human resources on the scale required to defeat the aggressor.

As for the threat from the superpowers, particularly from the US, the Islamic regime has found no difficulty in presenting American antagonism towards it as aimed against the Iranian nation as a whole.

Given the total identification of the US with the Shah and the mass revulsion against the monarch during the last years of his rule, this was not a difficult task. American policy after the revolution also played into the hands of Iran's revolutionary rulers, particularly the decision to admit the Shah into the US, and later Washington's portrayal of Bani Sadr as the 'rational' element in a predominantly 'irrational' decision-making apparatus. The former act led to the taking of American hostages in November 1979 and the end of the Bazargan period of government. The latter led to the near-total discrediting of Bani Sadr because the IRP utilised it to portray him as the new American surrogate in Iran.

If the Iranian threat perception is coloured to such a large extent by the ideological proclivities of its dominant elite, the Saudi case is not much different, except that in this case the ideological prism through which the Saudi rulers view the world is clouded by their assessment of what is good for the House of Saud, particularly for its leading princes. That the state and the royal family are equated in the minds of the Saudi rulers is evident from the very name given to the state – *Saudi Arabia*. There is probably no other state in the world that is identified so directly with the family that rules it.

Another, equally important, element in the creation of the Saudi state was the use of puritanical Hanbali Islam (popularly known in the West as Wahhabism after its principal exponent Muhammad Ibn Abdul Wahhab), both for purposes of mobilising the Najdi townsmen and tribes for the consolidation of the state and for its expansion, and later for according the state and the ruling house legitimacy within the peninsula, the Arab world and the larger Muslim world. The Islamic factor in the quest for Saudi legitimacy was augmented with the conquest of the Hijaz which made the Saudis the protectors of the holiest places in Islam, Mecca and Medina. In the 1950s, with the growth of pan-Arab nationalist sentiment in the Middle East symbolised by Nasser, the Arab factor in the Saudi legitimacy myth increased in saliency. This became particularly important in the context of the 'Arab Cold War' waged from 1956 to 1967 between the 'radical' (or 'progressive') Arab states led by Nasser and the 'conservative', pro-Western ones led by Saudi Arabia.[5] Saudi policy, particularly foreign policy, therefore, had to be justified by reference to pan-Arab ideals which in the 1970s came to be, at least in rhetoric, almost synonymous with the restoration of Palestinian rights.

The oil boom of the 1970s, with the Saudis cornering a large part of the OPEC market, formed the icing on this triple-layered cake (familial, Islamic, Arab) of Saudi political and security concerns. With the petrodollars pouring in, ambitious development projects were launched from above, including the building of two new industrial cities. Billions of dollars also were spent on the purchase of the most sophisticated weaponry from the US and its allies. According to most Western observers of the Saudi scene, this phenomenal growth of the 'modern' sector of the economy has created a dichotomy in the social structure of Saudi Arabia which may have destabilising effects on a political power structure based on the traditional pattern of royal and tribal authority. While this might be the case to some extent, the dichotomy thesis does not adequately explain the realities of political life in Saudi Arabia. A more satisfactory explanation is provided by Niblock, who argues that this thesis 'does not take into account the extent to which the old and the new are interlinked, with both "forces" serving common purposes. Those parts of the social structure which are usually termed "traditional" have often played a central role in creating a framework upon which "modern" economic development could proceed. Likewise these modernisation programmes have often constituted a key element in reinforcing the power of the traditional structures of authority. The large number of highly qualified personnel in the present Saudi government, while usually presented as an aspect of modernisation, is also evidence of the power of the traditional structures.'[6]

From this one can conclude, as Niblock does, that 'the key to understanding the direction of developments in Saudi Arabia – and to explaining the paradox of a traditional regime undertaking a vast programme of economic modernisation – is not to be found in competition between the forces of modernism and traditionalism, but rather in the attempt by leading elements (whether 'traditionalist' or 'modernist') to ensure the continued viability of the regime'.[7] This conclusion highlights the fact that the challenges to regime security in Saudi Arabia come not so much from the modernised section of the ruling elite as from those social groups that consider themselves at a disadvantage both as a result of the consolidation of traditional Saudi power and as a result of the process of modernisation which has created its own contradictions within the modern sector of Saudi society. For at the apex of Saudi society the traditional and the modern sectors complement, as well as use, each other to preserve the viability of the regime in which both sectors have a tremendous stake.

From the above discussion it becomes clear that for the Saudi rulers the various levels of security are interlinked, from the family to the state to the region, because Saudi Arabia is basically a family enterprise which is in the process of evolving into a joint stock company but with the large majority of shares securely held by members of the royal family. However, because of the peculiar nature of the Saudi state, which results from its origins and developments, its role as the guardian of the Islamic holy places, its small demographic but mammoth economic resources, and its inter-Arab and international alignments, the Saudi regime can ensure its viability and security only by ensuring its legitimacy not only within the kingdom but within the Arab and Muslim worlds as well.[8] This is why its foreign policy and security concerns go beyond the narrow confines of the Gulf and encompass most salient issues that dominate the political landscape of the Middle East heartland. Predominant among these is, of course, the Arab–Israeli conflict, particularly its Palestinian dimension. The Palestinian cause is still the touchstone by which the Arab credentials of regimes, particularly the oil-rich and pro-Western ones, in the Middle East are judged. William Quandt has summarised the dilemma facing the Saudi rulers on this issue by saying that

> The Saudis will remain committed to the Palestinian cause, for no other issue in the Arab world is potentially as divisive as this one. After a generation of nationalist agitation on behalf of Palestinian rights, no Arab regime is prepared to abandon the struggle entirely whatever the sentiments of the ruling elites may be toward Palestinians. To do so would be a sign of weakness, of abdication in the face of Israeli intransigence, of capitulation to American pressure.
>
> Unwilling to abandon the Palestinians, yet unable to take the lead in negotiating a settlement of the Palestinian issue with Israel, the Saudis are left with the unenviable task of trying to limit the negative consequences of the stalemate, while pleading with the United States to do something to ease the strain, to solve the problem for them. Much of the Arab world looks to the Saudis as holding the key to the Palestinian issue, a misconception perhaps, but one that adds to the kingdom's sense that it cannot remain aloof from inter-Arab politics, from the Palestinians or from Israel.[9]

Recent events in the Middle East, particularly the Israeli invasion of Lebanon, the devastation of Beirut and the massacre in the Sabra and Chattila camps, have made the Saudi dilemma more acute. The demonstrated impotence of the US, despite Reagan's initiatives, in restraining the Israelis either from invading Lebanon or, more important from the long-term point of view, from continuing with their settlement policies in the West Bank so as to create new realities in 'Judea' and 'Samaria', has detracted not only from US but Saudi credibility as well. The latter is, obviously, the result of the close Saudi connection in strategic and economic terms with Washington. While the Fahd and Fez plans might have done something to restore Saudi standing in the Arab world, the effect has probably not been more than marginal.

The Arab–Israeli conflict also has an overtly Islamic dimension related to the question of Jerusalem. Saudi Arabia, as the protector of the Muslim holy places in the Hijaz, cannot afford to be seen as compromising on the Jerusalem issue. Moreover, with the Israeli decision after the 1967 War to annex Arab Jerusalem, there has been no room left for compromise on this issue. Hypothetically, therefore, even if a *modus vivendi* is found with Israel on the issue of the West Bank and Gaza, the issue of Jerusalem's future would remain a zero sum game. With the Israelis unwilling to concede Arab sovereignty in East Jerusalem, the Islamic dimension of the conflict is bound to fester, even if a solution is found for the exclusively Palestinian dimension of the problem. In that event, the Saudi guardianship of the Islamic holy places and its self-proclaimed role as the defender of Islamic causes may turn out to be a delegitimising force rather than a legitimising one.

But that is not the only way in which politicised Islam can act to detract from Saudi legitimacy. There is evidence that the security and legitimacy of the Saudi regime have already come under increasing challenge from Islamic-inspired opponents of the royal house. The most dramatic manifestation of this challenge was, of course, the seizure of the Grand Mosque in Mecca in November 1979 by a group of people termed Islamic 'fundamentalists'. The very fact that there could be 'fundamentalist' opponents of a 'fundamentalist' regime was proof enough that the Saudi regime's use of Islam as a legitimising instrument could turn out to be a double-edged sword. As one observer of the Saudi scene put it, 'there can be no doubt that the action represented a mixed religio-sociological and political protest against the regime and its impious behaviour (made worse in the eyes of the believers by its lip service to Islam) and as such was typical of Traditional Islam. Undoubtedly elements of the army and of the National Guard were also involved.'[10]

Coming on top of all this unrest and helping to fuel it, the Iranian Revolution changed the regional and international environment which had so far afforded the Saudi regime a considerable degree of security. It therefore changed Saudi perceptions relating to security in a fundamental way. Until the Revolution, Saudi Arabia and Iran were considered the twin pillars of US strategy as it pertained to the Gulf after the enunciation of the Guam Doctrine by President Nixon in 1969. Although Saudi Arabia was much the weaker of the two pillars in terms of power and its rulers were wary of some of the Shah's grandiose designs, nonetheless the Saudi and Iranian roles complemented each other as far as the protection of American and allied interests in the region were concerned, and in staving off and containing the radical challenges that had emerged in the Gulf, such as those from South Yemen and the Dhofar region of Oman.

The cataclysmic events of 1978–9 changed all that. They affected Saudi perceptions particularly in two ways. First, the overthrow of the Shah, and the relative ease with which it was done, demonstrated the impotence of their superpower ally in terms of influencing internal change in Iran. American policy was seen to be both confused and ineffective during the anti-Shah upsurge. Certain lessons were driven home to the Saudis as a result. The foremost among them was that, given American impotence in meeting internal (and, in the case of Saudi Arabia, pan-Arab) challenges to allied regimes in the region, any reliance on the US security umbrella was not only unwise but also counter-productive. The latter worry stemmed from the assessment that, given the US commitment to Israel and its weak-kneed policy towards Israeli expansionism, the security of the Saudi regime was further endangered by its close connections with Washington. The Saudis also drew the conclusion that America's primary commitment was to oil supplies and not to the security of friendly regimes. If oil supplies could be ensured either by diplomacy or by force, the US would not be overly worried about the fate of the House of Saud. Congressional hearings and reports, prepared by experts, regarding US capabilities for take-over of Saudi oil fields in times of crisis added to such Saudi apprehensions. The strength of the Zionist lobby in the US on the issue of the sale of sophisticated weaponry to Saudi Arabia further convinced Saudi rulers of the lack of any basic societal commitment within the US either to Saudi Arabia or to its regime.[11]

The second major way in which the Iranian Revolution affected Saudi perceptions was related to the use of Islam as a bastion of regime legitimacy. The Iranian Revolution, as has been discussed above, demonstrated that Islam could be used for revolutionary as well as status-quoist ends.[12] Its anti-monarchial, anti-Western, anti-

American, anti-feudal, and anti-privilege thrust threatened all the major pillars on which the Saudi system rested. The impact of the Iranian Revolution was likely to be felt at various levels of Saudi society – the underprivileged *Shia* who provided a substantial proportion of the workforce in ARAMCO-run oil fields, the *Sunni* Muslim 'fundamentalists' whose revulsion of Saudi double-standards was expressed violently in the Grand Mosque incident, and the Arab nationalist and pan-Islamic opposition which resented the Saudi regime's role as a surrogate for a West that threatened Islamic and Arab values through its surrogate, Israel. It was no wonder, therefore, that the Saudi regime came to consider Iran under Ayatollah Khomeini as the gravest threat to its security.

The discontinuity introduced into the pattern of Gulf politics by the Iranian Revolution has also been responsible for the redefinition of the Iraqi ruling elite's security concerns. Iraq's security perceptions have been determined largely by four factors: (*a*) the regime's assessment of its own staying power in Iraq and the likely internal and external threats to the Baath Party and its strongman, Saddam Hussein; (*b*) the Iraqi rulers' assessment of Iranian ambitions and capabilities, particularly as they pertain to the Gulf; (*c*) their assessment of Saudi interests and capabilities both in the Gulf and in the larger Middle East arena, particularly any signs of a Saudi-Egyptian entente; and (*d*) Baghdad's assessment of superpower policies towards the Baathist regime, towards Iraq in relation to Saudi Arabia and Iran, and towards Iraq's ambitions to play a leading role in Arab affairs.

The Iranian Revolution upset a number of calculations that the Iraqi regime had made about its own security. While the Shah was in power in Tehran, he could thwart Iraqi ambitions in the region and even impose his will (as he did in 1975) on Iraq over the issue of navigation rights in the Shatt-al-Arab, but he posed no direct threat to the regime of Iraqi strongman Saddam Hussein. In fact, he contributed to the consolidation of Baathist power at home by playing the role of a credible whipping boy who could be accused, with some degree of truth, of trying to enforce his 'Persian' will on the Arabs of Iraq. The Shah's American connections also benefited Iraq's leverage with Moscow, for as long as Iran was the main Western surrogate in the Gulf, Iraq appeared a very desirable ally to the Soviet Union. With the Shah's departure and the collapse of the American position in Iran, Iraq could no longer maintain its earlier importance in Soviet eyes. The strains in Iraqi-Soviet relations increased as a result of the Soviet invasion of Afghanistan in December 1979 and Saddam Hussein's decision in 1978 to eliminate Iraqi communists from positions of influence within the Iraqi polity – a decision which culminated in the execution of twenty-one Iraqi soldiers in May 1978 for attempting to organise communist cells inside the Iraqi army.[13]

However, the greatest threat posed by revolutionary Iran to Iraq was in terms of the ideological and political challenge to the legitimacy of the Baathist regime in Baghdad. This regime represents not only a minority within a minority (the Baathist minority among the *Sunni* Arabs who in turn form only one fifth of the Iraqi population), but, what is worse, its base is further circumscribed by the regional character of its leadership.[14] It is in this context that the Iranian Revolution, which based its success on its capacity for popular mobilisation in terms of Islamic (and specifically *Shia*) symbolism, appeared so threatening to Saddam Hussein's leadership. Despite the socio-economic reforms introduced by the Baathist regime from 1968 onward which had certain beneficial effects on all strata of society and all regions of the country, the areas of *Shia* concentration continued to be relatively neglected and underdeveloped. The *Shia* population of southeastern Iraq continued to be, and considered themselves to be, economically underprivileged – a grievance which became very acute with the concentration of political and military power in the hands of the *Sunni* Takritis after 1968.

The successful operationalisation of Islam as a social revolutionary force in neighbouring Iran was a contagion that the Iraqi rulers felt they could not keep from affecting Iraq unless it was eliminated at its very source. The flow of people between Iran and Iraq, especially in the southeast, made it impossible to prevent ideas from flowing across the border. The Ayatollah Khomeini himself had spent most of his time in exile (from 1964 to 1978) at Najaf and issued his diatribes against the Shah from there, until the Iraqis expelled him to France in late 1978 under pressure from Tehran. Moreover, an Iran under the Ayatollah, which defined its basic character in ideological Islam (primarily *Shia*) terms appeared a much greater threat to the territorial viability of the Iraqi state (given its fragile nature) than an Iran under the Pahlavis, which defined its basic character in racial/Aryan terms and, thereby, alienated both *Shia* and *Sunni* Arabs. The influence of the Iranian Revolution was felt within Iraq in the form of the escalation of militant *Shia* political activity, bordering on terrorism. The main vehicle for the demonstration of *Shia* dissent and opposition was the religio-political party called *al-Dawa* (the Call). The Iraqi regime carried out a ruthless campaign of suppression against the party and its members, following the Iranian Revolution and the outbreak of the Gulf war.[15]

While the Iraqi decision to launch an invasion of Iran was taken largely as a result of this challenge posed by the Iranian Revolution to the Iraqi regime, a number of other factors converged to make the Iraqi military venture look both feasible and desirable. These included: the post-revolutionary chaos in Iran, and particularly the purge of the top leadership of the armed forces; the cut-off of Western, especially American, sources of arms supplies to Iran, including spare parts and ammunition; the low morale of the Iranian Army which many predicted would lead to its disintegration as a fighting force; the competition for power in Iran among various revolutionary factions and the lack of any central decision-making authority; and the political inexperience of Iran's new rulers. These factors combined to present a picture of Iran that would fall easy prey to the well-disciplined, although untried, Iraqi armed forces. The *casus belli*, if one was required, was also present: the Iran-Iraq Treaty of 1975 which had defined the boundary of the two countries in the Shatt-al-Arab according to the *thalweg* principle, thus overturning Iraq's traditional claim to the whole of the Shatt. This agreement was viewed by Baghdad as an 'unequal treaty', and when the power equation changed the Iraqis were not averse to repudiating the concessions they had made in 1975.

There were also factors not directly connected with Iran which led to the Iraqi decision to demonstrate its pre-eminence in the Gulf and its capacity to defend and protect what it portrayed as 'Arab rights'. The Egyptian defection from the Arab camp, as a result of its peace treaty with Israel, had left a vacuum in the leadership of the Arab world which Iraq was eager to fill. These Iraqi aspirations date back to the days of Nuri al-Said if not earlier, but it was the first time since the rise of Nasser that an opportunity had been provided to Iraq's rulers to translate such aspirations into reality. The Saudis, although forced to go along with the radical Arabs in their censure of Egypt, were apprehensive that the Egyptian defection would immeasurably weaken the moderate camp in inter-Arab politics and would allow the Arab consensus to be determined by the radical regimes of Syria and Libya. Therefore, they were looking for a partner who could help them neutralise the Syria-Libyan attempt to assume Arab leadership and give credibility to the Saudi efforts to preserve the moderates' ascendancy within the pan-Arab system based upon their anti-Israeli and anti-Western credentials. Iraq was the obvious candidate for the job, particularly since its disenchantment with the Soviet Union in the late 1970s had become obvious, as was its attempt to reforge its economic and military supply links with Western Europe.

The similar, if not identical, threat posed by the Iranian Revolution to both Baghdad and Riyadh further cemented the growing affinity between the Saudi royal house and the Takriti Baathists. Iraq's open condemnation of the Soviet inavasion of Afghanistan convinced the Saudis of the former's political reliability, as did Baghdad's attempts to strengthen ties with King Hussein's Jordan (which was apprehensive of Iraq's rival, Syria) and its diminished criticisms of the Arab sheikhdoms of the Gulf. Out of these converging interests there emerged a virtual Iraqi-Saudi entente with the twin purposes of curbing the spreading ideological influence of Revolutionary Iran and of preventing the Arab system from being 'hijacked' by the 'Steadfastness Front', led by Syria and Libya.[16] It was no wonder, therefore, that the Saudis and their allies in the Gulf underwrote Iraq's military campaign against Iran to the tune of US$1 billion per month until at least the end of 1982.[17]

A further form of Saudi-inspired response from the Arab countries of the Gulf to the Iranian challenge was the setting up of the Gulf Cooperation Council (GCC) in February 1981. The GCC, which brings together Saudi Arabia, Bahrain, Kuwait, Qatar, Oman and the UAE, but excludes Iraq, held its first summit meeting in Abu Dhabi in May 1981. While ostensibly aimed at achieving greater economic and social cooperation, the GCC's *raison d'être* is clearly the common security concerns of the Gulf regimes, with the Iranian ideological and political challenge heading the list. This was revealed when, following the discovery in December 1981 of a plot to overthrow the ruling family in Bahrain (attributed to *Shia* militants encouraged by Iran), the Saudis entered into separate security agreements with all members of the GCC, with the exception of Kuwait which considers such an agreement unnecessary. The Saudis had been pushing for a formal security pact amongst GCC members but ran into opposition from the smaller countries who seem to be anxious to maintain a semblance of military and political autonomy from the Saudi big brother. The Saudis, therefore, had to settle for bilateral agreements which, though unpublicised, 'are said to exclude the creation of any integrated military command or joint military planning or even full coordination in military activities'.[18] However, the Saudis did get the other members of the GCC to sign a secret agreement on the exchange of intelligence data, especially on political dissidents.

The earlier statement that each of the three major Gulf regimes suffers from feelings of insecurity needs to be qualified. There is a qualitative difference between the Iranian regime's feelings of insecurity and those of the other two powers. First, the IRP makes no bones about the fact that there is opposition to its rule from within, be it by the *munafeqin* (the 'hypocrites', i.e. the Mujahedin) or other 'misguided elements' in Iran, by the 'stooges' of the US and the USSR, or by remnants of the Shah's regime. While it does lay a part of the blame on the superpowers and their agents for stirring up trouble in Iran, it accepts the fact that there are economic and ideological divisions within Iranian society which have been inherited from the Pahlavi period. The very acceptance, in fact the active propagation, of the *mustazafin–mustakberin* (oppressed–oppressor) dichotomy thesis by the Iranian regime bears adequate testimony to its awareness and acceptance of socio-economic cleavages within Iranian society.

In Iraq and Saudi Arabia, on the other hand, a myth of unity within these societies is maintained that forces these regimes to continually find external scapegoats for problems facing their societies. Since internal fissures, whether socioeconomic, religious, ethnic or regional, are not only swept under the carpet but wished away, the Iraqi and Saudi regimes have to go to great lengths to demonstrate that the threats to their countries and regimes (which they equate) always arise from outside – either from a Zionist–communist conspiracy (Saudi Arabia), from the reactionary forces in the Arab world (Iraq), or currently, above all, from Iran which is portrayed as the historical Persian threat to the Arab world (Iraq) and as grossly misinterpreting Islam and all that an Islamic polity stands for (Saudi Arabia).

The difference between the sense of insecurity felt by the Saudis and the Iraqi Baathists on the one hand, and the IRP on the other, however, goes further than merely an unwillingness on the part of the former to accept openly the existence of fissures within their societies and to attempt to do something about it. It is, in one way, fundamentally related to the history of state formation in the three societies. Iran has long existed as a political entity. It is a historical fact that since 1501, when Shah Ismail established the Safavid state and proclaimed *Shia* Islam to be the state religion, the Iranian state has existed in more or less its present form and generally within its present boundaries. There is, therefore, no complex amongst Iran's rulers (of whatever hue) about the legitimacy of the state itself. This, however, is far from being the case with both Iraq and Saudi Arabia. Both came into existence in their present form only after World War I. The process of assimilation and political acculturation, as well as the habit of obedience to central authority (although oil wealth and sophisticated instruments of repression have helped much), has not gone far enough for Riyadh and Baghdad to be totally complacent about the continued existence of the states over which they rule.

The problem for the Saudis and Iraqis as compared to the Iranians becomes even more acute when one considers hypothetical situations where the peripheral areas of these states break away from the central core of rule in Tehran, Baghdad and Riyadh. It is clear that even without its peripheral areas of Kurdistan in the northwest and Baluchistan in the southeast, and even oil-rich Khuzistan in the southwest, the Iranian state will continue to exist in its Persian-speaking, predominantly *Shia* core, irrespective of the character of its regime. However, if the Hijaz (with the Islamic holy places) and al-Hasa (with all its oil and its *Shias*) should break away from the Saudi political core of Najd, and both have been under Saudi rule for only some fifty years, the Saudi core would be little more than a tribal principality.

Iraq, with its ethnic and religious division is, if anything, even more of a patchwork. As one analyst has pointed out:

A salient feature of the politics of modern Iraq is the inherent instability and violence mainly due to its origins and the fragmentation of its society. The country's borders have no historical basis and as a nation-state it has failed to evolve into a political community. ... None of [the] communities [in Iraq] accepts the State of Iraq in its present form, and to all of them it remains an artificial political entity.[19]

While the centre of its political gravity, especially the recruiting area for its ruling elite, lies in the predominantly *Sunni* Arab area to the north and west of Baghdad, the *Shia* majority (about 55 per cent) lives to the south and east of the capital and the *Sunni* Kurds (almost as numerous as the *Sunni* Arabs) are concentrated in the northernmost parts of the country. What makes things worse is that in economic terms this core is not viable when deprived of its peripheral areas, for the oil fields and facilities on which the Iraqi economy depends are concentrated in the Kurdish and *Shia* areas of the north and the southeast. Deprived of them, the political heartland of Iraq would not be much more than an appendage of Syria.

The problems of Saudi Arabia and Iraq are further compounded by the process through which elite recruitment in these countries takes place. The narrow recruiting base of the top decision-makers (the House of Saud and the Takriti Baath) has already been mentioned and does not need further elaboration. The recruitment system of both elites is 'closed' since one has to belong to the right parentage or town/area to obtain membership in them. While the Saudis have co-opted members of the technocratic elite into functions of decision-making, their participation is limited to issues of a technical rather than political nature. In comparison to the Saudi and Iraqi elites, the Iranian system of elite-recruitment is much more open and broad-based and does not restrict recruitment for reasons other than those of ideological commitment and shared political values (at least as far as the Persian-speaking and Azerbaijani communities are concerned, which together form over 70 per cent of the Iranian population). It is no wonder, therefore, that in comparison with the Saudi and Iraqi regimes, the Iranian one displays much greater capacity to absorb shocks of both a political and military nature. It also largely explains the greater confidence displayed by the Iranian regime in times of adversity, as in the first year of the war with Iraq and particularly after the assassination in June 1981 of sixty leading IRP figures.

PERSPECTIVES ON THE SUPERPOWERS

No discussion of security issues or perceptions in the Gulf can be complete without reference to external powers, particularly the superpowers. Since this chapter attempts primarily to analyse and explain regional perceptions of international security, what will be considered are the perceptions of the three major Gulf regimes of the role of the superpowers in the related arenas of regional and global security, and their identification with one or the other (or neither) of the superpowers.

If the international alignments of the major Gulf regimes is analysed, an interesting picture emerges. Saudi Arabia has close military and economic links with the West, particularly with the US, which is involved, among other things, in building a defence infrastructure for Riyadh worth tens of billions of dollars. Despite this close link with the US, however, the Saudis display a certain degree of wariness about overt American presence in the Gulf, largely because it tends to detract from their own legitimacy, particularly in the context of US economic and military support to Israel. Therefore, while the Saudis are interested in the US underwriting the stability of the conservative Gulf regimes, they prefer the American presence to be an over-the-horizon one. The US base in Diego Garcia, the presence of carrier-based US Task Forces off the Gulf, the planning for the RDF, and the recent establishment of the Unified Southwest Asia Central Command based at McGill Airforce Base in Florida, are welcomed because they enhance the American capacity to intervene in the Gulf in times of crisis. But US military presence at Masirah, Oman and at Ras Banas, Egypt are viewed with a greater degree of scepticism because they are considered to be major political liabilities and only marginal military assets.

Reference has already been made to Iraq's international alignments, particularly the ups and downs in its relations with the Soviet Union. However, since mid-1982, Soviet-Iraqi relations have improved quite visibly. The earlier strain was related to the Soviet invasion of Afghanistan, the Soviet support to Iraq's Arab rival, Syria, and Moscow's even-handed approach to the Gulf war. But as Iraqi Deputy Prime Minister Tariq Aziz stated recently, 'relations with Moscow are warmer now . . . because of a resumption of arms deliveries after a halt early on in the Gulf war, and because of improved political understanding'.[20] As far as Iraq's relations with the West are concerned, there has been a major improvement since the late 1970s, particularly with Western European countries such as France. Not only did the French supply the Osirak nuclear reactor to Iraq which was destroyed by Israel in 1981, but considerable quantities of sophisticated conventional weaponry, including F-1 Mirages, Frelon helicopters and AM-39 air-to-surface missiles were supplied by Paris. Moreover, in 1981 Iraq's total trade with the Eastern bloc amounted to only $499 million, as compared to a staggering $19 121 million in trade with the Western industrial countries.[21]

Iraqi perceptions of the US have also undergone change. This was most dramatically reflected by the way the Iraqi Ambassador at the UN cooperated with the American Ambassador after the Israeli destruction of Osirak to see that a resolution on the issue acceptable to the US was introduced and passed in the Security Council. Moreover, the Iraqi verbal attack on the US following the Israeli raid was much more muted than one would have expected in such circumstances. The imperatives of the Gulf war, in which certain Iraqi and American perceptions were shared regarding Iran, accounted at least partially for this rapprochement. Iraq's disenchantment with the Soviet Union and Saddam Hussein's bitter feud with the Iraqi Communist Party also contributed to America's improved image in Baghdad. The growing Saudi connection must have also forced Iraq to tone down its criticism of the Saudi's superpower ally. But above all, Iraq's economic and technological needs, particularly in the context of the Gulf war, have forced rethinking on US-Iraqi relations. The new approach was symbolised by Saddam Hussein's interview with *Time* magazine in July 1982, in which he said:

> I believe America has three fundamental interests in the region – commercial trade, improved economic relations and keeping countries from being attracted by [the Soviet Union]. These three considerations can be fulfilled. Take technology and expertise. Do these exist in the Soviet Union or in America? I will answer you. The technology we require exists in the United States, or in Europe and Japan.[22]

According to one report, US exports to Iraq, mainly agricultural, have reached $1 billion a year.[23] Apparently, Iraqi-US diplomatic relations, broken off during the 1967 War, also would have been resumed had it not been for the fact that this might have been misunderstood and misjudged as the Gulf war continued. Moreover, the growing detente between Iraq and the US is reflected in the fact that the Iraqis, once the most ardent of the 'rejectionists' in the Arab world *vis-à-vis* Israel, have now gone to the extent of endorsing peace negotiations between the PLO and Israel.[24]

Thus, Iraq's strategy now is to make the best of both worlds with its military dependence on the Soviet Union (although considerably reduced by purchases of French equipment) balanced by its dependence for economic subsidies on US-supported Saudi Arabia (and its Gulf allies) and for technology from Western Europe and the US. This involves some delicate tightrope-walking, although the task is made considerably easier by the increasing convergence in US and Soviet views of, and antipathy towards, Iraq's major regional adversary – Iran.

The basic Iranian stance regarding the superpowers is best summed up by the slogan 'neither East nor West', and while, for tactical reasons, Iran's rulers had been less harsh in their criticism of Moscow than of Washington (especially after the beginning of the hostage crisis), the rhetorical pendulum now seems to have stabilised at a dead-centre position. There were three major reasons for the earlier 'soft' attitude towards the Soviet Union. The first was related to the power struggle within Iran and the IRP's attempt to assure the neutrality, if not the support, of the pro-Moscow Tudeh Party as well as of the majority faction of the Fedayan in this struggle. A second major reason arose with the Iraqi invasion of Iran in September 1980 and was related to Tehran's attempt to keep the Soviet Union – Iraq's largest arms supplier – neutral in the war. The third, and possibly the most important, factor was Iran's need for a transit route for its exports and imports through Soviet territory as well as Moscow's importance as a trading partner for Tehran. This need became very pressing with the hostage crisis, the American threat to blockade Iranian ports and the Western allies' decision to cut trade ties to Iran. With the outbreak of the Gulf War and the Iraqi threat to Iran's ports on the Gulf, this factor further increased in importance. However, even in the context of increasing economic cooperation, the Iranians refused to permit the export of natural gas to the Soviet Union. They held out for a higher price, arguing that the price negotiated by the Shah was well below the market price.

Before mid-1982, the major strain on Soviet-Iranian relations had been the Soviet military presence in Afghanistan, Tehran's support of the Afghan insurgents and its near-total inflexibility on the issue of any contact, however unofficial or informal, with the Karmal regime. Subsequently, two other factors combined to increase Iranian hostility to the Soviet Union. The first was the Soviet decision of August 1982, following Iranian military successes which pushed the war into Iraq, to supply Iraq with modern weapons in order to prevent the total collapse of the Baathist regime and its likely substitution by an Islamic or, at least, a pro-Iranian one. From Tehran's point of view this meant that Moscow had made its choice between the two regional adversaries and that in the long term Iranian and Soviet regional objectives were sure to clash.

The second was the IRP's success at consolidating power and generating a degree of political and economic stability at home. This was partially linked to the military victories in the war, and partially to Tehran's success in boosting oil production to over 3 million barrels per day, thus making it once again the second largest oil producer in OPEC. But most of all, the IRP's success in neutralising, if not totally wiping out, the threat from the Mujahedin and other forces in Iran, provided it the opportunity to dump both the Tudeh Party and its superpower patron. The IRP's anti-Tudeh policy reached its culmination in February 1983 with the arrest of the party leader, Nureddin Kianouri, and several other top leaders on charges of spying for Moscow.

At the same time as Iran's relations with the Soviet Union were further deteriorating, the Iranian regime was seen to be sending out signals to the US that it was willing to return US-Iranian relations to near normality if the US accepted the IRP's predominance in Iran and Iran's primacy in the Gulf. These moves were facilitated by the American refusal to overtly take sides in the Gulf war, which now stood out in sharper relief against Moscow's decision to rearm Iraq.[25] However, there are limits beyond which US-Iranian relations cannot progress. These limits are set by US support to Israel on the one hand, and Washington's close links with Saudi Arabia (which the Iranians perceive as covert support for Iraq) on the other. Moreover, the basic anti-Western and anti-hegemonic thrust of the Iranian Revolution, coupled with the belief amongst the IRP leaders that neither superpower can be trusted, make for a relatively equidistant and distant relationship with both Moscow and Washington. This is best demonstrated in the orchestrated chanting of Iranian crowds to the Iranian leaders' exhortations to be aware of external and internal dangers to the revolution: 'Death to the Americans! Death to the Russians! Death to the Hypocrites (the Mujahedin)!'[26]

LINKAGES BETWEEN THE GULF AND CONTIGUOUS REGIONS

Beyond the linkages between regime security and national and regional security and the linkages between the regimes in the Gulf and the superpowers, there is yet another form of linkage which impinges upon the security perceptions of the ruling elites of the Gulf. This is the link between the security triangle of the Gulf (Iran, Iraq, Saudi Arabia) on the one hand, and the security problems of contiguous regions, the Middle East heartland and South Asia, on the other. There is a great deal of overlap in terms of shared problems and in terms of the membership of the three regional subsystems. In fact, in many ways the Gulf is an offshoot of the parent Middle East subsystem. Thus, the problems of the Gulf cannot be understood in isolation from the other two, particularly to the extent that the legitimacy of at least two of the three regimes in the Gulf (Iraq and Saudi Arabia) is directly affected by what happens in the larger Middle Eastern theatre. These linkages are also important in the context of superpower policies towards the Gulf and its contiguous regions. Superpower policies towards the Gulf both influence and are influenced by their policies towards the Middle East (especially the Arab-Israeli conflict) and South Asia (the India–Pakistan–Afghanistan triangle).

The linkage between the Middle East and the Gulf is easy to comprehend. After all, two of the three major Gulf actors are Arabs – as are all the smaller countries – and, therefore, form part of what Khalidi has called 'the Pan-Arab system'.[27] The Arab countries of the Gulf share the other Arabs' suspicion and distrust of Israeli policy and generally sympathise with the Palestinian cause. They are, therefore, parties to the central concern of Middle Eastern politics – the Arab-Israeli conflict. The presence of a quantitatively substantial and qualitatively crucial Palestinian population in the Gulf provides further evidence of the linkage between the politics of the Gulf and that of its parent Middle East subsystem.[28]

Since the Islamic Revolution of 1979, Iran has become one of the most militant supporters of the Palestinian cause. The only organised group of foreign volunteers which came to the help of the Palestinians besieged in Beirut was from Iran. Therefore, although Iran does not share the ethnic and linguistic affinity with the Palestinians which the Arabs of the Gulf do, in ideological terms it is far more uncompromising on the conflict with Israel and, in fact, has the potential to act with Palestinian militants to block any compromise settlement on Palestinian rights. Moreover, its ideological fervour on the foremost pan-Arab issue (which Tehran considers the foremost pan-Islamic issue) creates grave problems of legitimacy for Arab regimes, particularly those in the Gulf that appear as compromisers (and even defeatists) in comparison to the revolutionary militancy of Iran.

The relationship between security issues in the Gulf and those in South Asia was, until recently, not as direct or easily comprehensible. However, with the Soviet military intervention in Afghanistan shortly after the Iranian Revolution and Iran's denunciation of the invasion and its support to the Afghan insurgency against the Karmal regime, the connection has become clear. It has been argued that a major reason for the Soviet intervention in Afghanistan was related to its apprehension about the long-term influence of Iran on Soviet Central Asia as well as the short-term threat of American intervention in Iran following the taking of US hostages in Tehran.

However, there has been a longer standing connection between problems of regional security and regional conflict in the Gulf/Middle East and those of South Asia, namely the India–Pakistan confrontation. This linkage is mediated through Pakistan's role (central to South

Asia and peripheral to the Gulf) in the politics of the two regions. It should not be forgotten that the initial American decision to arm Pakistan in the 1950s was only marginally related to Nehru's disinclination to get involved in the bloc politics of the Cold War. It had much more to do with the emerging US strategy to safeguard Western interests in the Muslim world to the west of the sub-continent, particularly in the context of the refusal of the major Arab powers, with the exception of Iraq then under the Hashemite monarchy, to participate in either the still-born Middle East Defence Organisation scheme or the relatively more successful 'northern-tier' strategy. Pakistan, Iran and Turkey (along with Iraq) were then brought together to defend Western interests in the Middle East and the oil-rich Gulf.

Whatever the outcome of this strategy as far as the Gulf or the larger Middle Eastern region was concerned, it had tremendous impact on the power balance in South Asia, as between India and Pakistan, and was largely instrumental in determining the course of Indian and Afghan policies towards the Soviet Union. The former culminated in the Indo-Soviet Treaty of 1971 and the latter in the Soviet military intervention on December 1979. The fall of the Shah and the latest crisis in Afghanistan once again led to an American policy towards Pakistan which tends to strengthen the linkage between the conflicts in the Gulf and those in South Asia, as well as that between superpower policies towards the two continuous regions.[29]

CONCLUSIONS

Four broad conclusions emerge from this study. First, perspectives of regional (and, therefore, international) security in the Gulf vary quite widely, depending largely upon the nature of the regimes in power in the three major countries of the region. The character of the regimes seems to be the critical factor in these countries' perceptions of security problems in the region. Second, these perspectives are also dependent upon the nature of the Gulf regimes' relationships with each other and the nature of their relations, individually and collectively, with external powers, particularly the superpowers. Third, problems relating to security of the Gulf countries interact with the security problems of contiguous regions – both influencing the latter and being influenced by them. Finally, since superpower policies towards the Gulf are related to, influence, and are influenced by, their policies towards the contiguous regions, superpower involvement in the security issues of the Gulf tends to augment the linkages between problems of regional security in the Gulf and similar problems both in the Middle East heartland and in South Asia.

NOTES

1. For a perceptive analysis of the post-revolution power structure in Iran, see James A. Bill, 'Power and Religion in Revolutionary Iran', *Middle East Journal*, xxxvi:1, Winter 1982, pp. 22–47.
2. This came out very clearly in the author's conversations with members of the Iranian ruling elite in Tehran in March–April 1981.
3. For a discussion of Islam as the 'refuge of the dispossessed', see Mohammed Ayoob, 'Islam: New Grievances, Traditional Idioms', *Far Eastern Economic Review*, cxix:2, 13 January 1983, pp 14–15. For a discussion of the Iranian 'sub-proletariat', see Nikki Keddie, *Roots of Revolution: An Interpretative History of Modern Iran*, Yale University Press, New Haven, 1981, ch. 7. For the potency of the Mujahedin's appeal, see Shahram Chubin, 'Leftist Forces in Iran', *Problems of Communism*, xxix:4, July–August 1980, pp. 1–25.
4. For one report from Tehran, see R. W. Apple Jr, *International Herald Tribune*, 22 November 1982; for another, which implies similar conclusions, see Arnold Hottinger, *Swiss Review of World Affairs*, September 1982, pp. 14–17.
5. For details, see Malcolm H. Kerr, *The Arab Cold War: Gamal 'Abdul-Nasir and His Rivals, 1958–1970*, Oxford University Press, London, 1971 (3rd edn).
6. Tim Niblock, 'Social Structure and the Development of the Saudi Arabian Political System', in Tim Niblock, *State, Society and Economy in Saudi Arabia*, Croom Helm, London, 1982, pp. 75–6.
7. Ibid., p. 101.
8. For a detailed discussion of the relationship between the Saudi search for legitimacy in the Arab and Muslim worlds and the security of the Saudi regime, see William B. Quandt, *Saudi Arabia in the 1980s: Foreign Policy, Security and Oil*, Brookings Institution, Washington, DC, 1981, particularly chs 2 and 3; and Bruce R. Kuniholm, 'What the Saudis Really Want: a Primer for the Reagan Administration', *Orbis*, xxv:1, Spring 1981, pp. 107–21.
9. Quandt, op. cit., p. 35.
10. Arnold Hottinger, 'Political Institutions in Saudi Arabia, Kuwait and Bahrain', in Shahram Chubin, *Security in the Persian Gulf: Domestic Political Factors*, International Institute for Strategic Studies, London 1981, p. 16.
11. Some of these Saudi perceptions and American policies and actions leading to such perceptions are discussed in an interestingly titled article by a former official of the US Defence Forces who had served in the

region. See, Abdul Kasim Mansur (pseud.), 'The American Threat to Saudi Arabia', *Armed Forces Journal International*, September 1980, pp. 47–59.
12. See Mohammed Ayoob, 'The Discernible Patterns', in Mohammed Ayoob (ed.), *The Politics of Islamic Reassertion*, Croom Helm, London, 1981, pp. 271–90.
13. See John K. Cooley, 'Conflict within the Iraqi Left', *Problems of Communism*, XXIX:2, January–February 1980, pp. 87–93.
14. For details, see Hanna Batatu, *The Old Social Classes and the Revolutionary Movements of Iraq*, Princeton University Press, Princeton, NJ, 1978, p. 1088.
15. See e.g. Jean Gueyras, *Le Monde*, in *Guardian Weekly*, 12 October 1980; and Robert J. McCartney, *International Herald Tribune*, 3 December 1982.
16. For detailed accounts of Iraqi moves in inter-Arab politics, see Adeed Dawisha, 'Iraq: the West's Opportunity', *Foreign Policy*, 41, Winter 1980–1, pp. 134–53; Bruce Maddy-Weitzman, 'The fragmentation of Arab Politics: Inter-Arab Affairs since the Afghanistan Invasion', *Orbis*, XXV:2, Summer 1981, pp. 389–407; and Steven B. Kashkett, 'Iraq and the Pursuit of Non-Alignment', *Orbis*, XXVI:2, Summer 1982, pp. 477–94.
17. See e.g. Drew Middleton, *International Herald Tribune*, 29 November 1982.
18. Salamat Ali and Derek Davies, *Far Eastern Economic Review*, CXIX:9, 3 March 1983, p. 41.
19. Abbas Kelidar, 'Iraq: the Search for Stability', *Middle East Review*, XI:4, Summer 1979, p. 27.
20. Quoted in Nicholas Moore, *International Herald Tribune*, 25 February 1983.
21. Karen Dawisha, 'The USSR in the Middle East: Super Power in Eclipse?', *Foreign Affairs*, LXI:2, Winter 1982–3, p. 445.
22. Quoted in ibid., p. 444.
23. David Lamb, *International Herald Tribune*, 30 November 1982.
24. See e.g. *International Herald Tribune*, 8–9 January 1983.
25. For a rather optimistic account, see Amir Taheri, *International Herald Tribune*, 8 February 1983.
26. Quoted in Dawisha, op. cit., p. 447.
27. Walid Khalidi, 'Thinking the Unthinkable: Sovereign Palestinian State', *Foreign Affairs*, LVI:4, July 1978, pp. 695–6.
28. For details of the Palestinian factor in the Gulf, see John K. Cooley, 'Iran, the Palestinians and the Gulf', *Foreign Affairs*, LVII:5, Summer 1979, pp. 1017–34.
29. These issues are discussed in Mohammed Ayoob, 'India, Pakistan and Super-Power Rivalry', *The World Today*, XXXVIII:5, May 1982, pp. 194–202.

7 Afghanistan and International Security

ZALMAY KHALILZAD

The Soviet invasion of Afghanistan in 1979 generally has been regarded as a crucial development in contemporary history. There has been much discussion and analysis of this Soviet move. This essay focuses on several less explored dimensions of the conflict. Was the Soviet move a major change in Moscow's approach to risk-taking? What are the implications of the Soviet action, especially in affecting the relative balance of power in Southwest Asia and the Persian Gulf? What is the Soviet pacification strategy and what are some of the likely outcomes of the conflict?

AFGHANISTAN AND SOVIET RISK-TAKING

Unlike what is generally argued, it appears to this writer that Moscow's move into Kabul was not a departure from the low-risk pattern which has been the general characteristic of Soviet military operations against small neighbouring countries. In Afghanistan both the balance of interest and the relevant balance of power favoured Moscow. The Afghan case illustrates that the Soviet level of active involvement in small countries close to it geographically increases as ideological relations between such countries and Moscow become closer. The case of Afghanistan illustrates that Moscow uses indirect means such as military assistance, economic ties and links with sympathetic political groups to gain influence. When the gains are threatened, it uses more direct measures including the use of substantial force to prevent a setback. Because of territorial contiguity and the spread of ethnic groups across the common border, Soviet interest in Afghanistan has been persistent.

In addition, a number of developments after World War II shifted the balance of interest there significantly in favour of the Soviet Union. After Britain – which had played the role of the countervailing power against Soviet encroachment – had decided to withdraw from the sub-continent, Afghanistan felt more vulnerable to a Soviet threat. To gain protection against the perceived signs of Soviet expansionism and to build up the central authority in Afghanistan, the Kabul government sought a closer political, economic and military relationship with the United States.[1] In spite of Afghan efforts, a military relationship was not developed between Kabul and Washington. There were several reasons for this. First, American policy-makers were confused about the importance of Afghanistan. Unlike today, there was little conception of it being a possible barrier (or gateway) to Soviet access to the oil-rich region of the Persian Gulf. Another reason was the calculation that, in case of Soviet aggression, the US would not in fact be able to project sufficient military power to such a remote country to protect it. A third reason was the US fear that the Afghans might use American weapons against Pakistan, against whom Kabul had territorial claims in Pakistan's Pushtun and Baluch dominated provinces. Washington also assumed that the Afghans' fear of the Soviet Union would prevent them from turning to the Soviets for arms. This was to prove a miscalculation.

The intensification of the border conflict with Pakistan and the growth of security relations between Washington and Islamabad led to closer ties between Kabul and Moscow. Initially the Afghans moved very cautiously. In 1950, when Pakistan blocked the transport of goods to Afghanistan, Kabul faced many shortages, including petroleum. The Soviets offered Afghanistan petroleum and signed a four-year barter agreement. Moscow's aim was to encourage greater Afghan dependence on the Soviets and decrease Afghan incentives to move towards the West. In 1952, Kabul allowed Moscow to open a trade office in Afghanistan.

There was, however, some conflict within the ruling elite over policy priorities. Mohammed Daud's group saw the major priority as being the domestic state-building programme and the conflict with Pakistan. He had a much lower perception of the Soviet threat than others in the royal family. The US decision to provide military assistance to Pakistan in 1954 and the refusal to do the same for Afghanistan alienated Daud. Subsequent Pakistani membership in the Baghdad

Pact and SEATO also convinced him that the regional military balance was shifting against Afghanistan because of US-sponsored actions. Daud felt hurt and ignored and he even suspected that Washington and Pakistan might be planning his overthrow.[2] All this made him more receptive to Soviet offers of aid, which was opposed by the others in the ruling elite.

In sum, it was this combination of Daud's premiership in Afghanistan, the Afghan-Pakistan dispute, the American assistance to Pakistan, and the US reluctance to provide military assistance to Afghanistan that afforded Moscow an opportunity for greater influence in Afghanistan. Without any one of these circumstances, Afghanistan's relations with the Soviet Union might not have acquired the intensity that they did in the 1950s. The Soviet willingness to provide assistance not only served Daud's regional aims, but his domestic goals as well: to build a strong centre, with large armed forces.

In 1955, a major escalation in Soviet involvement in Afghanistan occurred. A loan of US$100 million was signed. Several projects including oil and gas exploration in northern Afghanistan and the construction of highways were launched. Moscow also signed a $25 million arms deal and Afghanistan became increasingly dependent on the Soviets for military training. Daud's acceptance of Soviet arms aid came as a surprise to the US. Paradoxically then, the Afghan slant towards the Soviet Union brought what all the efforts before had failed to achieve: active US interest. This increased American concern led to a phase of economic competition between the superpowers in Afghanistan. Between 1955–65, the Soviets provided Afghanistan with $552 million in aid. US aid in the same period was $350 million.[3]

However, while in the first decade after the Soviet-Afghan military agreement the US economic assistance was substantial, it decreased steadily during the second decade. Between 1965 and 1977, US aid totalled $150 million, less than half of the amount for the previous ten years. By 1975, US aid for Afghanistan had decreased to a symbolic level of less than $20 million. Paradoxically, this decrease took place at a time when Afghans were experimenting with 'democracy' by allowing greater freedom of the press and political activity and when high government positions were largely in the hands of American-educated Afghans. The decrease in American assistance also coincided with the period of detente in superpower relations and with US entanglement in Vietnam. Apparently a decision was made to recognise Moscow's greater interest in Afghanistan and not to compete there at the previous levels.

While Washington was reducing aid, Moscow sustained not only its military aid but also its economic interactions. Between 1965–77, it provided more than $700 million in economic aid. The inventory of Soviet-supplied arms in Afghanistan in 1977 included more than 700 tanks and 184 combat aircraft. While there had been little trade with the Soviets before 1950, in the 1970s more than 50 per cent of Afghanistan's trade was with its northern neighbour. Moscow became Kabul's principal supplier of capital goods, petroleum products and sugar. One indicator of the importance Moscow attached to Afghanistan was that by 1970 it had become one of the three largest recipients of Soviet economic aid.[4]

As the decline in American interest was reducing Kabul's bargaining power *vis-à-vis* Moscow, Afghanistan sought support elsewhere, including China. Beijing, whose rivalry with Moscow was intensifying in the late 1960s, was inclined to be responsive, although its aid resources were limited. In 1963 the two countries signed a treaty formally delimiting the 48-mile border between them. This agreement was followed by reciprocal state visits by King Zahir and Liu Shaoqi in 1966. The economic aid subsequently provided by China to Afghanistan in areas such as textiles and agriculture was modest when compared to that of the US and USSR. Beijing also tried to keep Afghanistan from becoming part of the Soviet satellite empire by encouraging improved relations between Kabul and Islamabad. From the late 1960s, the Soviets became increasingly worried about the prospects of growing Chinese influence in Afghanistan and Pakistan. The threat of a new challenge to their position in Afghanistan, after the apparent decline of such a threat from the US, could have contributed to the subsequent Soviet policies toward Afghanistan.

Domestically, while the pro-Soviet Percham and Khalq groups participated in parliament, they believed that because of the conservative and Islamic preferences of the majority of Afghans, it was unlikely for them to come to power through the parliamentary process. Thus, they infiltrated the armed forces, and by 1973 had gained considerable military backing. They also helped Mohammed Daud overthrow the Afghan monarchical regime. One reason for the successful infiltration of the armed forces was that Percham and Khalq maintained ties with the Soviet Union, as did the armed forces. Between 1956–70 the USSR trained some 7000 Afghan officers.[5] Some of these officers helped Daud come back to power in 1973. Daud had many pro-Soviet friends and had favoured pro-Soviet leftists during his premiership (1953–63). The leftists also supported Daud because they believed he would share power with them and that, in time, they would be his successors.

After the 1973 coup, Daud expressed support for Moscow's anti-Chinese Asian Collective Security Plan, appointed pro-Soviet leftists at all levels of government, followed Moscow in objecting to Iran's arms build-up, emphasised Afghanistan's support for Pashtun and Baluch nationalists in Pakistan, and agreed to infrastructure projects linking the two countries. He also increased the number of Soviet advisors in the country. The Soviets, in turn, increased their economic aid to Afghanistan, as in the February 1975 loan of 308 million rubles. Also, after the coup, trade between the two countries expanded substantially.[6] Daud's initial policies and close ties with pro-Soviet leftists led to several coup attempts by Islamic-oriented groups. However, once he had consolidated his rule, Daud broke with the pro-Soviet leftists, having become convinced that their support was tactical and fearing they would replace him at an opportune time.

Daud also shifted his foreign policy. In 1975, he sought improved relations with China. Despite initial Chinese reservations about Daud's assumption of power, relations between Beijing and Kabul improved significantly. In 1975, Beijing signed a $55 million aid agreement with Kabul. With US encouragement, Daud also sought to improve relations dramatically with Iran and Pakistan, and looked to the West for help in many projects, including oil exploration. He also made plans for training Afghan officers in India and Egypt.

The Soviets reacted to Daud's shifts with alarm. Reportedly, Brezhnev pleaded with Daud to change his policies, whereupon Daud responded that he would not allow the Soviets to 'interfere with the internal affairs of my country'.[7] As Daud's relations with the Soviets deteriorated, Percham and Khalq formed an alliance to overthrow his regime, which finally happened in 1978. Some Western analysts argued that the coup was as much of a surprise for Moscow as it was for Washington. However, according to a recent KGB defector, Khalq and Percham sought and received Soviet endorsement for the coup.[8] Once it succeeded, the new government expressed ideological hostility to the US and moved Afghanistan very close to the Soviet Union. The American reaction was low-key, probably because Washington did not appreciate the strategic implications of the change in Kabul. The American response continued to remain the same even after Kabul had signed a Friendship and Cooperation Treaty with Moscow in December 1978.[9]

After 17 February 1979, when American Ambassador Adolph

('Spike') Dubs was killed under peculiar circumstances that may have involved Khalqi and Soviet officials, the US evaluation changed significantly. On 29 February, President Carter declared that the 'trend' in Afghanistan had been against American interests. The US reduced economic aid to Afghanistan and eliminated the small military training programme.[10]

To Afghan–Soviet relations, the 1978 coup brought a dramatic change, even though the regime claimed to pursue a policy of non-alignment. Under Khalq, Afghanistan became an enthusiastic supporter of the Soviet role in international affairs.[11] Khalq also intensified bilateral relations with Moscow. The number of Soviet advisors increased. Moscow promised to provide $1 billion in aid between 1979 and 1984,[12] and deferred Afghanistan's payment of all loans and interest for a ten-year period.[13] The Afghan government hinted that it might seek associate membership in COMECON. Kabul and Moscow established a permanent inter-governmental Commission on Economic Cooperation. Soviet advisors were assigned to all Afghan ministries and were attached to the Afghan military units down to the platoon level and assisted in the establishment of party bureaus at all levels of the armed forces. Moscow also enlarged its influence in Afghanistan's education and mass communication institutions through an agreement providing for Russian language courses at Kabul University and other educational institutions. In September 1979, Amin revealed that 1500 students had been sent to the Soviet Union and that an agreement for sending 2000 to Bulgaria had been reached. Another indication of Kabul's rapid intensification of relations with Moscow was the 1978 treaty which called for the introduction of 'appropriate measures to ensure the security, independence and territorial integrity of the two countries'. These provisions provided the Soviets with justifications for dispatching troops to Afghanistan a year later.

Initially, the Chinese public response to the 1978 coup was low-keyed. Later, though, Beijing was quicker than Washington in recognising that Afghanistan had entered Moscow's orbit. Thereafter Chinese public displeasure became dramatic as Beijing described the insurgency against the Kabul government as a 'national struggle'.[14] The Chinese news agency, *Xinhua*, paid increased attention to the conflict in Afghanistan. Moscow charged on several occasions that the Karakoram highway was being used for supplying arms to the Afghan insurgents. Beijing in turn accused Moscow of using alleged Chinese support as a 'smoke screen' for Soviet interference in Afghanistan.

THE SOVIET INVASION AND ITS IMPLICATIONS

Although there is a great deal of uncertainty about the period immediately preceding the December 1979 Soviet invasion of Afghanistan, the most likely explanation involves a combination of two important factors. In Afghanistan itself, the invasion was part of a Soviet effort to prevent the possibility of the overthrow of a client regime in Kabul and its replacement by a hostile group. At the international level, the invasion took place after enormous growth in relative Soviet military power *vis-à-vis* the West, and the overthrow of the Shah had dramatically weakened the Western position in the region. Therefore, the 'correlation of forces' in the region favoured the Soviets.

Before coming to power, Khalq was already in conflict with several other urban-based groups over the desired future for Afghanistan. However, a more important development was the mobilisation of the rural population against the regime. This population had been rather apathetic in recent times, in large part because the local elites had preferred them to be. These elites were alienated by the new measures of the Khalqi government and roused their populations with appeals to traditional values (calling the new regime 'atheistic') and by employing a traditional authority structure. The rural population rallied around traditionalists and fundamentalists. Several political opposition groups established headquarters in Pakistan. As the opposition to the government increased, the Khalqis resorted to severe repression. As the conflict increased, it spread from the countryside to the cities. In March 1979, there was a major uprising in Herat. As the internal conflict escalated, the state apparatus began to fall apart, and there was a slow disintegration of the army (with the Bala Hissar garrison mutiny in Kabul on 5 August 1979 being reflective of this). The weakening of the state apparatus led to substantial areas of the country falling outside government control. Local leaders, both ethnic and tribal, as well as traditionalist and fundamentalist, gained in strength; rural areas began to refuse to pay taxes; government offices were closed down in a number of areas; and both the GNP per capita and the area under cultivation declined.[15]

Moscow must have recognised that its local clients had made major errors and faced serious threats. Given the state of Soviet–Khalqi relations, a Khalqi defeat might have dealt a severe blow to Soviet credibility regarding its ability to help allies in a timely fashion. The Soviets were faced with the risk that a client regime might be replaced by groups that were hostile to them and had strong ties with countries and groups unfriendly to the USSR. Such a defeat might have encouraged hostile groups elsewhere and discouraged those who were sympathetic. It would have decreased Soviet abilities to maintain pressure and influence developments in countries around Afghanistan, especially Pakistan. It could have also meant the loss of many years of economic, political and military investment in the country.

To avoid such a development, Moscow tried to convince its local clients to reconstitute the government and shift domestic policies rapidly. During his 13 September 1979 visit to Moscow, Taraki was persuaded that the excesses of previous months should be blamed on the Prime Minister Hafizollah Amin, and as a suitable scapegoat he should be eliminated. A new government with a broader coalition, including the Perchamis, should then be established and those policies that were 'unpopular' should be abandoned or revised. The Soviets also might have promised Taraki that they would increase military assistance, including military personnel, to protect the new government against its opponents. Moscow had already sent several delegations to Afghanistan to assess the situation there and plan for possible Soviet intervention. Two were of special importance. One, in April 1979, was headed by General Alexei A. Yepishev, who was in charge of morale, discipline and ideology in the Soviet Army. He had visited Czechoslovakia before the 1968 Soviet invasion. The other, during August 1979, was led by General Ivan G. Pavolvskiy, who had planned and led the Czech operations. Upon Taraki's return to Kabul, the Soviet-backed plan to eliminate Amin began to unfold in mid-September. As part of this plan, apparently, Moscow deployed some units on the Soviet-Afghan border and a 400-man airborne unit was sent to the Bagram air base near Kabul.[16] However, Amin apparently received a warning about his intended elimination and acted quickly to pre-empt Taraki's plan.

After eliminating Taraki, Amin then proceeded to put into practice some of the measures purportedly agreed to by his predecessor and the USSR. He attempted to cast Taraki in the role of a scapegoat, blaming the excesses of the previous government on the cult of personality that the regime had built up around him. Taraki had styled himself, among other things, the 'great teacher', the 'true son of the Afghan people', the 'father of the revolution', the 'leader', the 'teacher', and so on. Amin also introduced reforms such as the easing of restrictions on foreign travel and released some political prisoners. However, he baulked at a reconciliation with Percham. To show his displeasure with the Soviet role in the episode, he demanded that Moscow recall its Ambassador, Alexsander M. Pusanov, and appoint a new envoy. Amin, while suspicious of Moscow, believed that the Soviet Union had little choice but to support him and his regime. The Soviet view, however, was somewhat different. Moscow tried to deceive Amin by publicly expressing support for his regime while secretly planning his overthrow and the invasion of Afghanistan. For one thing, Amin was clearly the strongman of the regime in the eyes of the Afghan population. Even before Taraki's death, he undertook substantive functions while Taraki's role was largely a symbolic one. Perhaps more importantly, Amin had demonstrated his independence of action in a way that did not bode well for Soviet control. A more tractable person was desirable.

To implement their invasion plans, the Soviets took several major steps. First, Moscow gave refuge to military leaders and increased contacts with the Perchami exiles, including Karmal, in Eastern Europe. Second, Moscow tried to increase its military presence inside Afghanistan by persuading Amin that he needed increased Soviet assistance to combat the Afghan guerrillas. The Kremlin sent several delegations to Kabul to persuade President Amin of the importance of an increased Soviet presence. Officially they were to help the government with counter-insurgency, but their real mission was to mobilise Amin's opponents within Khalq and Percham and pave the way for the Soviet invasion. Third, Moscow increased its capability near the Afghan border for massive and rapid intervention.

A different account supplied by a recent Soviet KGB defector claims that by September 1979, Moscow had come to a decision that Taraki should be replaced by Amin, who was judged as too weak and ineffective to deal with the mounting crisis.[17] Initially after the coup, he had been appointed as the country's Foreign Minister. After the Herat uprising, he was named the country's Prime Minister, a post previously held by Taraki himself. In July 1979, Amin also took over the Defence and Interior ministries. According to this account, Moscow subsequently began to doubt Amin's sincerity and his ability to deal with the opposition forces. It began to look for alternative solutions which led to the invasion and the installation of Karmal.

At the international level, the invasion took place at a time and place where the relative configuration of military and political factors favoured Moscow. The Soviet move came after the overthrow of the Shah which dealt a devastating blow to the American security framework for the region. After the British withdrawal from the Gulf in 1971, Washington adopted the Nixon Doctrine consisting of security cooperation with key states in the region, Iran and Saudi Arabia (two-pillar policy). Of the two pillars, Iran was the far more important one. The US relied heavily on Tehran to protect its interests in the region. It adopted a low profile as far as its own presence in the area was concerned, although after the oil price increase of 1973–4, there was greater recognition of the need for a higher level of American military presence in the area (even though the policy remained fundamentally unchanged).

The revolt in Iran not only undermined the two-pillar policy in the Gulf, it also led to the disintegration of the Central Treaty Organisation (CENTO). Iran's hostility to the US was demonstrated amply when American diplomats were taken hostage on 4 November 1979. By the time of the Soviet invasion, the United States did not even have an embassy in Tehran. The decline in America's position in both Iran and Pakistan must have been recognised as a positive development by the Soviet Union. In Moscow's hierarchy of preference, non-aligned states, even hostile ones, are preferable to those allied with the West. With the revolt in Iran and other developments in the region, there was a widespread perception of American power in disarray and retreat.

The Soviet invasion took place after dramatic changes favourable to Soviet military strength relative to that of the US. At the global level, past US strategic superiority had been replaced with essential parity. As far as relative capability to project power in the region is concerned, the Soviet position had also improved significantly as a result of several factors. First, shifts in the regional policy and power constellations, such as the upheaval in Iran and the infrastructural changes in the area, favoured Soviet power projection capabilities. Moscow increased its power projection capability through expanding its overseas 'base structure', and strengthening its airborne troops.[18]

It is clear that in Afghanistan both the balance of relative power and interest favoured Moscow. The US did not have the capability to meet the Soviet threat on its own terms in Afghanistan, nor did it regard Afghanistan as vital to its interest. As we have seen, Washington's responses to various internal changes and reports of possible Soviet invasion were rather muted. On the other hand, clearly Moscow had considerable interest in Afghanistan. With the pro-Soviet coup of 1978, Kabul's relations with Moscow fundamentally changed. Moscow became highly involved in the country politically, militarily and economically. Because of these considerations, it is likely that Moscow discounted the likelihood of an American military move against them in Afghanistan. The Soviets probably expected a degree of international condemnation and isolation, similar to what followed in the aftermath of its moves against Hungary (1956) and Czechoslovakia (1968). The Soviet invasion, therefore, *conformed* to the low-risk pattern, the general characteristic of Soviet operations.

Although involving little risk of a military confrontation with the West, the Soviet invasion nevertheless had far-reaching implications. At the international level, in one sweep the Soviet invasion of Afghanistan overturned a number of assumptions and significantly changed the situation in the region. It eliminated a buffer state, brought Soviet forces to the Pakistani border, and set a new precedent in the massive use of Soviet forces in an area outside its satellite empire. On the strategic level, it reduced the distance between the Soviet forces and the entrance of the Persian Gulf, putting the ports of that region within the range of a number of Soviet tactical aircraft. It thus increased Soviet capabilities to threaten vital NATO and Japanese interests, and it impressively demonstrated Soviet capability for the rapid deployment of forces.

To Washington, the invasion reinforced the growing sense of threat to its interests in the region. The Soviet move was seen as part of a Soviet global challenge to US interests. At the regional level, the Carter Administration feared the Soviet action would raise serious questions about American reliability among its friends in the Persian Gulf and could lead to increased regional instability and Soviet expansionism. The US encouraged political opposition to the Soviets from the Moslem countries, non-Islamic non-aligned states and its own allies. Washington hoped that Afghanistan would become a point of conflict between these countries and the Soviet Union.

It also launched a major effort to shore up its military capability around Afghanistan. In January 1980, the President declared what has come to be called the Carter Doctrine: 'An attempt by any outside force to gain control of the Persian Gulf region will be regarded as an assault on the vital interests of the United States of America and such an assault will be repelled by any means necessary, including military force.'[19] By engaging vital American interests, Washington hoped to deter Soviet aggression beyond Afghanistan and reassure local states in Southwest Asia.

Some of the measures taken by Washington to increase its military capability in Southwest Asia were under consideration before the invasion, but were largely at the conceptual stage. The US military effort in the region had two elements: seeking limited presence in the area and increased capability for projecting US forces to the area. A Rapid Deployment Joint Task Force was established. However, the US effort to increase its military capability was hampered at least in part by the reluctance of the countries which the US would want to protect the most, namely Saudi Arabia and Iran. There are several reasons for this. First, there is considerable fear of becoming entrapped in a superpower conflict. For example, the Saudis have argued that such an American presence will increase Soviet incentives to seek more facilities in the area.[20] It is unclear how much of the reluctance on the part of those sympathetic to Washington is due to their lack of confidence in the long-term staying power of the US. Local actors, especially Saudi Arabia, were unsettled by the inability or unwillingness (or both) of the US to help the Shah overcome his internal problems. Second, some states in the area fear that increased American capability in the region might also increase Washington's propensity to intervene in internal and regional conflicts, especially when they were seen as endangering the flow of oil. Third, the forces who seek dissociation from big powers politically and militarily have grown in the countries of the region. Accepting foreign bases exposes the regime to internal and regional pressures. The states of the area are thus caught in several contradictions. Most of the conflicts they face are internal and regional, and with the change in internal and regional configuration, it is believed that a foreign presence would only accelerate these conflicts.

Washington also faced substantial difficulties in gaining the support of its industrial allies for its policies in the region in the aftermath of the Afghan and Iranian crises. These two crises produced new strains within the Western alliance, both between Europe and the US and to a lesser extent amongst the Europeans themselves. Because of clashes in priorities between Europe and the US in policy towards Southwest Asia, Washington was largely isolated from its allies, Britain being the only exception. The response to Afghanistan re-emphasised some of the underlying problems in alliance relations. The Europeans have also established an independent and growing economic relationship with the Soviet Union and Eastern Europe. American policy was seen as creating unnecessary risks to these relations and as failing to acknowledge the Europeans as more equal partners than they had been in the past. Afghanistan was not viewed in the same light and the Europeans instead chose to stress the importance of saving detente. Several US allies, including France, refused to provide military assistance to the Afghan partisans.

However, despite these disagreements, several European countries have helped Washington to increase support for some critically located states in the region. Germany took the lead in providing economic assistance to Turkey. They have also tried to provide an alternative Western avenue of association to local actors whose internal politics or ideology make open association with Washington difficult.

Third, the US has sought improved relations with regional actors, especially Pakistan, and has tried to sustain a low-level Afghan resistance against the Soviets. The Soviet invasion brought a change in policy priorities towards Pakistan. In April 1979, because of nuclear proliferation concerns, all US military and economic aid to Pakistan had been suspended. In the aftermath of the Soviet move, Washington reaffirmed its 1959 security agreement with Islamabad and offered military and economic assistance to that country. It wanted to discourage Pakistani accommodation towards Moscow and help in supplying weapons to the Afghan resistance forces. The US offer consisted of a two-year package worth $400 million and included the sale of F-16s. Pakistan rejected this offer as inadequate, in view of the threats the country faced. Under the Reagan Administration, the two countries agreed to a five-year programme of economic aid and military sales. Although following a cautious policy towards the Soviets, with US support, Pakistan has led the diplomatic opposition to the Soviet move at the UN, non-aligned and Islamic meetings. In coordination with Pakistan, Egypt, and perhaps some other states, the US apparently also started a covert operation for helping the Afghan resistance.[21] Since the Afghan programme is covert, it is difficult to be confident about the size of the effort. Afghan resistance leaders insist it is very small. Since Washington does not transfer these weapons directly, it is also possible that much of what is intended for the Afghans does not reach them.

While it is clear that without cooperation from local actors, especially Iran and Pakistan, there would be severe limitations on the US ability to provide large-scale military assistance to the insurgents, it appears that Washington itself has not sought dramatic or substantial improvement in Afghan insurgent capability. Washington's policy appears to consist of providing only meagre assistance in the hope of keeping low-level resistance alive for an extended period. Washington fears that increased Afghan capability might lead to a more forceful Soviet response against the insurgents and/or Pakistan, leading to rapid deterioration in the relative position of the Afghans and a Soviet military victory. Pakistan has similar concerns. It is possible, however, that increased Afghan military capability might increase Soviet incentives to seek a political settlement and withdraw. For Washington, a sustained low-level struggle in Afghanistan would provide evidence of Soviet aggressiveness against a small Islamic and non-aligned country. The US also benefits from the Afghan conflict by appearing to support a national liberation movement; something that previously has been almost a Soviet monopoly. At the same time, Afghanistan provides the political and military justification for Washington's own military efforts in the region and bogs down a large number of Soviet soldiers who might otherwise be available for other contingencies more threatening to US interests elsewhere.

To the Chinese, Afghanistan was neither an isolated act nor a regional phenomenon, but yet another step in Moscow's sustained offensive towards global expansion. It was part of the Soviet grand design for dominating the Indochina peninsula in the east to the Persian Gulf in the west. The Vietnamese invasion of Kampuchea was seen as part of this design. In order to encourage a firmer anti-Soviet line in Washington, Beijing emphasised the threat to vital Western interests in the Persian Gulf resulting from Moscow's Afghan invasion. According to the Chinese, Afghanistan was 'another gate through which the Soviet Union could enter the Persian Gulf'.[22] Immediately after the invasion, there was considerable speculation about possible Sino–American military cooperation to meet the Soviet threat. Both sides agreed on the need to strengthen Pakistan. There were concurrent reports that China had allowed American facilities for tracking Soviet missile tests which were closed in Iran after the overthrow of the Shah.

While the Chinese have called for international support of the Afghan resistance and have opposed any compromise with the Soviets, as far as material support for the Afghan resistance is concerned only a very limited amount of assistance has been provided by Beijing. China has indicated an interest in normalising relations with the Soviets and thus seeking an equal distance between the two superpowers. The Chinese have emphasised that before normalisation can be achieved Soviet troop withdrawal from their common border, Vietnamese withdrawal from Kampuchea, and the Soviet withdrawal from Afghanistan must be accomplished.

CONCLUSIONS

More than three years have passed since the December 1979 Soviet invasion of Afghanistan. To all parties involved, the occupation has been costly. Afghanistan's population has been most affected. More than three million refugees, or some one-fifth of the country's population, have fled to Iran and Pakistan; a state of war governs life in the cities, with curfews, food shortages and occasional fighting; badly needed experts, from diplomats to airline personnel, have left the country; and substantial civilian and partisan casualties have been sustained. Despite the cost of maintaining some 85 000 troops, Moscow has not yet succeeded in pacifying the country and has had enormous problems in extending the authority of the centre, which it largely controls, over the countryside.

The Soviet invasion marked a major escalation in the USSR's long and persistent involvement in Afghanistan. Once in Afghanistan, the Soviets initiated a multipronged strategy for pacification of the country. This has included the accommodation of Islamic feelings, a propaganda blitz to win support for the Soviet position both in Afghanistan and abroad, and blaming the Afghan crisis on the Americans, Chinese, and the Pakistanis. Another element has been attempts at harmonising relations between Khalq and Percham and broadening the base of government by forming the National Fatherland Front, an umbrella organisation representing the various elements of the population. Moscow is also trying to train hundreds of new cadres to help not only in maintaining law and order but in running the country. The Soviet-installed regime has also attempted to win popular support by undoing some of the 'radical' policies of the previous government. Moscow has tried to build loyal armed forces so as to turn the Russian–Afghan war into an Afghan–Afghan conflict. The Soviet military strategy appears to be one of holding on to major cities and highways while applying force intermittently against resistance in the countryside. This policy aims at minimising Soviet loss of life, and rests on a belief that in time they will either discourage the population from supporting the resistance or force them to leave the country.[23] Moscow appears to be counting on the international community to forget about the Afghan crisis.

The Soviet strategy has not been successful so far and Moscow is far from pacifying the country. The Soviets have not deployed enough troops in the country to permanently extend the centre's control over the countryside in a short time. Violent opposition to the occupation has spread all over the country. The Karmal government controls the country's capital, but even Kabul is not very secure. A 10.00 p.m. curfew continues and gunfire and explosions often can be heard. Serious fighting has taken place continuously in nearby towns such as Paghman less than seven miles away. Regime opponents using guerrilla warfare and urban terrorism techniques have assassinated party members, Soviet officials, and military men in the city itself. The resistance has also attacked the gas pipeline taking gas to the Soviets, and briefly cut off the gas supply. The major roads linking Kabul to other parts of the country also have been subjected to harassment and interruption.

Soviet forces foresee a long struggle and have constructed permanent underground storage facilities for fuel and ammunition, completed a road and rail bridge across the Amu Darya, constructed permanent communication facilities, upgraded several Afghan airfields, enlarged existing helicopter gunship maintenance workshops, and begun construction on new airports. To 'legitimise' the Soviet presence, Moscow has signed a status-of-forces agreement with the Karmal regime which is similar to those in effect between the USSR and several East European countries.

Several factors will be crucial in determining whether the Soviet Union succeeds in liquidating or neutralising the Afghan partisans. These include the policies adopted by Pakistan toward the insurgents, the extent of external support for the partisans, the success or failure of Soviet attempts to convert divisions among the insurgents into open conflict, Soviet efforts to establish a government in Kabul which commands a large armed force and has a wide base of support, and the scope and duration of the Soviet military commitment.

There are a number of conceivable outcomes to the Afghan crisis. These include a Soviet-dominated, pacified Afghanistan in the near future; a protracted war lasting many years leading to a Soviet military victory; a neutral Afghanistan resulting from a compromise involving some voluntary Soviet withdrawal and international guarantee of Afghan neutrality, either in the near future or after a protracted war; or even the spread of the Afghan war to the neighbouring countries, especially Pakistan.

As long as Moscow believes that it can win the war in Afghanistan and that time is on its side, it is unlikely to work towards a political compromise. Should Moscow insist on the domination of the Afghan political system by pro-Soviet communist groups, with or without their current leaders, a compromise between the Soviets and the Afghan resistance forces appears unlikely. There are, however, a number of possible arrangements which could satisfy both Soviet security concerns and the requirements of Afghanistan's sovereignty. A state of permanent neutrality for Afghanistan provides one such framework. Such an arrangement is acceptable to the Afghans, and might also become so to the Soviets. Immediately after its invasion of Afghanistan, Moscow argued that its move was caused by Washington's efforts to bring Afghanistan under its control. For example, an authoritative article in *Pravda* argued: 'Having lost their bases in Iran, the Pentagon and the US Central Intelligence Agency were counting on . . . approaching our territory more closely through Afghanistan.'[24] Brezhnev gave personal sanction to this view by arguing that there had been a real threat that Afghanistan would lose its independence and be turned into an imperialist bridgehead on the USSR's southern border.

Afghanistan's military neutrality should satisfy these alleged fears. It will also deal with current Soviet concerns that the resistance groups might enter into a military alliance with blocs hostile to Moscow should they come to power. Since none of the major partisan groups advocate such an alliance they can go a long way toward satisfying such Soviet worries. It will be in the interest of both the Afghans and the Soviets if Kabul's neutrality is guaranteed by the major powers and the neighbouring countries. Moscow is likely to reject this approach in the near future, as it still appears to be hoping to gain legitimacy for a Soviet-dominated regime in Kabul. But Moscow is capable of a *volte-face*, especially if the resistance becomes more effective and Afghanistan remains a source of international embarrassment to it.

NOTES

1. For details of the Afghan effort to seek American economic and military assistance, see Zalmay Khalilzad, 'The Struggle for Afghanistan', *Survey*, xxv:2, Spring 1980; H. Negaran (pseud.), 'The Afghan Coup of April 1978, Revolution and International Security', *Orbis*, xxiii:1, Spring 1979, pp. 93–114; and Leon Poullada, 'Afghanistan and the US.: the Crucial Years', *Midle East Journal*, xxxv:2, Spring 1981, pp. 178–90.
2. Poullada, op. cit.
3. Walles Hangen, 'Afghanistan', *Yale Review*, 56, October 1956, p. 61.
4. Borys Lewytzkyi (ed.), *The Soviet Union: Figures, Facts, Data*, Saur, New York, 1979, pp. 348–55.
5. R. Newell, *Politics of Afghanistan*, Cornell University Press, Ithaca, New York, 1972; and Hasan Kakar, 'The Fall of the Afghan Monarchy in 1973', *International Journal of Middle Eastern Studies*, May 1979.

6. For details, see Lewytzkyi, op. cit., p. 355; and *The Economist*, 3 August 1970.
7. Afghan National Liberation Front, 'The Appeal of the Afghan People to the United Nations', New York, September 1979, p. 2; and interviews by the author.
8. *Time*. 22 November 1982, pp. 33–4.
9. See e.g. comments by a State Department spokesman in the *Baltimore Sun*, 7 December 1978.
10. *Department of State Bulletin*, Washington, DC, LXXIX, pp. 6ff.
11. For details, see Zalmay Khalilzad, 'The Superpowers in the Northern Tier', *International Security*, IV:3, Winter 1979/80, pp. 6–30.
12. *New York Times*, 28 April 1978.
13. *Foreign Broadcast Information Service, Daily Report – Middle East and North Africa (FBIS–MENA)*, 161, 17 August 1979, p. 53.
14. Garsi Dutt, 'China and Developments in Afghanistan', in K. P. Misra (ed.), *Afghanistan in Crisis*, Croom Helm, London, 1981, p. 42.
15. *Anis*, 28 February 1980; and *Kabul New Times*, 28 February 1980.
16. Jiri Valenta, 'The Soviet Invasion of Afghanistan: the Difficulty of Knowing Where to Stop', *Orbis*, XXIV:2, Summer 1980, pp. 201–18. Also see his 'From Prague to Kabul: the Mode of Soviet Invasions', *International Security*, V:2, Fall 1980, pp. 114–41.
17. *Time*, 22 November, 1982, pp. 33–4.
18. For a detailed discussion of this, see Albert Wohlstetter, 'Meeting the Threat in the Gulf', *Survey*, XXV:2, Spring 1980.
19. *New York Times*, 24 January 1980.
20. *New York Times*, 27 February 1980.
21. President Sadat of Egypt disclosed in September 1981 that Washington was buying Soviet arms in Egypt for use by Afghan insurgents. *New York Times*, 23 September 1981.
22. *Beijing Radio*, 29 December 1979, quoted in Dutt, op. cit., p. 48.
23. On Soviet strategy, see Zalmay Khalilzad, 'Soviet Occupied Afghanistan', *Problems of Communism*, XXIX:6, November–December 1980, pp. 23–41.
24. *Pravda*, 13 January 1980, in *FBIS – Soviet Union*, 14 January 1980, pp. A1–6.

8 Pakistani Perspectives on International Security

PERVAIZ IQBAL CHEEMA

Security perceptions of most nations are directly linked with the real or perceived threats confronting them. Threat is a geopolitical environmental condition for which the price and penalty will have to be paid by the target state if it fails to build its own effective warding-off mechanism. To obviate real or perceived threats, nations seek power (economic, political and military). Power can lead to prosperity, and prosperity may generate more power. This process is continuous under the operative international political system, primarily because it breeds insecurities and is unable to enhance security for all. Given its inability to evolve an effective collective security arrangement, coupled with operative economic and power disparities and inequalities, the system has left nations with no option but to rely upon the age-old principle of self-help. Thus, one witnesses the phenomenon in which almost all nations are constantly striving to create that kind of power equilibrium–disequilibrium which affords them maximum security. Periodic changes in equilibrium–disequilibrium directly affect the security perceptions of nations.

Pakistan's security perceptions have largely been influenced by regional developments. More specifically, the most crucial determining factor has been the continuous state of hostile relations between India and Pakistan. The Soviet invasion of Afghanistan in 1979 and the consequent massive influx of refugees into Pakistan not only added another dimension to its security perceptions but also led to a further deterioration of the regional security environment. This chapter initially examines Pakistan's perceptions of the superpowers' involvement in South Asia, and then concentrates on Pakistan's regional perceptions.

THE SUPERPOWERS AND SOUTH ASIA

The involvement of the superpowers in any region of the world is primarily the product of two principal categories of interests: those related to their global position as a superpower and those associated with their regional policy. For a small power like Pakistan the major considerations for forging close relations with either of the superpowers often stem from a desire to correct the regional imbalances and to accelerate the pace of economic development. The ideological proximity and the complementarity of interests make it easier for both the superpowers and small powers to come closer to each other. However, close association between a superpower and a small power may not prove to be lasting because of the inherent inequality of the relationship and competing interests. Shifting perceptions of global and regional interests not only vitally affect the durability of a given set of relationships, but also give birth to new sets of relationships. Pakistan's relations with the superpowers have been changing in order to accommodate the new geopolitical realities that were partly the product of the shifting perceptions and policies of the superpowers and partly the result of changes in the regional environment.

For the Americans, South Asia has always remained an area of peripheral interest in terms of strategic planning. American policy towards the region flowed partly from the Cold War considerations of the 1950s and early 1960s and partly from the role local states play *vis-à-vis* other regions and powers, including China and the Soviet Union.[1] The initial American involvement in Asia was primarily the product of the globalisation of its containment policy. It was to be achieved through an American-sponsored system of security alliances. The Americans were willing to sign up all those who exhibited some interest in checking the onward march of communism. They did not bother to analyse the factors and compulsions that induced the local players to sign up with the Americans. Each local player had his own set of reasons influencing the decision to opt for closer association with the Americans. Take, for example, the case of the Southeast Asia Treaty Organisation (SEATO). Admittedly, the American objective was to foster collective efforts in the region to check the perceived expansion of communism, but the objectives of the local members of SEATO were all different. Thailand's reasons for joining SEATO were perhaps closer to the American objectives of securing help and protection against external and domestic communist forces. For the Philippines the major influencing factor was to gain partnership with a wide group of regional and great powers. Pakistan participated in SEATO to procure much-needed arms and to gain a kind of psychological defence against India.[2] The other outside powers joined SEATO to pursue their own objectives, which were not identical to those of the Americans. The French joined to gain protection of their remaining colonial interests and the British saw an opportunity to provide security to Malaya's northern flank.[3]

This conglomeration of varied objectives manifested in a collective defence arrangement was basically the product of the vastness of Asia and its complex and divergent problems. The initial major American objective in Asia was the containment of communism, which seems to have evolved over the last three decades to a current focus upon the containment of Soviet expansionism. The security of shipping lanes in the Indian Ocean, coupled with the regular flow of oil from the Gulf region and the protection of American investments and trading interests, remain associated objectives. The reduction of tensions and the securing of peace in various areas evoke a certain degree of American interest, but not much enthusiastic effort. The American policy in South Asia is geared to the attainment of its own objectives rather than to seeking a genuine peace and stability there.

The acute sense of insecurity and helplessness during the earlier years of independence compelled Pakistan to embrace the West. Without giving much thought to its immediate geopolitical realities, it threw in its lot whole-heartedly with the West so as to avert the perceived Indian threat and to acquire much-needed economic and military aid. Although both Pakistan and the US entered into an alliance with a view to serve their national interests, both did not fully try to understand the implications and consequences of an alliance between unequal partners. This was shown when two test cases eventuated. The Americans never committed, or even contemplated the deployment of, US forces or the use of American-supplied equipment against India. The Pakistanis, on the other hand, expected that the Americans would not only extend diplomatic support to Pakistan's case on Kashmir but would also actively back Pakistan in the event of a war with India. The Pakistani expectations, though a little on the high side, were somewhat natural as they thought that the Americans were not only fully conscious of the Indian threat to Pakistan's security but also realised that this was the main factor that induced Pakistan to land itself in the Western camp. Maybe it was a somewhat naive view, but this naivety could have been the product of ignorance about world politics and lack of experience in diplomacy.

Equally ignorant were the Americans whose experience as the world policeman was extremely limited and who, on the one hand, could not properly judge the implications of an alliance between a superpower and a small power deeply locked in a local conflict and, on the other hand, failed to comprehend the psyche of a people of totally different stock. Subsequently, the Sino-Soviet rift and the Sino-Indian border conflict, beginning in the late 1950s, were followed by nearly a decade of parallel Soviet and American efforts to build India as a counterpoise to China, which in turn gave birth to a Sino-Pakistan *entente cordiale*.

The American failure to come to Pakistan's assistance in the 1965 and 1971 Indo-Pak Wars completely disenchanted the Pakistanis. This disenchantment with the West is understandable, especially when viewed within the context of Indo-Soviet relations and the support that the Soviets have given to India over the years. The Pakistani's sense of insecurity brought the Americans to South Asia, and the quick Indian reaction to this introduced the Soviets into the area. The Indians interpreted Pakistan's alignment with the West as an attempt to upset the existing power equilibrium and to challenge its over-riding authority in sub-continental affairs. India had assigned for itself a central role not only in South Asian affairs but in Asian affairs generally. Consequently, enraged over Pakistan's membership of SEATO and CENTO, India invited the Soviet leaders to visit the area. The Soviets, who were equally annoyed over Pakistan's participation in Western defence alliances, were in a punitive mood and thus immediately committed themselves to support both India on Kashmir and Afghanistan on Paktunistan issues. While it may be true that the initial Soviet thrust into South Asia was a reaction to Pakistan's involvement in the Western-sponsored defence alliance system, recent research indicates that Moscow had anticipated the deterioration of Sino-Soviet relations in the mid-1950s and was 'already looking for an alternative Asian power to play one of the roles that had been projected for China in Stalinist foreign policy – that is, to serve as a channel to the non-aligned or reluctantly aligned nations of Asia and Africa'.[4] At the time, India seemed to be the most attractive replacement. Perhaps this explains why the Soviets, who were initially extremely critical and disdainful of Indian leadership, responded to Indian overtures so quickly and so enthusiastically.[5] To woo India, Moscow not only abandoned several fundamental features of Stalinist policy towards non-communist Afro-Asian states and influenced the Communist Party of India to tone down its attack on the Indian ruling group, but also considerably, and quickly, expanded economic and military aid to India. Thus, the Indian reaction to Pakistan's membership in SEATO and CENTO merely provided further opportunities for the Soviets to enhance their influence in India, but was not the sole cause of Soviet entry into South Asian affairs.

The thaw in the Cold War during the early 1960s, the introduction of intercontinental missiles, the Sino-Soviet rift, and the Sino-Indian War of 1962 caused dramatic changes. Despite the warnings and protests of Pakistani leaders, the West rushed arms aid in response to an Indian request following the Sino-Indian border war. Pakistan became disenchanted with the West and began to drift away in search of new friends to maintain the balance *vis-à-vis* India. China readily fulfilled this need.

Since the early 1960s, Chinese and Soviet policies have exhibited a remarkable degree of consistency in their dealings with South Asian states. Moscow's support for India and Afghanistan has remained essentially unaltered. Chinese relations with Pakistan continue to be fairly high on the Chinese priority ladder. Despite the dramatic changes in the international and regional environments, Indo-Soviet and Sino-Pakistan relations continue to enjoy cordiality and basic continuity. This basic continuity suggests that not only their primary interests have governed the policies of Beijing and Moscow but also that the continuity itself was the best option for both of them. Although Sino-Pakistan relations are based, to a considerable extent, on mutual trust and confidence, the main Chinese interest in the region is to prevent the extension of India's control or influence over Pakistan. Just as China has an interest in containing India, India and the Soviet Union have a common interest in containing China. Although India and the Soviet Union have formally signed a mutual defence treaty, Sino-Pak ties continue to grow without formal linkage. Despite the dynamic nature of world politics, both the USSR and China enjoy the reputation of being a reliable friend to others. Whether or not this reliability will be the same once the Soviets and the Chinese work out a better mutual relationship remains to be seen.

Although Sino-Soviet and Sino-Indian relations have shown no significant improvement in the 1970s, no one can be certain that this will be the case in the 1980s. On the contrary, if one is to go by the trends of the mid-1970s, a modest change is likely to take place. In many ways Soviet and Chinese policies are likely to continue, though in a somewhat modified form, in almost the same manner as in the 1970s. This is primarily because each set of relationships is primarily linked with other sets of relationships between the superpowers and the South Asian states. If Indo-American relations improve without adversely affecting Indo-Soviet relations, Beijing might interpret it as Soviet-American collusion with India against China – especially if progress is made in Soviet-American detente while Sino-American relations do not register any improvement over the Taiwan issue. Similarly, if Pak-American relations improve, as it seems at present, India is likely to draw even closer to the Soviets and may even intensify its efforts to normalise relations with China. An Indo-Chinese detente is likely to influence Pak-Soviet relations, which in turn would improve Pak-Afghan relations. Perhaps that is why it seems reasonable to assume that in this decade the Soviet Union will continue to attach priority to its ties with India, while concomitantly trying to improve relations with Pakistan so as to broaden its role in the sub-continent.[6] But it seems quite reasonable to say that while all sets of superpower relationships have either directly or indirectly affected South Asian affairs, the Sino-Soviet rift had the most profound impact on regional security.

Detente heralded the superpowers' recognition of each other's legitimate interests and accommodation, at least in areas of vital concern. Competition continued in the grey areas, but with caution so as not to upset the whole arrangement. Compared to the Americans, the Soviets have been much more active and responsive to situations that provided an opportunity to encourage sympathetic parties to bid for power. Local conflicts, political instability and separatist movements coupled with vacillating US policy and the lack of timely American response created situations ripe for Soviet moves. The Soviets, being more vigilant and active in peripheral areas, cautiously moved in and tilted the momentum in their favour. Afghanistan has been no exception to this general style of Soviet operation. Detente might have provided the much desired breather and helped the Americans to disengage from Asia, but it has certainly undermined the security of South Asians who were once closer to the Americans than to the Soviets.

THE REGIONAL BALANCE

Pakistan's perceptions of the regional balance are fundamentally influenced by India's hostility coupled with India's own vision of being a great power. The ongoing Afghanistan crisis has not only further deteriorated Pakistan's security environment, it has also injected a sense of urgency in checking the worsening security dilemma. Sandwiched between Soviet-occupied Afghanistan and the Soviet's close friend India and confronted by a difficult internal situation, Pakistan finds itself uncomfortably placed in a three-front threat scenario which is much worse than India's two-front threat scenario of the 1960s. In order to place Pakistan's security perceptions in proper perspective, it is necessary to discuss briefly the India factor and the Afghanistan crisis.

Since the partition of the Indian sub-continent, Pakistan's security environment has been conditioned by its perception of a security threat from India. The two nations have fought four wars and have experienced countless border clashes since then. The Indo-Pak War of 1971 resulted in the dismemberment of Pakistan. At the time of partition, the Pakistanis were convinced that the overwhelming majority of the Indians were not reconciled with the division of the sub-continent and favoured reintegration, if necessary by force. This belief was confirmed by the bellicose statements of important Congress leaders.[7] Moreover, Mountbatten's desperate surgery had left many grave issues unsettled.[8] Among these, the Jammu and Kashmir question survived as the main cause and symbol of Indo-Pakistan animosity and intransigence. It was this sense of insecurity which compelled Pakistan to align itself with the West. The Indians interpreted Pakistan's membership of Western-sponsored defence alliances as attempts to attain parity with India and to challenge the natural power-hierarchy in the sub-continent. India envisaged for itself a place of pre-eminence in the region and expected to be acknowledged as such by its regional neighbours. Pakistan's drive for security was regarded as a dangerous pursuit aimed at distorting the existing regional power balance.[9]

During the 1950s and the early 1960s, Pakistan's main efforts were directed towards the attainment of two major objectives: how to deter possible Indian aggression; and how to influence India to resolve the Kashmir dispute. Pakistan was able to attain the first objective, not only modernising its forces with the help of Western military assistance but also maintaining a near parity with India. However, the attainment of the first objective adversely affected the second one. The flow of Western arms hardened India's attitude on Kashmir. Instead of resolving the issue, India accelerated the erosion of Kashmir's special status and gradually integrated Kashmir into the Indian Union. Pakistan's repeated protests were ignored by India. Strangely, Pakistan's Western allies were not as forthcoming on the Kashmir dispute as expected.

It was not until the Indo-Pak War of 1971 and the subsequent signing of the 1972 Simla Accords that Kashmir began to play a relatively less significant role in Pakistan's India policy and the Indian attitude towards Pakistan became much more relaxed. Not only did the Indians begin to be much more realistic in their appraisal of apprehensions emanating from Pakistan's quest for security, but the average Indian also began to shed his obsession with the Pakistan factor.[10] Similarly, with Pakistan's dismemberment and its disillusionment with the West, the Pakistanis began to acknowledge the vastly improved position of India in the region.[11]

Mutual accommodation was shown at Simla when both sides discarded the UN cease-fire line in Kashmir and a mutually acceptable 'line of control' was worked out.[12] For India the new line meant that it could delink the line of control from the old UN line and also keep few strategic posts in the Kargil area. For Pakistan the new line symbolised its successful resistance to Indian efforts to solve the Kashmir issue on the basis of a *status quo* favouring India. It thus kept the issues alive in some form.[13]

Following the Simla Accords, Pakistan's external security environment gradually began to improve. While the East Pakistan crisis demonstrated the military superiority of India, the separation of East Pakistan in fact improved Pakistan's security situation by making the state geographically more compact. However, this state of affairs did not last long. In 1974, India exploded a nuclear device and demonstrated its technological superiority. In a nation acutely conscious of past Indian attitudes regarding Pakistan, the Indian nuclear explosion generated a new wave of fear about possible future nuclear blackmail. Former Prime Minister Bhutto's often quoted remarks that the Pakistanis will 'eat grass' if necessary to match the Indian nuclear capability reflected the intensity of the Pakistanis' 'helplessness and insecurity'. The explosion meant that the Pakistanis will not only have to forget about the Kashmir issue but will also have to learn to live under the shadow of a hostile and powerful nuclear neighbour. For them this was a bitter pill to swallow. Besides, the memories of the East Pakistan débâcle were still fresh.

Mrs Gandhi's assurances in May 1974 that India remained committed to only peaceful uses of nuclear energy did not alleviate Pakistan's apprehensions. Bhutto suggested that India should commit itself, along with other nuclear states, to protect the non-nuclear states against nuclear attack or alternatively publicly commit itself never to make nuclear weapons.[14] Given the past history of mutual animosity, Mrs Gandhi's assurance did not seem credible at the time, but with no new nuclear explosions during the years 1975–8, India's claim began to acquire some credibility. But during late 1982, Mrs Gandhi began to drop hints about another nuclear explosion in the near future, and deals she made to acquire missile technology from France and the sophisticated MiG-27 from the Soviets were also revealed. There also were American newspaper reports based on satellite-derived intelligence that India might explode a second nuclear device.

Pakistan made frantic efforts to secure a protective nuclear umbrella from the major nuclear powers, especially from the Americans, but no guarantees were forthcoming. The Soviets could not provide such an umbrella because of their special relationship with India, while Chinese nuclear capabilities had not developed to an extent that it could extend its umbrella to a non-communist country. The Americans did not provide a guarantee to Pakistan because the region as a whole had never figured high on Washington's priority list. It was only after the introduction of Soviet combat troops in Afghanistan in December 1979 that the region in general and Pakistan in particular became an area of increased American interest. The recent Pak-American aid package invoked somewhat traditional reactions from India. Despite having a fair idea of the implications of the Soviet invasion of Afghanistan for Pakistan's security and Pakistan's urgent need for modernisation of its equipment, India both vehemently criticised and failed to encourage Pakistan's offer of a 'No War Pact'.

Given the existing disparities in size, population, resources, technological development, military strength and defence production capabilities, and considering the somewhat non-conciliatory Indian attitude, the threat from India has not yet really receded. In fact, the current Indian reactions to Pakistan's efforts to modernise its forces, the muted response to the Soviet invasion of Afghanistan, the discouraging attitude towards Pak peace moves in the area, and the existing high degree of imbalance in capabilities provide ample evidence to civilians and soldiers alike that the threat from India has not yet faded and should not be underestimated.

The threat emanating from Afghanistan did not acquire serious proportions until the Soviet occupation. Previously, Pakistan's military strength was more than adequate to cope with the Afghans alone. Pakistan has never really enjoyed friendly relations with Afghanistan, mainly because of Afghani irredentist claims on Paktunistan.

Before 1976, the Paktunistan issue often reduced Pak-Afghan relations to breaking point and led to the sealing of borders. However, the years 1976–8 saw a significant rapprochement with President Daud visiting Pakistan twice and Pakistani leaders making return visits. The outcome of these visits was that Kabul dropped its insistence on Paktun self-determination, hostile propaganda in both countries ceased, and an active search for an amicable solution of the Paktunistan dispute was well under way when the Marxist takeover in April 1978 immediately reversed the trend. The birth of the resistance movement and the subequent violent clashes between Afghan forces and resistance groups led to a large-scale refugee influx into Pakistan. The introduction of Soviet combat troops into Afghanistan not only alarmed the Pakistanis but also generated fears and apprehensions for the Indians. Both Iran and Pakistan began to calculate whether or not their long-standing fears of a Russian desire to gain access to warm-water ports through their territories was about to materialise.

The Soviet invasion of Afghanistan has produced a situation which has all the essential ingredients of a long-term guerrilla movement. One essential element is the availability of sanctuaries. The Afghan guerrillas are using both Pakistani and Iranian territories without the approval or, in some cases, even the knowledge of the neighbouring governments. The nature of the geographical terrain around the Afghan borders with Iran and Pakistan is such that neither the Pakistanis nor the Iranians would be able to completely destroy these sanctuaries. Not only are the tribesmen extremely familiar with all the passes along the border but they also have their kinsmen living across the border. In addition, the governments in Iran and Pakistan have neither the capability nor the manpower to plug all the routes of infiltration. This inability of the two governments is often interpreted as deliberate encouragement and support for the Afghan guerrilla cause.

For Pakistan, the Soviet invasion has introduced many disturbing elements in its strategic environment. First, the invasion itself has generated fears and apprehensions among many Pakistanis that their country would be the next target. Many Pakistanis believe that having consolidated its position in Afghanistan, Moscow will try to extend its influence beyond Afghan borders. The argument that the Soviets are likely to use Afghanistan as a springboard to destabilise Pakistan in order to gain access to the warm waters of the Indian Ocean, is still held valid by a sizeable section of Pakistanis. Sandwiched between Soviet-occupied Afghanistan and Soviet ally India, such anxieties do not seem too far-fetched, especially if viewed within the context of past Soviet attitudes toward Pakistan.

Second, because of the presence of large numbers of Afghan refugees on Pakistani soil and the continuous Afghan civil war, the possibility that Pakistan may be drawn into the Afghani turmoil willingly or unwillingly cannot be overlooked.[15] Given the nature of the Afghan civil war and the activities of the resistance movement, it can be assumed that the crisis will be protracted. If the civil war persists and the Soviet casualty rate becomes intolerable, the Soviets might seriously contemplate undertaking hot pursuit and sanctuary-busting operations. Once this happens, Pakistan would be dragged more deeply into the Afghan crisis unwillingly. When Pakistan decided to accommodate a large number of refugees on compassionate grounds it became involved indirectly in this struggle. However, this noble Pakistani gesture could provide a pretext for the Soviets to accuse Pakistan of helping and providing sanctuaries to the Afghan guerrillas. What the Soviets appear to have failed thus far to recognise is the fact that the massive refugee influx has presented the government of Pakistan with an irresolvable dilemma. If it organises help and provides the bare minimum facilities to these refugees on humanitarian grounds, then Moscow accuses Pakistan of aiding, abetting and encouraging what it terms counter-revolutionary elements. If it does not look after them, then the danger of refugee camps becoming hotbeds of insurgency appears even more threatening.

Third, the Soviets may be tempted to exploit the internal problems arising from subversive activities in the bordering Northwest Frontier Province (NWFP) and Baluchistan by dissident elements within Pakistan. It is often reported that the Baluchis feel 'they have never had a fair deal and are still not getting one'.[16] The Punjabi-dominated Army and bureaucracy is unable to understand the gravity of the Baluchi problem. Similar feelings, though on a much reduced scale, also exist in other minority provinces such as the Sind and the NWFP. The problems of the NWFP and Baluchistan have been further compounded by the massive influx of Afghan refugees.

While it is true in strategic terms that, because of Afghanistan's internal problems and relative military inferiority, Kabul cannot pose a serious threat to Pakistan's security, the danger of possible fall-out from Afghani political instability into the restive neighbouring provinces of Pakistan cannot be discounted either. The NWFP and Baluchistan are extremely prone to such an eventuality because of the existence of dissident elements, which in the past were actively encouraged and materially supported by Afghanistan. For the Iranians, there is even a greater danger that the movement for a greater Baluchistan (which includes Iranian Baluchistan) might now be revived and developed with the help of the Soviets as well as the Afghanis. The resulting destabilisation of the region would provide ample opportunities to the Soviets to gain at least partial, if not complete, control of the Gulf and its oil resources.

The Soviets have not only deployed some 100 000 or more combat troops (roughly divided into eight divisions, including mechanised infantry and airborne divisions), but have also employed more than 300 helicopters and aircraft in Afghanistan (including the MI-24 helicopter gunship, MiG-21, MiG-23 and MiG-25). Perhaps the most disturbing aspect of the Soviet presence in Afghanistan for the security planners of Pakistan is that they have not only upgraded the existing airfields but are also constructing many new ones with a view to deploying all types of Soviet aircraft. Besides, the reported occupation of the Wakhan strip has made the strategic Karakoram highway into southwestern China much more vulnerable.

SECURITY PERCEPTIONS

Pakistan's current perception of the central balance seems to be much closer to reality than was the case during the early days of independence when regional developments were far more important than any calculated analysis of the long-term intentions of the superpowers. The India factor virtually had a blinding effect on Pakistan's perceptions. Security relationships were contemplated but with a singular objective in mind, how to deter the Indian threat. Similarly, American security perceptions were largely influenced by the communist threat to the 'free world'. Initially, attempts were made to draw both India and Pakistan into the security network that the Americans envisaged for the area. Pakistan responded positively to American overtures, primarily because Indian irredentism was far more dangerous than the non-existent communist threat. Aware of the major motivating force behind Pakistan's response, the Americans saw Pakistan's cooperation as useful in establishing a northern tier (CENTO) and a southern tier (SEATO) to counter communist aggression: 'Pakistan was the point at which the alliance system geographically converged, and thus a linchpin in their continuity.'[17] Apart from strengthening local self-defence capabilities, the Americans secured certain specific privileges from Pakistan, such as facilities for launching high altitude reconnaissance aircraft over Soviet or Chinese territory, which were significant privileges in the era before spy satellites.[18]

While rejecting American offers perceived to divide the world into two armed camps and opting for non-alignment as the best form of security, India reacted strongly to Pakistan's participation in the Western alliance system and responded enthusiastically to Soviet overtures. Not only did she invite the Soviets into the area in 1955, but the intensity of India's enthusiasm provided an opportunity to the Soviets to penetrate South Asia. The Sino-Soviet rift and the Sino-Indian border clash further facilitated this process and eventually led to the signing of the Treaty of Friendship and Cooperation.

While appreciating the American role in strengthening Pakistan's economy and defence, especially during the early phase of the post-partition period, Islamabad subsequently was disappointed by three major let-downs. The first blow was struck in the aftermath of the Sino-Indian border clash of 1962 when President Kennedy decided to rush military aid to India disregarding his earlier commitment to Pakistan. President Kennedy had promised to consult President Ayub before deciding to send military aid to India.[19] Besides Pakistan's obvious disenchantment, the subsequent military imbalance in the area was most disturbing. The second major let-down was the arms embargo which the Americans imposed on South Asia after the outbreak of the 1965 Indo-Pak War. The third let-down came during the 1971 Indo-Pak War in which not only was India regarded by most nations of the world as an aggressor, but the Soviets became actively involved in the proceedings. The USS *Enterprise* mission was seen as nothing more than a symbolic American gesture which made no serious effort to prevent the dismemberment of Pakistan.[20]

Apart from the three major let-downs, two more factors have contributed substantively to the eventual erosion of American influence in Pakistan. First, the Pakistanis felt that the Americans had not pursued an even-handed policy regarding the quest for nuclear technology in South Asia. As compared to its tough and uncompromising policy toward Pakistan, the American policy regarding India's nuclear quest seems much milder despite the fact that it was India which used American and Canadian supplied material to explode a nuclear device in 1974.[21] Second, American policies in the Middle East often have hurt the sensitivities of the people of Pakistan, particularly its concern for the security of Israel.

American policy in South Asia has been mostly reactive to events and has lacked coherence and consistency. It has shown scant regard for the feelings and interests of its ally. Not only have American policies been unable to prevent Soviet expansion but they also have influenced Pakistan to view its relations with the Americans in more realistic terms. Pakistan has learned the hard way that where there is little identity of interests between two parties, often a treaty is not kept.[22] Thus the Americans came to be viewed as undependable partners by the Pakistanis. Perhaps this explains why Pakistan is treading its path cautiously with the Americans following the Afghanistan crisis, despite the fact that a congruity of interests now exists. Compared to the Americans, the Soviets and the Chinese are regarded as much more dependable allies. Although the Soviet image has been tarnished by its invasion of Afghanistan, its consistency in relations with India, though generating fears for the Pakistanis, is in many ways appreciated, particularly in non-official circles. Some influential groups even advocate the recognition of the dictates of geography and assert that the best way out is to evolve a working relationship with the Soviets. To ascertain any non-official view in Pakistan is a rather difficult task because the government-controlled media rarely encourages debates on issues or policies of any significance. It is thus difficult for the thinking population (whatever little there may be) to make contributions.

CONCLUSIONS

As mentioned at the outset of this essay, Pakistani security perceptions are largely determined by regional developments. It perceives the security of South Asia as being linked to the involvement and power interplay of the superpowers in the region. Although it may be possible to insulate the region from superpower rivalry, it is not a desirable objective for the smaller regional powers. To insulate the region implies a recognition of India's predominant position there, a prospect with which the Pakistanis have not yet fully reconciled themselves. While recognising India's pre-eminent position in the region, the smaller nations fear that the insulation of the area from superpower involvement would only remove the balancing mechanism and promote Indian hegemony. India, on its part, has not made concerted efforts to alleviate such fears. Instead, its muted reaction on the Soviet invasion of Afghanistan and mixed response to Pakistan's efforts to advance normalisation reinforced the old fear.

Pakistan's current dilemma is that while it theoretically opposes superpower involvement in the region, it needs a superpower's assistance to counter the moves of others. As long as the Soviets continue to maintain their military presence in Afghanistan and India does not realistically view the developments in Afghanistan or encourage the normalisation process, the chances are that Pakistan will not feel compelled to translate its theoretical opposition to superpower meddling into a more practical opposition, at a time when there is a greater identity of interests between Pakistan and the US.

Pakistan views itself as a small power with limited resources that are rapidly devoured by its own security needs. Its major security concern is India but recently an Afghanistan crisis coupled with closer Indo-Soviet links has adversely complicated its security environment. To improve its security environment, Pakistan has once again been compelled to renew its ties with the Americans, albeit cautiously and reluctantly. Pakistan realises the futility of entanglement in the superpowers' power game and has opted to stay as far away as possible from it. It has joined the Non-Aligned Movement and has strengthened its ties with the Islamic world. But its security perceptions are largely the product of the existing geopolitical environment. Neither the participation in the Non-Aligned Movement nor the close ties with the Islamic world have so far really helped to resolve its security predicament. Thus, one witnesses a situation in which Pakistan is left with no option but to seek favours with those who severely disappointed it in the past. However, the renewed linkage is based on a realistic appraisal of each other's interests rather than on the misperceptions and inflated hopes that often accompanied alliance partnerships in the Cold War era.

NOTES

1. See Stephen P. Cohen, 'US, Weapons and South Asia: a Policy Analysis', *Pacific Affairs*, XLIX:1, Spring 1976, p. 67.
2. T. B. Millar, 'America's Alliance: Asia', *America's Security in the 80s*, Part II, Adelphi Paper No. 174, International Institute for Strategic Studies, London, 1982, pp. 28–9.
3. Ibid.
4. See, Leo E. Rose, 'The Superpowers in South Asia: a Geostrategic Analysis', *Orbis*, XXII:2, Summer 1978, p. 401. See also Geoffrey Jukes, *The Soviet Union in Asia*, Angus and Robertson, London, 1973, pp. 99–112; and Pervaiz Iqbal Cheema, *Conflict and Cooperation in the Indian Ocean: Pakistan's Interests and Choices*, Canberra Papers on

Strategy and Defence, No. 23, Strategic and Defence Studies Centre, Australian National University, Canberra, 1980, p. 37.
5. Jukes, op. cit.; and Cheema, op. cit.
6. William J. Barnds, 'The USSR, China and South Asia', *Problems of Communism*, XXVI:6, November–December 1977, pp. 14–16.
7. Leaders like Acharya Kripalani (President, Indian National Congress) said that 'neither Congress nor the nation has given up its claim of a United India', while Sardar V. B. Patel (Home Minister) asserted that 'sooner than later, we shall again be united in common allegiance to our country'. Cited in M. Ayub Khan, *Friends Not Masters*, Oxford University Press, London, 1967, pp. 115–16.
8. Among the unsettled issues which generated distrust were the division of financial and military assets, the massive refugee influx, evacuee property problems, the question of Indus waters, the minorities issue, and the question of the integration of princely states like Juna-gadh, Hyderabad, and Jammu and Kashmir.
9. For details, see S. D. Muni, 'South Asia', in Mohammed Ayoob, *Conflict and Intervention in the Third World*, Croom Helm, London, 1980.
10. Mohammed Ayoob, 'India and Pakistan: Prospect for Detente', *Pacific Community*, VIII:1, October 1976, pp. 156–7.
11. S. Irtiza Hussain, 'The Politico-Strategic Balance in South Asia', *Strategic Studies*, I:2, July–September 1977, p. 36.
12. Ayoob, op. cit., pp. 156–7 and 165–6.
13. Ibid.
14. *Dawn*, 19 January 1974.
15. *Pacific Defence Reporter Yearbook, 1978–79*, pp. 160–1.
16. For detailed analysis of winds of change, see Lawrence Ziring, *Pakistan: The Enigma of Political Development*, Westview Press, Boulder, Colorado, 1980, pp. 248–57. See also, Atizaz Ahsan, 'In search for political order', *The Muslim*, 16–17 May 1982.
17. Rodney W. Jones, 'Mending Relations with Pakistan', *Washington Quarterly*, Spring 1981, pp. 17–29.
18. Ibid.
19. For detailed exchange of notes and statements, see Khan, op. cit., pp. 129–53. See also, G. W. Choudhury, *India, Pakistan, Bangladesh and Major Powers*, The Free Press, New York, 1975, pp. 11–122; and P. I. Cheema, 'Pakistan–American Relations: a Question of Credibility', *The Muslim*, 2–4 December 1982.
20. Cohen, op. cit., p. 67.
21. Cheema, 'Pakistan–American Relations: a Question of Credibility'.
22. David Formkins, 'Entangling Alliances', *Foreign Affairs*, XLVIII:4, July 1970, pp. 688–700.

9 An Indian Perspective on International Security

K. SUBRAHMANYAM

INTRODUCTION

The security perspective of any nation is largely determined by its historical memories and its perceptions of current conflicts of interests with other nations. Ideology no doubt has played a role in sustaining conflicts between nations in recent decades, but its role has been very limited. Ideological differences tend to be played down whenever conflict and identity of interests among nations supervene in international relations. The Western nations and the Soviet Union overcame their ideological gap when faced with the Hitlerite threat. The United States and the Soviet Union, in spite of all their antagonisms, rivalries and ideological differences, have never fought against each other, except for one incident of a limited character during the Bolshevik Revolution. China and the US did not permit differences in ideology to stand in the way of the normalisation of their relations, particularly in light of the mutuality of their strategic interests regarding the perceived threat posed by the Soviet Union. Therefore, while ideological differences have to be taken into account in determining mutual security perspectives they cannot be considered the sole or even the crucial determining factors in international perspectives.

Systemic differences in terms of political, social and economic values have not always prevented nations from collaborating with each other nor has affinity in values prevented them from fighting with each other. Nor has there been any consistency between values practised by a country domestically and externally. The biggest empires of the world were established by Britain and France even as they were becoming liberal democratic societies. These factors are emphasised here to highlight that the Cold War, which has been renewed, is more a struggle for power than one for ideology.

A major influence on Indian security perceptions is the experience of colonial subjugation. The earlier invaders of the sub-continent were absorbed into India but the colonisers who came across the ocean remained colonial masters for over two centuries. While other invasions did not affect India's economy or technology, colonial rule exploited India for the benefit of British industrialisation and put India's economy and technology into a deep freeze. It is noteworthy that the occupation of India was justified in the initial stages in terms of the global struggle of Britain against France.

The Indian fears of the new Cold War are reinforced by the behaviour patterns of the two superpowers. According to a study conducted by the Brookings Institute in the United States, in the period 1945–75 the US had demonstrated the use of force without war on 215 occasions and the Soviet Union on 195 occasions. At least one major US exercise of the use of force without war was during the Bangladesh war when the US task force headed by the USS *Enterprise* was sent into the Bay of Bengal. It is commonplace to cite the fact that out of nearly 130 instances of major acts of international and intranational violence since World War II, nearly 120 took place in the developing world. What is usually not publicised is that in two thirds of these there were interventions by the industrialised nations. Interventionism by great powers has thus become a major source of insecurity for developing nations.

Similarly the arms build-up in the developing world is much talked about and it is often pointed out that the rate of growth of military expenditure in the developing world is higher than that in the industrialised world. But a detailed analysis of the facts would lead to a different perspective. According to the *SIPRI Yearbook 1982*, out of the global defence expenditure of US$518.7 billion (in 1979 prices) the developed market economies spent 50.6 per cent. The centrally-planned economies, the Warsaw Pact countries, Albania, North Korea, Mongolia, China and Cuba, spent 33.5 per cent. The other developing countries spent 15.9 per cent of the global military expenditure. In this latter group, the OPEC countries (including six West Asian, four North African, one Latin American, and one ASEAN country) were responsible for 8.9 per cent of the global expenditure. Of the remainder in this group, the high per capita income developing countries, thirty-five in number (eighteen in the

Western Hemisphere, four in West Asia, five in East Asia, two in Oceania and six in Africa), spent 3.9 per cent. Out of the balance, some twenty-four developing countries with per capita incomes of $300–700 spent 1.4 per cent, while the rest of the developing world (over fifty countries, including all countries of South Asia) spent about 1.7 per cent. India and South Asia are surrounded on all sides with areas having higher rates of defence spending. This factor is bound to have an impact on the Indian security perception.

The sub-continent by itself is perhaps not an area of high vital stakes to the three major nuclear powers, but the surrounding areas of Southeast Asia and Southwest Asia, including the Persian Gulf, are deemed to be areas of vital interest. The extra-regional powers have, however, intervened in the affairs of the sub-continent because of their interests in the surrounding areas. The US supplied arms to Pakistan in the fifties and sixties and entered into an executive agreement in 1959 mainly on account of its interest in securing an airbase at Peshawar and an electronic surveillance base at Badber, both of which were directed against the USSR. Pakistan was incorporated into the SEATO military alliance directed against China. The US attempt to intervene in the Bangladesh Liberation War in 1971 was inspired by its anxiety to please China with whom it was entering into a new relationship. The Soviet interest in the sub-continent is also largely attributable to its anxiety to keep the US and China out of an area close to its southern borders. The Chinese had a natural interest initially in excluding US presence from the sub-continent and subsequently had a stake in attenuating Soviet influence in the area. Therefore, India has reason to be concerned about problems of security that could be created by the secondary impact of the confrontations among the major powers in its neighbourhood.

THE SUPERPOWERS AND THE INDIAN OCEAN REGION

Security in the Indian Ocean region has to be viewed against the background of superpower confrontation in the Indian Ocean littoral that has come about as a consequence of the new Cold War. Even as the first Cold War came to an end with the Helsinki Declaration, it was pointed out that a detente limited to Europe alone would not be viable or long-lasting. This fear was realised by 1978 when the Indian Ocean and conventional arms transfer talks between the two superpowers were broken off by the US. This was followed by the NATO decision to step up defence expenditures by 3 per cent of real growth rates, the continuous deployment of an American carrier task force in the Indian Ocean following the fall of the Shah, Washington's decision on the Rapid Deployment Force, the strengthening of the Diego Garcia base, the seeking of facilities for military deployment in the Indian Ocean region, the NATO announcement on Euromissiles, and, lastly, the Soviet intervention in Afghanistan. The last event did not trigger off the new Cold War, but was a culmination of a series of developments which had been initiated in 1978 and 1979.

In parallel to these developments came the thesis which sought to establish a linkage between the allegedly increased Soviet proclivity for intervention in Third World countries and their achievement of parity in strategic nuclear weaponry and their building of a blue water navy. This, it was argued, was evident from their support to Angola and Ethiopia. But, this interpretation does not fit the known historical facts. The Soviet Union, as a global power, had always attempted to intervene in a situation when an opportunity presented itself. In the 1950s, as Indonesia came under Western pressure, the USSR supplied arms to that country (as it also did to Egypt's President Nasser). In 1962 it came out in strong support of Cuba. Similarly the Soviet air bridges to resupply Ethiopia in 1977–8 and Vietnam in 1979 were not new developments but were preceded by a similar operation in the 1973 Arab-Israeli War. The Cuban support to Angola backed by the Soviet Union was a response to the combined intervention of the CIA, Zaire, China and South Africa in favour of the Angolan factions of UNITA and FNLA. The Soviet support to Ethiopia was fully endorsed by the Organisation of African Unity (OAU) which held Somalia responsible for violating the basic principle of the OAU charter by trying to alter the territorial *status quo* by force. These were instances where Third World countries under pressure from one superpower sought the help and countervailing power of the other superpower.

Underlying the behaviour patterns of the two superpowers is the basic perception that the international system is a bipolar zero-sum game in strategic terms. This incorrect perception even leads them to interpret developments brought about by indigenous factors as having been caused by the adversary, and to conclude that if a particular development is seen as not beneficial to one's interest then it must result in gain to the rival and thus justifies counteraction. This counteraction usually takes on the form of intervention in the area by selective arms supplies to a rival of the Third World nation where the original development took place, various kinds of covert and overt actions, and the acquisition of facilities in an adjoining country. This sets off a chain reaction in the region exacerbating the insecurity of all states there.

In quite a few cases, the superpowers' predictable behaviour pattern has been manipulated for parochial gain by the rulers of some developing nations. South Africa and Israel are classic examples of smaller nations holding a superpower hostage to their regional policies very much against its own larger national interests. Somalia attempted to play this game. While the US reacted in the Cold War pattern by keeping silent on Somali aggression, the Soviet Union was more flexible and switched sides. This again triggered off the standard Cold War response from the US which moved to support Somalia.

The developing nations are largely new nations and in most cases do not have broad-based elite participation in formulating their national interests or foreign policy. In the first Cold War in Europe there was a structured confrontation within the discipline of military alliances, with fairly good communication between the leaders of alliances and the members acting within a broadly common political culture. The new Cold War rivalry pursued in the Indian Ocean littoral does not have these features that otherwise contribute to confrontation stability. Hence, this Cold War is more inchoate and risk-prone than the earlier one. This is a major rationale for the plea to declare the Indian Ocean as a zone of peace.

Often it is argued that the US is stepping up its presence in the Indian Ocean area mainly as a response to the request of a number of littoral states who, though they may vote for the Indian Ocean Peace Zone resolution, privately urge the US to step up its presence so as to balance the impact of the vast Soviet land mass and its awesome military capability at one nation depth from the Indian Ocean. These arguments cut both ways. If the Soviet land mass at one nation depth from the Indian Ocean has an impact on the security of the area then conversely the presence of the rival superpower navy equipped with nuclear weapons deployed in the Indian Ocean would have an adverse impact on Soviet security and justify its various actions including intervention in Afghanistan. Secondly, if the US were to accede to the allegedly private requests of some littoral nations to maintain a presence in the area, then Soviet counter-presence will follow. The Soviet Union is building nuclear-powered aircraft carriers and *Typhoon*-class submarines, and the continued US naval presence in the Indian Ocean will legitimise the eventual entry of these Soviet weapons systems into the region. If the 'zero option' is deemed a viable one in Europe in respect to Euromissiles (though there are different interpretations of what zero implies to rival sides), it is not quite clear why zero presence in the Indian Ocean area is considered an impractical proposition.

The situation in the Indian Ocean region has been complicated by American nuclear war doctrines and by the spatial proliferation of nuclear weapons into it. There have been discussions on the need to use nuclear weapons in defence of the Persian Gulf area. Nuclear weapons are standard equipment on board US aircraft carriers continuously stationed in the Arabian Sea and dual capable B-52 bombers reported to be operating from Diego Garcia. The US declaration in regard to the use of nuclear weapons is full of ambivalence. It guarantees

> not to use nuclear weapons against any non-nuclear weapon state party to the non-proliferation treaty or any comparable international binding commitment not to acquire nuclear explosive devices, except in the case of an attack on the United States, its territories or armed forces or its allies by such a state allied to a nuclear weapon state or associated with a nuclear weapon state in carrying out or sustaining the attack.[1]

The phrase associated with a nuclear weapon state can be interpreted according to one's own convenience and it is to be noted that the attack itself need not be a nuclear attack to justify the US resorting to nuclear weapons. Secondly, the declaration is vague as to whether the attack on the US armed forces would also include a counter-attack by a country when the US forces launch an attack on it. This ambivalence should be considered against the background of the proclaimed US policy not to commit itself to 'no first use', unlike the Soviet Union and China.

Therefore, the Indian Ocean Peace Zone proposal has to be looked at from the point of view of the risks of a nuclear war and not merely from the point of view of the parochial interests of the leaderships of some littoral states. Most of the nuclear weapons deployed on nuclear weapon carriers in the Indian Ocean can only be tactical ones capable of being used primarily in situations of conflict *vis-à-vis* the littoral states. Consequently, this spatial proliferation of nuclear weapons in the Indian Ocean significantly adds to the sense of insecurity of the states in the area. Also, along with clandestine nuclear proliferation by nations like Israel and South Africa, it generates pressures for further nuclear weapon proliferation.

A central US command covering nineteen nations of the Indian Ocean littoral has been announced. Additional military appropriations running into several hundred millions of dollars are being sought in the FY 1984 budget to expand the facilities in the Diego Garcia base and improve the facilities for deployment of US forces in Ras Banas in Egypt, Berbera in Somalia, Mombasa in Kenya and Masirah in Oman. There are also reports of US interest in electronic surveillance facilities in Pakistan, as a contingency if US facilities in China's Xinjiang are lost as a result of an improvement in Sino-Soviet relations. There are reports of Soviet interests in developing facilities in Aden and at Dahlak in Ethiopia. There are thirteen US ships with equipment prepositioned near Diego Garcia. There is no secret that the Rapid Deployment Force is designed to secure the Middle East oil not so much against a Soviet threat as from threats likely to be posed by domestic developments in the Middle East oil-producing countries. Once this capability is established, the possibility of various other kinds of intervention in the littoral states cannot be ruled out. Such interventionist capability can also be used selectively in local conflicts between littoral nations. In 1967, US Defence Secretary Robert McNamara proposed stationing a Fast Deployment Logistic Ship Force in each of the three oceans of the world. This was vetoed by the US Senate after its Armed Services Committee said that there was concern about creating an impression that the US had assumed the function of policing the world and would consider intervention in any strife-ridden nation of the world. What was feared in 1967 has now come about.

New weapons technologies are under development which will make such intervention operations less costly to states having high technological capabilities. A preview of future high technology intervention operations was provided in the Lebanon invasion by Israel. Precision guided munitions linked with airborne surveillance and target tracking capability, airborne warning and control systems directing air strikes, sense and destroy anti-armour munitions, area weapons such as cluster bombs and fuel air explosives, and such will make future intervention operations by industrialised countries against developing countries less costly in lives and expenditure. While there is so much talk about arms being acquired by developing countries it is very likely that the technology gap between developing and developed countries will widen to the disadvantage of the former.

Very few developing countries will be in a position to absorb the sophisticated technologies of these new generation weapons. Therefore, it is highly probable that countries threatened by intervention by one superpower will seek the countervailing presence of the other superpower. In view of the difficulties involved for most developing countries in handling such sophisticated weaponry, they may have to *depend upon* relatively more advanced developing countries like Cuba and Pakistan for technical manpower assistance.

The thesis that the Soviet Union would be running short of energy resources and therefore it would need the Middle East's oil has been thoroughly discredited. Also, the significance of Middle East oil for the industrialised economies is eroding. Today the Gulf provides only 20 per cent of the total world demand, and a number of new sources with very large potential are under development elsewhere. Given the elasticity in supply that is now available, it will be difficult to maintain that even a Saudi Arabia supplying currently 10 per cent of world's demand can strangulate the industrialised economies by shutting off its supplies. The stoppage of Iranian and Iraqi supplies, which once constituted 7 per cent of world supply, did not stop the wheels of industry in the developed world. It formerly was said that the Suez Canal was the jugular vein of Western Europe and its closure would mean disastrous consequences. However, the world adjusted to the disuse of the Suez Canal. Thus, it is time there was a dispassionate reassessment of the risks involved in any closure or suspension of Middle East oil.

The countries of the Indian Ocean littoral, especially the Middle East and Persian Gulf countries, are simultaneously subject to pressures of a number of conflict systems. The impact of the East–West conflict has already been referred to. The North–South conflict also has its impact. The oil-producing countries aim at having optimal prices for their primary commodity in order to accelerate their own development. The industrialised countries have seen a non-military threat in the cartelisation of the oil-producing countries. They followed a strategy of increasing the sense of insecurity of the oil-producing developing nations in the Middle East and at the same time offering them security through the sale of military hardware and various kinds of reassuring commitments. However, the Iranian revolution exposed as fallacious the assumption that the US would be able to guarantee the domestic security of a ruler. The post-Iranian revolution environment has led to the creation of the Rapid Deployment Force as an instrument of intervention to ensure domestic security of the rulers threatened not by external threat but by domestic turbulence. This only shows that the lessons of the Iranian revolution have not been learnt. While it may be possible for an intervention force to keep law and order in the small states of the Gulf, it is not going to be easy to do it in more populous states. While the cost of intervention may come down because of new weapons technology, the cost of occupation of a foreign country and policing it will go up. Once such a process of intervention starts it may end up quite negatively by triggering off forces of nationalism in neighbouring countries or leading some of the neighbouring countries to invoke the countervailing power and presence of the rival superpower.

A major factor having an impact on the domestic security of the rulers is the conflict between tradition and modernisation. The enormous oil profits have led to an accelerated process of modernisation, while the political structures remain generally archaic. The oil prosperity is now likely to slow down as a result of a fall in oil prices and demand. The burst of prosperity and its demise are likely to create new tensions and turbulence in these countries. Also, fundamentalist Islamic revivalism is bound to result in sectarian conflicts. Only secularisation leads to ecumenical unity. Already one sees the impact of this adverse development of sectarianism in the Gulf area. Given all these conflict systems, West and Southwest Asia are bound to be turbulent and unstable and any intervention in this area is likely to result in wide-scale repercussions.

THE INDIAN VIEW ON CHINA

To India's north is China, which is attempting to stabilise itself after the turbulence of the Cultural Revolution. It has been successful to some extent, although many crucial questions about China's future remain, especially what will happen with the departure of the present leadership. From the reports emanating from China it would appear that there is still considerable resistance to the pragmatic reforms introduced by the Deng Xiaoping leadership, and that this has exacerbated unresolved controversies between the Chinese Communist Party and the People's Liberation Army. The impact of such unresolved controversies on the Army–Party relationship is difficult to predict, but they do introduce an element of uncertainty for China's neighbours. It will be remembered, for instance, that the Chinese attack on India took place at a time when Lin Biao was helping Mao

Zedong stage a comeback to topple the Liu Shaoqi–Deng Xiaoping leadership.

China has defence modernisation as one of its Four Modernisations objectives. As of now, the programme is not being pushed vigorously in conventional weaponry, though in nuclear weapons China has tested an ICBM and a SLBM in the last three-year period. It could be argued that this combination of obsolescent and obsolete conventional weapons and a nuclear arsenal has the risk of lowering the nuclear threshold in the event of conflict. With the development of a Chinese SLBM the issue of the location and likely deployment of the submarines arises. If they are to perform a second strike role *vis-à-vis* the Soviet Union, they need to be deployed in an area from which the European and Central Asian Soviet cities could be targeted. The only area from which this could be done by such first generation missile submarines is the Arabian Sea. To deploy the missile submarine in the Indian Ocean the Chinese will need a home port in the Indian Ocean region, otherwise most of the time between crew changes will be spent by the submarine transiting from China to the deployment area. There have been some recent reports, including testimony before the US Congress, about a China–Pakistan nuclear relationship. The *quid pro quo* for China helping Pakistan with nuclear technology could be in one of two ways. First, some speculate that Pakistan may pass on some of the sophisticated conventional weapons technology of its US-supplied weaponry to China. The US has therefore amended the Arms Export Control Act to prohibit the transfer of sensitive equipment to any country which receives arms from a communist country. Senator John Glenn made it clear that this amendment was aimed at Pakistan. The second possibility could be for Pakistan to provide the homeport for Chinese missile submarines deployed in the Indian Ocean as a *quid pro quo* for help in the development of nuclear weapons.

While there has been no spectacular development, there is general acceptance of the assessment that China is attempting to normalise its relations with the Soviet Union and attenuate the degree of hostility between the two countries while distancing itself from the US. The Soviet Union has repeatedly expressed its desire to improve relations with China. Any improvement in Sino-Soviet relations will be a stabilising factor in the Asian strategic environment so long as it does not lead to a sharp deterioration in the Sino-US relationship. A balanced relationship between China and the two superpowers is more probable than China once again leaning to one side or the other. There is also likely to be great pressure on China to improve its relations with its neighbours. While there is reasonable justification for an optimistic outlook on China's impact on the Asian security environment, it will take quite some time for nations like India and Vietnam to overcome their inherent distrust of China. Until Deng Xiaoping came to power in 1978 and publicly recognised China's limitations, the motive underlying China's international relations was power and dominance. China had attempted to project a big power image through its ideology, large-scale arms transfers, prestigious economic aid projects, nuclear armaments programme, support to the Pol Pot genocidal clique, and, lastly, military clashes with the US, Soviet Union, India and Vietnam. In the current Indian perception there is optimism about China's impact on the Asian strategic environment, tempered with vigilant caution. While a number of positive signals have emerged on China's stake in a stable environment, its nuclear relations with Pakistan and its attempt to impose Pol Pot are causes for uneasiness and concern.

THE AFGHAN IMBROGLIO

The Soviet intervention in Afghanistan marked a qualitative change in that country's behaviour pattern. There is no doubt that the presence of Soviet forces down to the Khyber Pass has had an adverse impact on the sub-continental security environment that is somewhat similar to Chinese occupation and annexation of Tibet and the US permanent naval presence in the Indian Ocean. The Soviet move did not initiate the new Cold War but constituted a development in the Cold War unleashed in 1978. There is a considerable body of opinion that views the Soviet move into Afghanistan as a paranoid over-reaction to the series of US moves in the Indian Ocean area. The Soviet action in Afghanistan has been a costly mistake both in terms of men and material in Afghanistan and political costs in the non-aligned world. The intervention has been against a non-aligned nation and goes beyond the Yalta framework. The Soviet Union could have lived with the chaotic and turbulent situation in Afghanistan, as it has had to in the case of Iran or as India has had to in northern Burma. Even if one were to concede that the Soviet motivations were defensive, yet there has been a gross miscalculation on the costs and benefits of its action. Now Moscow is stuck in a situation from which it is difficult to extricate itself without loss of face. There also appears to be a consideration in the Soviet calculation that any appearance of weakness in the case of Afghanistan will be taken advantage of by the Western powers to apply pressure on the Soviet Union elsewhere, especially in Poland.

Whatever initial impressions the Soviet intervention may have had on other countries it is now obvious, after a lapse of three years, that there is no immediate adverse security impact on the nations in the immediate neighbourhood of Afghanistan. Neither Pakistan nor Iran have attempted to reinforce their defences *vis-à-vis* the Soviet Union. Pakistan keeps, according to General Zia ul Haq, 80 per cent of its armed forces on the Indian border. It has not initiated any significant steps to bolster its defensive capabilities in the northwest. Foreign Minister Aga Shahi said at the Lahore seminar of 30 June 1981 that if the Soviet Union were to move against Pakistan it would mean a superpower confrontation. He pointed out that the Soviet Union had assured that it posed no danger to Pakistan and that Islamabad had to take the Soviet Union at its word. He argued that Pakistan should be able to defend itself against an attack from any quarter but needed to strengthen its defence accordingly. It is quite obvious from this that Pakistan does not look on the Soviet Union as the principal threat. Rather it is India that remains the primary threat in the minds of the Pakistanis.

THE SITUATION IN SOUTHEAST ASIA

Among some Western and Southeast Asian observers, Vietnam is regarded as a proxy of the Soviet Union. Those who espoused the domino theory of the 1950s and 1960s and who once regarded China as a proxy of the USSR and Vietnam as a proxy of China now argue that Vietnam is a tool of Soviet interests. It does not make sense why a country which fought such prolonged and costly wars successively against France, the US and China should be a proxy for the distant Soviet Union. In the Indian view the shortsighted and revanchist policy pursued by the US and Thailand, China's attempt to pursue a hegemonistic policy towards Southeast Asia, and the joint efforts of these countries to apply all-round pressure on Vietnam left Hanoi with no choice but to invoke countervailing Soviet power and support. It is ironic that those who talked about the billion Chinese swamping Southeast Asia are today aiding and abetting the Chinese attempt to dominate the Indochinese peninsula. Those who kept silent when Prince Norodom Sihanouk was overthrown and the US forces occupied Kampuchea are today very eloquent in supporting Prince

Sihanouk as a front to cover the ugly reality of Pol Pot. Those who stood in the way of Sihanouk who had just been deposed by a puppet regime supported by external military forces attending the Lusaka Non-Aligned meeting are talking of principles in support of Sihanouk attending the Seventh Non-Aligned Summit. In the name of non-intervention in the internal affairs of a state, Pol Pot is today proclaimed as the legitimate ruler of a population three million of which he exterminated. When China talked of punishing other nations and teaching lessons in 1979, those who previously trumpeted about the Chinese threat to South and Southeast Asia in the 1950s and 1960s were eloquently silent. In the Indian view, Vietnam is a fiercely independent country which has undergone sufferings with little historical parallel. The Vietnamese are fully justified in their extreme sensitivity to security threats posed by their neighbours and their actions have largely been motivated by defensive considerations. The countries which espouse an anti-Vietnamese posture and support the Chinese pressure on Indochinese states are adopting a shortsighted and counter-productive policy detrimental to their own long-term interests.

INDIA AND REGIONAL SECURITY

Against this overall perspective about the Asian strategic environment, the security-related developments within the sub-continent have to be viewed. India is one of seven countries in South Asia but it is the largest, most populous and relatively more industrialised. India in terms of population, size, GNP, industrial production, science and technology dominates the other six South Asian states all taken together. India and Sri Lanka are the only two democratic countries in the region. India and Bangladesh are the only two secular nations, while the other five are theocratic states with established state religions. India is the only federal polity with a degree of autonomy for the constituent states and the various languages are used as official languages for administration at the state level. Two of the countries, Pakistan and Bangladesh, were carved out of a single polity of British India. The countries surrounding India share with India common languages, ethnicity, religions and culture and there are divided families in significant numbers living across international boundaries. All these factors contribute to the very complicated and dissonant political, economic and security relationships between India and its neighbours.

Once a nation-state has been created by partition from a larger entity, strong vested interests are bound to develop among the elite of the new state who wish to preserve its separate identity. One can see this phenomenon in operation in East Germany, South Korea and Taiwan. This is equally true of Pakistan and Bangladesh and they are under continuous compulsion to assert and further develop their separate identities. Unlike the other instances cited, in India there is total acceptance of the fact of partition and very few would favour the reversal of it today. India has publicly, and repeatedly, proclaimed that it has absolutely no desire for reunification, unlike the other cases mentioned. But it is natural for the smaller states to have certain fears, especially when they do not have a superpower to guarantee their survival and when the equation in regard to size and capabilities is far more disproportionate than in the case of the two Germanies and the two Koreas. For the elites in the smaller countries, a visible and publicised threat to separate identity is a convenient instrumentality in new nation-building. In the absence of such a visible threat, it becomes necessary to create a contrived one. It is therefore understandable for the elites of Pakistan and Bangladesh to entertain and build on fears about India to help in their own nation-building process. For Pakistanis, 1971 was a traumatic experience. The separation struggle was a case of a majority of a nation seceding because it was not allowed to play its rightful role in the polity by a minority which used military force against it. However, the Pakistanis stress that theirs is the only nation which was forcibly bifurcated in a war in the post-World War II period.

This problem does not exist to the same extent for the other neighbours of India in South Asia, as they have other problems. India continues to function as a federal state and Tamil, being an official language in India, Malaysia and Singapore, creates certain problems for Sri Lanka which is faced with the demand from its Tamil minority for a federal polity and official status for the Tamil language. The King of Nepal is under pressure to convert the Panchayati system into a multi-party democratic system. The dissidents of Nepal have always taken asylum in India. All these elites are also influenced by their readings of the history of nation-states in the West where larger states have always tried to dominate the smaller ones. Consequently, they are extremely sensitive to what they perceive as the capability of India to force its own views on them. The fact that they are unable to cite any specific instance of such conduct on India's part seems to them as being irrelevant. Their argument is 'if you have not so far done it you may start doing it sometime in future'. Most of these fears are psychological and are therefore difficult to resolve by rational means.

In India, too, there are deep-seated complexes. Indian history is replete with instances of kings and princes in the sub-continent collaborating with extra-regional powers and thereby bringing about the occupation of India. The extra-regional linkages of the smaller nations are therefore viewed with suspicion. Comparisons between India's relations with extra-regional powers and those of the smaller neighbours with them are not acceptable. In the Indian mind the relationship of India with extra-regional powers cannot be equated with those of the smaller powers with them in view of India's size and capabilities. India is also sensitive to what the Indians believe to be attempts at 'Balkanisation'. This fear arises not only out of memories of a long history punctuated by only limited periods when India was united under a single ruler, but also by the partition and by the attempts by China to intervene in support of insurgencies in the 1960s and 1970s. The four wars which India had to fight have left deep scars on the Indian psyche. Most Indian decision-makers have come to adopt the view that military strength is essential to shield the Indian developmental process from turbulence all around.

In light of the above considerations, realistically one must expect the process of regional cooperation to be a time-consuming process. None the less, recent developments in the sub-continent justify an optimistic view about the possibility of regional cooperation. The fall in oil prices and consequent reduction in the influence of the oil-producing West Asian countries, however transient the phenomenon may be, are likely to steer the nations of South Asia towards greater regional cooperation. As time goes by the fear of India is also likely to attenuate. Even Pakistan's quest for a nuclear weapons capability need not necessarily come in the way of such a development. No doubt when Indians come to believe that there is adequate evidence of Pakistan having reached a nuclear weapons capability there will be enormous pressures within India for a nuclear weapons programme. At this stage it is difficult to say whether both nations would become explicitly nuclear or would adopt the strategy of ambivalence successfully practised by Israel. The strategy of ambivalence has enabled the US to turn a blind eye on the Israeli nuclear capability. There is no reason why the Pakistani and Indian cases should not also be treated in the same manner so long as neither goes in for a nuclear weapons test. In any case, at any time of its own choice India is in a position to overtake the Pakistani nuclear capability and establish a clear deterrence equation *vis-à-vis* that country. There is no reason why symmetric nuclear capability of Pakistan and India should not stabilise the situation in the subcontinent. One tends to agree with Kenneth Waltz's observation that

> New nuclear states will confront the possibilities and feel the constraints that present nuclear states have experienced. New nuclear states will be more concerned for their safety and more mindful of dangers than some of the old ones have been. Until recently only the great and some of the major powers have had nuclear weapons. While nuclear weapons have spread, conventional weapons have proliferated. Under these circumstances, wars have been fought not at the centre but at the periphery of international politics. The likelihood of war decreases as deterrent and defensive capabilities increase. Nuclear weapons, responsibly used, make wars hard to start. Nations that have nuclear weapons have strong incentives to use them responsibly. These statements hold for small as for big nuclear powers. Because they do, the measured spread of nuclear weapons is more to be welcomed than feared.[2]

CONCLUSIONS

We are at present in a situation when the current generation of weapons is being replaced by a new generation of weapons. The third generation of sophisticated supersonic aircraft is replacing the second generation. Tanks with 115–125mm calibre are replacing those with 105mm calibre. New generation anti-tank missiles, air defence missiles and other precision-guided munitions are being introduced. The new technological revolution in micro-electronics is affecting every area of armaments. So long as nation-states feel the need for armed forces it logically follows that they have to equip them with current armaments. It is not possible for developing countries to continue with obsolete and obsolescent armaments because the industrialised countries which produce them will close down their production lines and spares will no longer be available. A developing country will not be able to ensure the serviceability of its weaponry unless it changes over to the current generation. Therefore, the arms race in conventional armaments in the developing countries is only a reflection of the arms race in the developed world. One must therefore expect that the countries of South Asia will also incur expenditures in modernising their armaments as the new generations of equipment are deployed by the industrialised countries and are spread by them in the developing world.

From the above account, it is obvious that today's globe has shrunk so that it would take only thirty minutes from the time of firing of a warhead to its impact in any part of the world. Thus, it is not realistic to talk merely about regional perspectives. Security is international and indivisible. The most important aspect of the insecurity of the nations is the Cold War between the two superpowers and its consequences. Therefore, the appropriate way to promote security is to bring the collective pressure of the international community to bear on the two superpowers and their allies to reverse the present Cold War. In this effort there is a general consensus among all the non-aligned nations as witnessed in the 7th Non-Aligned Summit.

NOTES

1. ' "Security Assurance" by the Nuclear-Weapon States as Presented to the Committee on Disarmament in 1980' (CD/139), quoted in *Comprehensive Study on Nuclear Weapons*, United Nations, New York, 1981, vol. I, Appendix II, p. 172.
2. Kenneth N. Waltz, 'The Spread of Nuclear Weapons: More May be Better', *Adelphi Papers*, 171, International Institute for Strategic Studies, London, 1981, p. 30.

10 Chinese Perspectives on International Security

DONALD HUGH McMILLEN

Since communist liberation in 1949, the international relations of the People's Republic of China (PRC) have fluctuated between introspection and interaction, reflecting variations in the priority assigned to the more revolutionary dimensions of its 'great experiment'. This study will assess the fundamental factors that condition Chinese foreign policy and security perspectives, often in subtle (but always complex) ways.[1] It will be argued that Chinese policy-makers currently view their polity as an unfulfilled (and long humiliated and frustrated) emerging nation-state in search of its own territorial, political, and socioeconomic form and pursuing its national development and interests as a socialist entity in a world of dynamically interacting states. While the concept of national interest fuels this basically balance-of-power perspective, ideology helps to shape and colour, as well as legitimise, it. For the immediate future, and during a time of crucial leadership-generation and 'techonomic' transition, Beijing's leaders believe that national security is to be found in a domestic prosperity and stability based upon a developmental rather than purely revolutionary approach to modernisation. This requires an active, but balanced, foreign policy emphasising the maintenance of national independence and sovereignty and the promotion of a stable global and regional environment. At the same time, it demands a cautious 'open door' to foreign techonomic inputs which will contribute to the building of a strong, modern Chinese state.

FOUNDATIONS OF CHINESE PERSPECTIVES OF THE WORLD

Geodemographic features, including location, size, natural resources, vast population and ethnicity, have long been of great importance to China's world view. In the evolution of traditional Chinese thought, the orthodox view was of an ethical and universal world order based upon a conflictual model which portrayed the forces of harmony and disharmony as being governed by the degree of imperial virtue. Morality, rather than law *per se*, was the basis for a hierarchial system of rule that extended, at least ideally, over a vast culture realm. But, this moral order also had political and ethnic dimensions, as reflected in the sinocentric tribute system. Thus, within the concept of a Chinese cultural imperium there emerged notions that could be called 'nationalistic', whether or not the people of China were yet aware of them. With the arrival of the technologically more advanced West at the turn of the nineteenth century, many of China's traditional institutions broke down, along with most of the assumptions which had underlain them. While it can be over-emphasised, the bitterness, suspicion and frustration caused by 'unequal treaties' and foreign meddling in China has not been forgotten by the present generation (nor, it might be added, has the memory of former Chinese domination died in the minds of many neighbouring Asians). It has contributed to the still basically conflictual Chinese view of the international order, which is dominated by the notion of 'contradiction' at all levels and is accompanied by the ever present prospect of universal disharmony and war.

When Chinese nationalism was awakened there was confusion and debate over its nature. In part it came to represent a drive for China to catch up with other nation-states and catch on to the evolving international system by rectifying its status inconsistency in the power-influence structure of that system. To some, this was to be achieved by retaining the 'essence' (*ti*) of the Confucian moral order while grafting on the 'utility' (*yong*) of the West's 'Mr Science and Mr Technology', especially modern weapons. Of course, the flaws in this 'self-strengthening' view included the inevitability that the utility would undermine the essence. Furthermore, there remained a strong strain of xenophobia in the evolution of Chinese nationalism. This continued to coexist, however uneasily, with the more xenophilic tendencies of Chinese modernisers who recognised the need for foreign dealings, even if they were wary of the potential dangers of such activities to their own ideologies and institutions. As Chinese nationalism eventually began to find focus around such Marxist-Leninist concepts as class struggle and anti-imperialism, there remained a basic duality of Chinese self-reliance and proletarian internationalism. Mao's emphasis on contradictions, with its associated notion of 'uniting temporarily but struggling absolutely', fed into this duality. Also, there may have been little popular understanding or agreement concerning the term 'nationalism' itself (*minzu zhuyi*), particularly because it was not always clear just what 'the people' (*minzu* or *renmin*) meant politically or ethnically. There perhaps was a wider appreciation of a sort of Chinese 'patriotism' (*aiguo zhuyi*, or 'love of country-ism') which traced its roots primarily to the proud culturalism/proto-nationalism of the pre-Western impact period.[2]

In sum, one cannot deny the dynamic character of change in Chinese thought and institutions over the last 150 years or so. Nor can one deny that this change occurred at differing rates at various sociopolitical levels in China, and that there may have even been many kinds of change occurring simultaneously. Undeniably, there have been basic continuities as well. How, then, will change and continuity interact in the future? Where does stability fit into the still evolving Chinese order? Will the Maoist legacy of sudden and periodically convulsive change be muted by efforts to implant a less frenetic yet still determined style of pragmatic readjustment? How resilient will the system be when confronted by old, new, or perhaps external, challenges? How will China be perceived by others, and in what ways will China respond to or play upon others' images of it?

By definition, an ideology is a set of beliefs which establishes the basic intellectual framework through which reality is perceived. While it provides an image of the ideal state of the world and thus determines the long-term goals of foreign policy, it also serves to rationalise and justify shorter term strategies and tactics. Ideology also posits a set of norms and criteria for assessing past failures and successes, and, for some, sets the limits of the permissible at any given time. Ideological formulae may thus affect the way in which events are perceived and the kinds of policies that are consequently adopted. A choice of policies is normally available to decision-makers, even with regard to such a central goal as national survival, and what they may choose will depend upon many factors, including their ideology. The problem is, however, that perception may or may not accord with reality, or that there is often a gap between a state's expectations and aspirations and its actual performance (which may also be crucially influenced by the availability of resources that can be marshalled to support it).

While the Chinese assert that their perspectives on international relations and security derive from Marxism–Leninism–Mao Zedong Thought, there is a wide range of theoretical assumptions in Western scholarly literature about the role of ideology in Chinese foreign policy formulation and behaviour. On the one hand, it has been argued that ideology is simply window-dressing for foreign policy decision-making and behaviour which is solely concerned with questions of power, security and traditional national interests. This view perceives ideology as simply the means which all national leaders use to legitimise their policies (and wage their party room battles), with ideology playing a very minor role or none at all in determining the actual direction of policy.[3] At the other extreme is the view that ideology is the primary explanation of communist foreign policy behaviour. It asks if national interest (which is said to be a vague term) is separable from ideology, or if it is a function of a system's ideology. It contends that the Beijing leadership both perceives the international environment and behaves within it in terms of a well defined yet non-dogmatic ideology which defines China's notion of its national interest and prescribes the means for pursuing and securing that interest under changing conditions and in relation to differing issues. Thus, in the perception of these decision-makers, there is no dichotomy between ideology and national interest.[4]

The position held in this chapter recognises the nationalist motivations of communist regimes, but believes that ideology is essential to a full understanding of the dynamics of actions in the international system. The argument here is that the Chinese communists are both Chinese and communists, and therefore their foreign policy pursues both national and ideological interests, albeit to varying degrees at different times.[5] The Chinese perspective shows the influence of both an ideological conceptualisation of the world and the persistent concerns of the *Realpolitik* world of power, security, prestige, and so forth. This interweaving of ideas and interests produces a shifting, mosaic-like blend of elements which contribute to policy formulation. While ideals or doctrine may occasionally be in the forefront, at other times they may fade into the background so as to make room for persistent interests which are independent of the espoused ideals. In fact, it can be argued that China's national survival and development is a crucial precondition for the effective pursuit of any ideological interest, and as such has priority in time.

It must be recognised that the perspectives and policies under scrutiny here have, like their counterparts elsewhere, both a declaratory and operational dimension. Often, what may be considered a reflection of Chinese perceptions might well be mere propaganda or misinformation. It must also be pointed out that Chinese relations with the outside world are carried out at several levels, often with quite different objectives. These levels include state-to-state, party-to-party, and people-to-people. Furthermore, it should be noted that policy debate does occur within the Chinese leadership. For example, some analysts in China interpreted Soviet actions in Afghanistan as part of a larger strategic design, while others saw it as a sign of Soviet weakness and desperation. There have been signs of disagreement between those who would have China pursue a more globalist course and those who believe Chinese interests lie closer to home in the Asian region. Some have emphasised purely strategic military security perspectives, while others have advocated a broader view which includes sociotechonomic concerns for China and the world. There has also been dissonance over the degree and type of contacts with foreigners and foreign ideas. The voices of self-reliance versus interdependence are on a spectrum that runs from freedom from foreign influence to the more relaxed position of freedom from foreign control. The 'nativists'[6] tend to be inward-looking and somewhat xenophobic, adhering closely to ideology and hoping to set China off from the corrupting influence of the outside world. For them, strength is to be found in the hearts and minds of the people and security is to be derived more from political than objective military considerations. They have seen the two 'superpowers' (*chaoji daguo*),[7] the United States and the Soviet Union, as colluding against China and other progressive world forces and they have championed the interests of the Third World. Lin Biao and the 'Gang of Four' were representative of this perspective, which was committed to a dual adversary conception of and a more militant approach to China's relations with the two superpowers. This viewpoint may still have some influence within China's defence and security establishment. The more eclectic 'selective interactors' emphasise China's modernisation and recognise the importance of techonomic factors as components of national strength. But they view outside (especially capitalist Western) society as inferior and corrupting and thus try to minimise cultural and political spill-over effects from dealings with outsiders. They view the superpower balance as one of world-wide contention, and adhere to the basic view that the Soviet Union is on the offensive while the US is on the defensive and therefore the former is the principle enemy to world peace and the main threat to China. While this view has recently shifted somewhat, it has basically retained its ascendancy amongst Chinese decision-makers since Zhou Enlai advocated it nearly a decade and a half ago. It would be incorrect to say that these two perspectives are mutually exclusive and absolute, however, for there may be elements of both that combine on a given issue at a particular time.

CHINA'S CURRENT STRATEGIC VIEW AND FOREIGN POLICY INTERESTS

As the author has pointed out elsewhere,[8] several events combined to give impetus to a major shift in Chinese perspectives in the late 1960s. The 'dual shocks' of the Soviet intervention into Czechoslovakia in August 1968 and the armed clashes along the Sino-Soviet border between April and August 1969 were particularly important in pointing out the immediacy and primacy of the Soviet threat. The subsequent rapid growth in Soviet military might behind the façade of detente and its expansionism in Africa, with the aid of the Cuban mercenaries, was also set against the perceived waning of American power, particularly in light of its failed policies in Indochina. Moscow's behaviour was thus held as a rationale to adjust China's policy toward the US through rapprochement, thereby constructing the 'broadest united front' from above to counter-balance the threat. This shift toward a balance of power stance was indicative of the dynamic quality of Chinese strategic assessment.

In the early 1970s, both Zhou Enlai and Deng Xiaoping argued that the international system would remain unstable due to superpower contention centred in Europe. In the short term, it was speculated that superpower competition in more vital and vulnerable spheres of interest than Asia might provide China with the international 'breathing space' required to resurrect itself politically and economically from a decade of turmoil. However, after the spring 1975 collapse of the Saigon regime, Chinese analysts began to argue that Soviet power was moving beyond a wholly Eurocentric orientation:

> Soviet social-imperialism, like a hungry tiger coming out from its lair in the mountains, poses an even greater danger to the states and peoples in Southeast Asia than decaying US imperialism. That is why it is far more important to heighten vigilance against the Soviet

Union . . . [which is] trying its best to replace the United States as the overlord in Asia.⁹

By November 1977 it was unequivocally stated that the USSR was the most reckless and treacherous of the superpowers as well as the most dangerous source of future world war, but that China urgently needed a long period of peace to achieve the gigantic task of modernisation.¹⁰ The possibility of delaying or otherwise impeding the outbreak of world war was raised for the first time since Zhou had first suggested it at the Tenth Party Congress in 1973:

> So long as the people of all countries heighten their vigilance, close their ranks, get prepared and wage unrelenting struggles, they may be able to put off the outbreak of war, or will find themselves in a favorable position when war does break out.¹¹

PRC policy proceeded from the assumptions that the USSR considered the US to be its chief enemy and that Soviet build-up in the Far East was directed mainly at America and Japan, rather than China. This had earlier been described as 'feinting to the east while attacking the west'.¹² The appropriate strategy was deemed to be that of emphasising China's long-term techonomic development rather than opting for an abrupt, and by implication illusory, quick fix to deal with the threat.¹³ Indeed, by insisting that the Soviets were occupied with the West and Middle East (a critique substantiated by Moscow's intervention in Afghanistan), Beijing gained a degree of freedom from domestic criticisms about the priority it began to put on techonomic improvements over military modernisation, as well as its diplomatic rapprochement with the US.

With the dramatic escalation of Sino-Vietnamese tensions in early 1978 and the Soviet invasion of Afghanistan in December 1979, a somewhat different Chinese strategic view emerged. Emphasis on an approaching frontal confrontation between the superpowers subtly gave way to a perception of Soviet strategic encirclement aimed at strangling the West through a dominance over the world's energy sources and supply routes. Moscow's goal was seen as an outflanking operation whereby it was pushing into Southwest Asia and, with the help of its Vietnamese and Cuban surrogates, was seeking to expand its hegemonic control from the Horn of Africa and Persian Gulf to the Strait of Malacca and the Pacific Ocean (the so-called 'dumb-bell strategy').¹⁴ Because the Soviet Union was effectively blocked in terms of taking Europe by force, it had developed the concept of 'seizing Europe by stratagem'. This involved on the one hand, exerting military pressure to compel Western Europe to seek detente with Moscow, thus neutralising it, disintegrating NATO, and squeezing out US influence. On the other hand, it attempted a breakthrough in the Middle East and Africa, 'the extended backdoor of Europe' – thus re-enacting Tsarist Russian postures. The Chinese pointed out that the USSR had reinforced its strategic position in the Asian-Pacific region. It had backed Vietnam's policy to establish regional hegemony, while building up its own military strength and gaining access to naval, air and other facilities at Da Nang and Cam Ranh Bay.

Since late 1981, China's view has shifted from the neo-bipolar one described above to one which is much more multipolar.[15] Its previous tilt toward the US, which was based upon a combination of 'strategic cooperation' against the Soviets and a desire to tap the techonomic reservoirs of the 'developed world' for its own domestic Four Modernisations[16] programme, has eroded significantly. While the mutual security interests of the two have persisted, their strategic dialogue has largely lapsed as each has become suspicious of the other's intentions. In fact, Beijing has returned to its earlier practice of denouncing both hegemonisms,[17] Soviet *and* American (as well as their regional manifestations), while at the same time initiating a dialogue with Moscow.[18] It has also expressed its worry about the dangers of intensified superpower contention in the Third World, including its own Asian region. As Beijing sees it, the world is entering a period of greater turmoil characterised by a superpower contest marked by an unending arms race amidst deepening economic recession. The bipolarism of the superpowers is being challenged by centrifugal forces within the two alliance systems. The 'guns or butter contradiction' has fed the peace movement and caused policy disagreements between the US and its Western European allies and amongst the Soviet Union and its COMECON comrades. While Europe remains central to superpower contention and the Soviets are still seen to be trying to outflank the West by gaining control over the resources and trade routes from the Middle East to Asia, the scramble for strategic points in the Third World has widened. The shifting of the burdens of the economic crisis and the hegemony struggle onto the Third World has affected the unity amongst Third World states by resurrecting 'old historical differences' that allow further superpower meddling.[19] While this is said to have awakened some states to the need for an alliance against superpower encroachments, it is admitted that ceaseless partial wars in the Third World could easily evolve into a conventional or nuclear global conflict.[20] China has called upon the superpowers to destroy their nuclear weapons and undertake real cut-backs in conventional arms as preconditions to such moves by others.[21]

China's relations with the US have cooled significantly, largely as a result of a lack of American subtlety over the highly sensitive issue of its support to Taiwan (and by the implicit partial return to a 'Two Chinas' or 'One China–One Taiwan' policy underscored by the 1979 Taiwan Relations Act and continued weapons deals). Other irritants have included trade disputes (particularly involving textile quotas and tariffs), Chinese disappointment with the slow pace of technology transfers, and the nettlesome decisions to grant political asylum to Chinese tennis star Hu Na and to support claims by American investors in the Huguang Railroad bearer bonds court case. Underlying all of these issues are the long extant and fundamental ideological and cultural differences between the two states.[22] Beijing has openly criticised Washington's 'superpower complex' and scored its backing of Israel and South Africa, and its actions in El Salvador, on the Falklands conflict, and on the Law of the Sea Treaty. China recently has been more reserved about President Reagan's confrontationist posture toward the USSR, given China's need for a stable environment and its wish to devote more attention and resources to its domestic modernisation drive and to questions of domestic reform and leadership (and policy) succession. The Chinese shift can also be traced to its on-going assessment of relative superpower strengths and weaknesses, with recent estimates of American power being more positive. The rough military parity between the US and the USSR, as seen from Beijing, has inspired a more 'balanced' Chinese position between them. It has also allowed China greater flexibility in terms of policy options. There was a recognition that more distance between Beijing and Washington would silence domestic critics who continued to be anxious about the negative consequences the closer relationship might have on internal politics, China's relations with Third World states, and the Party's prestige amongst revolutionary-insurgent groups abroad. Finally, there are those in China who reckon that the Soviet expansionist offensive has been stalled for a number of reasons. It is bogged down in Afghanistan, has serious problems in Poland, has long-term and expensive commitments to Cuba, Ethiopia and Vietnam at a time when it is experiencing economic difficulties at home, and is wary of running foul of the international peace movement. As a result, the Soviet strategic threat is less immediate than it was in 1978–80, during the honeymoon period of Sino-American relations. There does remain, however, a recognition that Soviet military strength has dramatically increased in Asia and that the primary military threat to China is still the USSR.[23] But overall it appears that developmental-economic priorities at home have become equally, if not more, important in the eyes of Chinese policy-makers than strictly strategic military-security ones.

Of the currently declared principles underlying Beijing's foreign policies, undoubtedly the most important are those of independence and sovereignty. Beyond indicating China's preference for a position of implied non-alignment, these principles emphasise the crucial importance of national interest[24] in the practice of Chinese foreign policy. Emphasis is given to security in the broadest sense, including domestic economic prosperity (and thus sociopolitical stability) as well as the survivability of the state in terms of external threats. The current domestic policies of the Deng Xiaoping leadership, in fact, stress the notion that security is to be found in economic growth and general modernisation as well as in military security – that insecurity is rooted as much, if not more, in non-military vulnerabilities.[25] Thus, taking into account China's geopolitical and geodemographic realities, and considering the global context in which Beijing sees these realities, there is a recognition that national interest must be equated with domestic stability and harmony amidst economic sufficiency, rather than identified with the politics of turmoil and economic sacrifice, and that non-military means of deterring external threat are preferable to the more expensive military ones. The PRC's recent 'consultations' with the USSR and its renewed dialogue with India, both of which have treated the border question as a central issue, are reflective of this thinking. There is a concern not only to maintain the nation's territorial integrity but to exploit the vast continental and ocean/ seabed resources that are so vital to its modernisation. Also, Beijing must go beyond a mere defence and stabilisation of its borders to realise concurrently the integration (*de novo* in some cases) of its own vast, distant, and traditionally non-Han frontier lands.

Of immense importance to China is the completion of the process of national reunification (or revolutionary reintegration), namely the application of Beijing's sovereignty over Taiwan and Hong Kong. Although this process is considered by the PRC to be a domestic one, it none the less is clouded by the involvement of US, British and other regional interests. The depth of Chinese sentiments on these matters of 'fundamental principle' should not be underestimated. Indeed, the very claim to leadership and policy legitimacy within Beijing will be linked closely to this ambition. These facts are reflected in the downturn in Sino-American relations despite the August 1982 Shanghai II communiqué which exhibited only notional progress on the questions of a timetable ending American arms supplies to Taibei and a basic agreement by Beijing to pursue reunification peacefully.[26]

China's support for world peace and stability as well as for a new world economic order through a sort of international reformism (as opposed to its earlier espousal of international armed struggle) serves both its own domestic policy objectives while not wholly forsaking its more internationalist moral and ideological principles. Thus, while Beijing roundly condemns the de-stabilising features of global superpower contention, it also publicly assumes a redistributionist stance on world economic issues. However, this does not mean that China's own national security interests and its support for world peace and reform coincide absolutely. A basically pacific world environment, however, is seen to be essential for China's Four Modernisations drive at home. While Beijing believes that economic independence is the key to consolidating its own political independence (and it applies this principle to other developing countries as well),[27] in practice it is compelled by circumstance to adhere to a policy of *relative* self-reliance whereby it maintains 'open door' economic ties with other more developed states (including those in the Asian region) so as to channel trade and investment, technology, and talent into its developmental endeavours. This has led to a greater coordination of China's foreign and trade policies, as well as to a more active role by the PRC in world financial organs (such as the International Monetary Fund and the World Bank). But it has not been forgotten how political values and economic tasks often tend to tug against each other both within China and in dealings with foreigners, particularly those from capitalist states. Thus, while opening its doors to techonomic exchange, China's leaders have warned against 'worshipping things foreign, fawning over foreigners, and falling victim to the corrosive effects of capitalism and other decadent ideas from abroad'.[28] China's devotion to its own modernisation, though, has demanded that it assign and *attract* vital human and material resources to this undertaking and has meant that its aid and assistance programmes abroad generally have had to be cut back.

Currently, the revolutionary dimension of Chinese foreign policy is being put on hold as Beijing gives priority to security and techonomics rather than politics and class struggle. Although Mao's value-oriented world view, with its emphasis on proletarian internationalism, is retained as an overlay, and perhaps a long-term ideal, its present utility seems to lie in providing a degree of ideological legitimisation for the pursuit of what are in fact pragmatic policies generated by Deng's more power-oriented perspectives on national interest. China's emphasis on Third World unity in opposition to the political and economic hegemonism of the superpowers reflects, in the view of some analysts, a degree of opportunism whereby the moral and practical support of developing states is sought regardless of their internal class nature.[29] While revolutionary content may be voiced so as to retain China's respectability amongst radicals overseas or, as recently, to placate similar elements at home, Beijing has been actively portraying itself as a responsible and peace-loving actor in international affairs seeking to normalise its state-to-state relations – even at the cost of playing down, in the short term, its ties with and support for revolutionary-insurgent groups.[30] This is especially true of China's activities in Asia, where its most immediate security interests are and where it seeks to minimise the rise or penetration of hostile powers while concurrently optimising its own influence.

CHINA AND ASIA: THE PRIORITIES OF REGION

One of the most potentially volatile and insoluble problems for China in Asia, and one which is instructive about the PRC's concerns in the whole region, is its continuing confrontation with the Socialist Republic of Vietnam (SRV). For Beijing, the Hanoi problem is as much a worry about an expansionist SRV, which destabilises Southeast Asia and challenges Chinese interests, as it is a fear of a Vietnam acting in the service of or being used by an encircling Soviet Union. The 1979 war was launched by the PRC as much for reasons of long-term security as it was for more immediate purposes, and was aimed at compelling both Hanoi and Moscow to exercise future restraint. The venture was also undertaken to maintain China's credibility in the world – that its words (and warnings) were not to be taken lightly, particularly regarding the proximate region of Asia. Beijing's pride and prestige had been damaged by Hanoi's rough treatment of the ethnic Chinese community in Vietnam and by its toppling of China's ally in Kampuchea. It had been both angered and frightened by the formalisation of an SRV–USSR alliance. For its part, the SRV had felt betrayed by the PRC's rapprochement with the US, insulted by China's 1974 takeover of the Paracel (*Xisha*) Islands, and embittered by Beijing's withdrawal of aid and assistance. Underneath it all was the legacy of nearly 2000 years of enmity, half of which was marked by Chinese imperial rule over the Vietnamese.

On balance, the results for China in its 'punishment' of the SRV were unfavourable. Beyond high costs in terms of casualties and expenditures, the hostilities only drove the SRV further into reliance upon the USSR and allowed the latter to substantially enhance its presence in the region. While some Southeast Asians inwardly welcomed China's intervention against the Vietnamese, to others its aggressive handling of Hanoi and its perceived willingness to rush to the support of the radical (and, to many observers, barbaric) Pol Pot regime as well as its ethnic kingsmen in the region only confirmed its reputation for inscrutability and bellicosity. For some, such as the Indonesians, it rekindled worries about the long-term nature of the Chinese threat, with the implied feeling that a viable and satiated Vietnam would be a bulwark against inevitable Chinese communist expansionism. China has persisted in believing that Vietnam can be compelled to withdraw its troops from Kampuchea and Laos by a combination of internal insurrection and external military pressure. Beijing has funnelled arms and supplies to resistance groups in all three Indochinese states, and has also supported the formation of a tripartite coalition of these resistance groups, although its backing is undoubtedly conditioned by the continued integrity of the Khmer Rouge and that group's dominant role in the coalition.

To a significant degree, the Soviet Union has been the big winner in the Sino-Vietnamese conflict to date. It has gained a valuable ally on the southern flank of China as well as use of Vietnamese facilities. This foothold confers upon Moscow two substantial advantages: a means to further relieve its own perceived encirclement and contain China; and a bridgehead for further penetration into the Southeast Asian and Southwest Pacific regions. Its presence also has made a significant political and psychological impact on regional states and actors. Stated simply, the Soviet Union is no longer a *remote* power there (even though its primary interests may lie elsewhere).

While recent signs of strain in the Moscow-Hanoi alliance, such as reported Soviet complaints about Vietnamese impotence, corruption and misuse of aid and Vietnamese grumblings about Soviet failures to fulfil their needs, have suggested that the USSR-SRV relationship can be manoeuvred into one of distance, some have predicted that the current Sino-Soviet dialogue may lead to normalisation between Moscow and Beijing, and that as a result some improvement in Sino-Vietnamese relations might also occur. One of the three steps that Beijing has said the Soviet Union must take before any such normalisation can be considered, however, is the end to Moscow's direct and indirect support for Vietnamese aggression in Indochina.[31] It is doubtful that the Soviet Union would (or could) overtly agree to such a condition on 'third-party issues' since doing so would jeopardise its present rights of access to Vietnamese facilities. China has repeatedly stated that deeds, not words, are a prerequisite to any progress toward normalisation, and while there have been reports of greater quiet along the Sino-Soviet borders, there have been no indications of even token troop withdrawals.[32] A full Sino-Soviet reconciliation is not feasible owing to historical reasons (legacy of mutual resentment, suspicion and fear), the realities of geopolitics, and China's continuing commitment to modernisation which now carries with it a basic reliance on the West and Japan. The temperature of their relations, however, may change, and it must be recognised that while China has no permanent enemies it also has no permanent friends. None the less, any perceived cooling of the Sino-Soviet conflict, which has been a central feature of the global and regional strategic environments for two decades, could have immense impact. For Hanoi, the initial reaction was a fear that relaxation along the Sino-Soviet borders might allow China to devote more of its resources (and troops) to its ambitions in Asia. It was only a decade ago, the SRV undoubtedly recalled, that Beijing dumped Vietnam in favour of a rapprochement with Hanoi's enemy in conflict, the United States.

Privately, even the Chinese believe that the partnership between Moscow and Hanoi is an unnatural and incompatible one. Publicly, Beijing argues that these differences will not lead to the two allies falling out completely. They are, China says, joined together by their common goal of expansion in Asia, and neither third-party offers of economic aid nor other inducements will wean them apart. China has suggested that Vietnam is merely being used as a Trojan horse to bring the other regional states into a Soviet sphere of influence. The problem for Vietnam is to try to disengage itself from both Soviet control and Chinese pressure. However, it is doubtful that any Soviet leadership would watch such a development passively, particularly when concurrently Chinese power is seen to increase with some support from the West.

Thus, while the current Sino-Soviet dialogue may produce some hope for a negotiated solution, or at least a lessening of tension, in Indochina, to date neither Hanoi nor Beijing has shown much enthusiasm for moving beyond propaganda statements towards a real settlement. In fact, there are indications that their dispute over territorial and resource claims in the South China Sea has become increasingly militarised. Furthermore, there is a real chance that fighting along the Thai-Kampuchean border will intensify, bringing with it renewed Sino-Vietnamese border hostilities and little prospect for detente. Also, it may be felt that the maintenance of a focus on the 'enemy' contributes to a higher degree of unity on domestic policies and issues than might otherwise be the case.

There are also the important issues of Beijing's support for revolutionary-insurgent movements and the overseas Chinese. Deng Xiaoping's November 1978 statement in Malaysia that China was interested in good relations with regional states was followed by the remark that the Communist Party of China still supported the outlawed communist parties of the region.[33] His point was that party-to-party relations should be kept separate from state-to-state ties – a distinction that is not accepted (nor has it won any friends) in the region. When similar comments were made by Premier Zhao Ziyang during his August 1981 visit to all ASEAN states except Indonesia, it prompted curt responses from local leaders despite his assurances that these party-to-party relationships were confined to a political and moral realm and that China itself 'wanted no hegemony or spheres of influence in any part of the world now or in the future'.[34] The Malaysian Foreign Minister, Ghazali Shafie, derisively labelled this China's 'sweet and sour policy', while the Malaysian Prime Minister, Dr Mahatir Mohamed, retorted that 'my own political party has no counterpart in China and has no intention of interfering in Chinese domestic affairs. This idea that you can have both party-to-party and government-to-government relations is not really acceptable to us.'[35]

Beijing later attempted to show that it was encouraging local revolutionary movements to adopt a more anti-hegemonist and less strident anti-government line, but these were generally viewed as being cosmetic gestures. They did, however, have a demoralising and debilitating effect within the insurgent groups, and increased bickering led some to argue in favour of alternative patronage. It must be emphasised, however, that Beijing still feels obliged for the latter reason to provide some support for these revolutionary groups, and at no time has it gone so far as to completely disavow its relationship with any of them. This is so, in part, because it is an important issue in the domestic party politics of China itself, as well as a reflection of the leadership's stated commitment to its long-term power interests and revolutionary struggle.

While the overseas Chinese comprise only 5 per cent of Southeast Asia's population, they hold an economic position of strength far beyond their numbers. Although they are by no means a wholly cohesive cultural-linguistic group, they have traditionally tended not to assimilate readily into the regional societies. While this may be changing somewhat, among the ruling elites of the region the presence and activities of ethnic Chinese, however much a functioning part of the indigenous society, continue to be suspect. These feelings have been fed by the statements of PRC leaders supporting revolutionary movements and Beijing's ambiguous policies on the legal status of the overseas Chinese, as well as by policies of regional states that overtly discriminate against them. Moreover, Islamic extremists and ultra-nationalist groups have sometimes capitalised on anti-Chinese sentiment to provoke trouble or cast them as scapegoats for various social ills, while Soviet (and Vietnamese) propaganda tries to sustain the myth of the dangerous Chinese fifth column.

China's appeal for the overseas Chinese is now primarily economic rather than political.[36] They are among the top investors and traders in China's modernisation drive and play an important middleman role in re-exporting and selling China's products to the world. Their remittances also provide a useful influx of foreign currency to fuel China's development and they are a reservoir of professional expertise and skilled manpower which has helped to introduce advanced technology and methods. However, because of the frequency of their contacts at the more personal level of PRC society, the overseas Chinese are often seen to be the bearers of decadent values and habits which might undermine the moral fabric of the state. In sum, the overseas Chinese constitute both a source of strength and an encumbrance to Beijing's interests in the region, and whether links to their motherland can be compatible with loyalty to their nations of residence will continue to be a matter of concern.

Significant tensions between China and its neighbours will be generated by competing claims to resource-rich offshore areas. When it is deemed opportune, Beijing can be expected to pursue its claims to the Spratly (*Nansha*) Islands and the Daoyutai (*Senkaku*) Islands with Vietnam, Japan and other states in the region. China has already shown its intentions by occupying the Paracel Islands. These stepping stones of Chinese presence also have strategic value at a time when Soviet naval activities are on the increase. Beijing's recent opening up of Hainan Island and the seabeds west of it to joint-venture explorations with foreign companies reflects the importance attached to such developments. It is worth noting that by involving various Western, Japanese and overseas Chinese-owned firms in endeavours undertaken in areas of dispute with Vietnam, the PRC is indirectly involving them (and their home countries) in its own security-development concerns.

China's future interests in the region will also be affected by competition in industrial production, particularly as the PRC improves the marketing and marketability of its goods. There already is the problem of a continual trade imbalance which, with the exception of Japan, favours the PRC. For the longer term, there appears to be little recognition within China of how unsettling the process of its modernisation could be or of the threat it will pose to future patterns of political power in the region. The question in the minds of many regional leaders is what will happen if/when the PRC passes from the stage of national construction to a more outward-looking variety of power nationalism.

China's major concerns in East-Northeast Asia are the volatile security situation there characterised by the rapid build-up of Soviet military strength and the development of economic trade and resources for the PRC's modernisation efforts. Beijing has indicated its desire for stability in the area based largely on the status quo. Describing its fraternal ties with Kim Il Sung's North Korea as a 'lips and teeth relationship', China has recently made significant efforts to court Pyongyang, possibly with the intent of reaching an understanding whereby China will support the succession of Kim's son, Kim Jong Il, as the next North Korean president in exchange for pledges that no immediate steps be taken to achieve Korean reunification by force of arms. Beijing may have thrown in a shipment of 20-40 Chinese F-7 (MiG-21) jet fighters, both to counter the American decision to put F-16s into South Korea and to offset the increased Soviet naval and air capabilities southward from the Sea of Okhotsk, and agreed to Kim's request to cut off China's indirect trade with Seoul. The Chinese also publicly increased their calls for an immediate pull-out of American troops from South Korea following President Kim's visit to the PRC in late 1982. While this was done largely to mollify their visitor, it also constituted a signal that China would like to see a reversal of the present trend of militarisation in this sensitive region. It also reflected

Beijing's concern about the vulnerability of its own northeastern provinces, as well as its keenness to protect China's newly established offshore petroleum facilities and its important trade routes to Japan.

In Sino-Japanese relations, the economic dimension will continue to dominate, with China according Tokyo a special place due to its ranking as Beijing's number one trade-technology-development partner. An earlier Chinese assessment of Japan as an economically strong country, but an illusory power dependent on raw materials from abroad and reliant for its defence upon one of the superpowers is still basically held in Beijing. But there are subsurface anxieties about the re-emergence of radical right-wing nationalism in Japan at a time when considerable American pressure is being applied on Tokyo to increase its defence budget and capabilities. This unease was heightened in 1982 by China's protests over the publication of textbooks in Japan which sought to soften accounts of Japanese brutality in China from 1931 to 1945.

On the one hand, some Chinese leaders have implied concern over rifts in Japanese-American relations. For example, the Chinese Ambassador to Japan, Song Zhiguang, said in December 1982 that the US-Japan Security Treaty was 'acceptable' because it was no longer aimed at the PRC.[37] On the other hand, recent public statements from Beijing have been more critical of US-Japan security ties and activities. Chinese media commentary on proposals to extend Japan's maritime defence perimeters some 1000 miles along its southwestern sea lanes of communication has been cool, possibly because such operations might clash with Beijing's own regional ambitions. All of these indicators point to a continuation of Chinese worries over the extent of any Japanese remilitarisation as well as mixed feelings about diminishing American commitments or strength.

CHINESE GLOBAL AND REGIONAL LEVERAGE

What resources can China bring to bear in support of its global and, particularly, its regional interests and influence? There is at present very little the PRC can or will do to buy leverage through its aid and assistance programmes. It cannot compete with others in the giving of large sums of money to other states, nor will its economy allow it to do so. In terms of military power, China still must rely upon its vast numbers (4.2 million in uniform) rather than technological sophistication. In comparison to the other major military powers in Asia,

Beijing's forces are qualitatively inferior and thus do not allow it to project force far beyond its own borders or coasts.[38] China's naval and air forces lack technically trained manpower; its existing surface-to-surface missile system is obsolete; it has no operational surface-to-air missile system; its electronic equipment is minimal and largely dated; its anti-submarine warfare capability is primitive; it has no over-the-horizon radar or airborne warning and control system aircraft; its long-distance supply and communications facilities remain weak; its land-based naval air force is restricted in terms of its reach and its technology; it has no operational submarine-launched ballistic missile (SLBM) capacity; and its submarines are noisy and lacking in sting. Moreover, until recently, Chinese military strategy emphasised Mao's theory of people's war and its attendant 'luring the enemy in deep' approach. There was little emphasis within this continentalist posture on building up a naval capability that would allow China to defend or assert itself beyond its coastal environs.

While China will continue to adhere to the policy of denying the enemy the ability to win, as opposed to the concept of deterrence by threat to inflict unacceptable punishment (as in the doctrine of 'mutual assured destruction'), there are reasons to believe that subtle doctrinal refinements are under way. First, within policy planning circles in Beijing there has been a renewed debate on the 'luring deep' versus forward defence and continentalist versus maritimist viewpoints. This is reflected in allegorical media articles using historical events and persons to elucidate various positions. Typical was a rehash of the great strategic debate of the late nineteenth century over whether funds should be given to defend the western border province of Xinjiang against Russian encroachments or to increase China's abilities to counter Western imperialism along the coast.[39] These imply a partial turn away from previous strategies by China, or at least a serious questioning of their continuing viability and relevance.

Secondly, while China continues to emphasise the rapid development of its nuclear weapons capabilities to cope with the strategic threat of both superpowers and has brought some border military regions up to a higher state of readiness and capability,[40] there are increasing signs that the PRC would like to inject new life into its navy, particularly the South Seas Fleet headquartered at Zhanjiang. It is clear that Beijing's objective is to build a regional navy that can show the flag, protect offshore oil exploration operations, monitor merchant marine and other traffic and guard China's fast developing port facilities and seaside economic zones, and reinforce its territorial claims (which in the south stretch nearly 1000 miles into the South China Sea).⁴¹ In its May 1980 intercontinental ballistic missile tests in the South Pacific, China displayed a fledgling, but not wholly unsophisticated, bluewater naval capability, and its successful October 1982 firing of a submarine-launched ballistic missile in the East China Sea shows that it has mastered that highly advanced technology. A thorough evaluation of hostilities in the Falkland Islands contributed to the PRC's November 1982 decision to purchase more than $100 million worth of advanced naval equipment from a British consortium.⁴² Included were Sea Dart surface-to-air missiles (which also have a surface-to-surface capability), sonars for anti-submarine warfare, and navigational and fire-control radars for China's *Luda*-class destroyers. Defences on Hainan Island are being strengthened by the installation or upgrading of naval, air and missile facilities, and the South Seas Fleet is being reinforced by additional destroyers and landing craft.

While it is conceivable that the development of an operational SLBM force, coupled with the modernisation of other selected naval and air elements, might alter China's military reach in the region over the long term, in the short term it will be capable only of undertaking a somewhat extended coastal defence, and may even find itself hard pressed to defend such vulnerable sites as the Paracels. China maintains regular air patrols over most of its claimed island territories, but it would have difficulty in controlling the airspace. This would be particularly crucial if any attempt were made to push the Vietnamese off the five islands they occupy in the Spratlys (where the Philippines has also occupied seven islands and Taiwan has garrisoned Itu Aba). There already have been serious skirmishes between Chinese and Vietnamese vessels in the Tonkin Gulf and off the Paracels, as on 3–4 March 1982. This raises the question of whether the Soviet Union would intervene if any large-scale hostilities occurred. Other claimants in the region undoubtedly would take an ominous view of such events.

As China goes about its modernisation, with emphasis on the domestic side, techonomics will be the lodestone for all policies and activities. Beijing will feel compelled to divert its vast energies but limited financial resources away from defence toward its overall developmental programme, and in this context defence modernisation will be realised only as a consequence of the latter. There will be continued emphasis on defence self-reliance and, where it can be afforded, the acquisition of production capability rather than the outright purchase of large amounts of military equipment.⁴³ It may buy selected military items, such as anti-tank and anti-aircraft missiles and high technology electronics and radars, with the aim of augmenting its existing defence capabilities. It might seek to partially finance the purchase of such key items by selling off some of its superannuated, but none the less durable and simple to operate equipment to regimes in developing states. The hard currency obtained from such sales, which reportedly total nearly $5 billion to date in the Middle East alone,[44] is important enough, but of even greater significance are the samples of more modern Soviet equipment and other technologies not already in its own inventories that Beijing has procured as part payment. One may also speculate that military advice and assistance accompanies Chinese arms to some recipient states.

In general, Beijing would prefer to maintain a low profile and avoid the use of force if possible. It does not want to feed the existing regional perceptions of its aggressiveness. In a more practical sense, China's economy (and probably its current social mood as well), could not sustain a viable military machine in any prolonged conflict situation far outside its own frontiers nor could it afford to become involved in any race for arms. While its modernisation process moves slowly ahead, Beijing may seek to strengthen its posture by political and diplomatic manoeuvring and by manipulating the perceptions of others in the region through such devices as 'psychological deterrence' and 'image management'. These will be strikingly reminiscent of the tactics discussed by the classical Chinese military strategist, Sun Zi (Sun Tzu):

> If we do not wish to fight, we can prevent the enemy from engaging us. ... All we need to do is to throw something odd and unaccountable in his way.... Though the enemy be stronger ... we may prevent him from fighting. Scheme so as to discover his plans. Rouse him and learn the principle of his activity.[45]

CONCLUSIONS

China's world view has recently become more multipolar as its relations with the superpowers have shifted towards greater 'independence'. Its foreign policies emphasise security in the broadest sense, with priority given to promoting a stable international (and domestic) environment that will allow it to proceed with its national modernisation. Greater attention has been given to techonomic and national reunification objectives than was the case before 1981 when strategic military-security interests prevailed and when Beijing's perceptions were more dominated by the immediacy of the Soviet threat. By coincidence, most other Asian states also accord top priority in policies to economic development (and to spreading its benefits evenly throughout their societies).

China will remain primarily an Asian great power that seeks to enhance its global influence. As far as its objectives in the Asian region are concerned, a crucial issue for the near future may not be whether it will rapidly acquire the military assets to conduct distant battles or undertake complex offshore air and naval campaigns in support of its claims and interests in the region, although these will be important enough, but whether the actions of others will force its hand on issues its leaders would prefer to defer to some more opportune time. That Beijing prepares for both contingencies is clear.

In the short term, the PRC's foreign and defence policy options will be limited by economic constraints and by anxieties over leadership and policy transition. Beijing will only be able to exert limited physical leverage in the Asian region and will seek to pursue its interests there, and globally, through a low-key approach involving a broad, active diplomacy, the cautious cultivation of ethnic kinsmen, and the selective and quiet endorsement of revolutionary-insurgent movements working in an avowedly broad united front with other antihegemonist elements. As (or if) China's military capabilities become comparatively better, it will publicly emphasise the non-aggressive aspects of its intentions in the region. The longer China can continue its economic and military modernisation without facing a showdown with any of its potential enemies or witnessing the erosion of its position in the region, the better are its chances for playing the global and regional balance of power to its own advantage. In essence, this means that China's strategy will be one largely of denial, whereby it strives to deny its enemies basically the same things that it seeks for itself. In its 'dual dialogue' strategy, one would not expect China to come to a full accommodation with the Soviets, although it will assume an even more distanced stance with the US. Its basic outlook will continue to be affected by the existence of a two-way military threat from Moscow in the north and west as well as from Vietnam in the south, although there will be worries about American interference in Asia and anxieties about the future of Japanese defence policies.

For the longer term, the horizons of Asian international relations appear somewhat cloudier. The region tends to be one of comparatively rapid economic growth and burgeoning population where the phenomenon of rising expectations is on the move. It is a dynamic area of still maturing nation-states trying to find their own expression at a time when cooperation and confrontation domestically and within the region as a whole are pushing and pulling at their viability. It is also an ethnically complex region and one where differing sociopolitical systems based upon divergent ideological-religious traditions compete openly and, often, violently.

In the future, China and its neighbours will increasingly find themselves seeking the same fruits of development in a region, and a world, characterised by diminishing natural resources and shrinking markets. Their competing economies will likely face growing trends toward protectionism and increasing gaps in levels of technology. There will be greater strains over territorial sovereignty and exploitation of seabed resources, as concurrently extra-regional actors continue to intrude into the area for economic or strategic gain.

The growth of Japanese economic strength and the rapid increase in Soviet military presence in Asia have been accompanied by a decline in American economic and military power bringing with it calls by Washington for the regional states to shoulder more of the burdens of their own defence. As pressures increase in the US for more resources to be poured into its domestic economy, strains will be placed on the developing economies of Asia (and on that of Tokyo) who would rather not deflect vital growth capital to defence and security. If this results in an increasing militarisation from within the region, the probabilities for tension, destabilisation and conflict may also grow.

The evolution of such an uneasy environment would have ominous ramifications for Chinese domestic affairs and foreign policies. While the very process of modernisation itself will create stresses within Chinese society, a failure to modernise and share the fruits of that process with the various sectors of the state would bring even greater problems. These include the loss of leadership legitimacy and basic policy continuity, with one possible consequence being the return to a more radical, revolutionary perspective and policy line at home and abroad.

Thus, in the long term there are at least two possibilities for China's global and regional role, both of which suggest that it will be a power to be reckoned with (and, to some, *the* major threat). One is a China that has basically succeeded in its initial modernisation efforts and has begun to pass from the stage of national construction to a more outward-looking, assertive variety of power nationalism possibly tinged with revolutionary intentions. The other is a China that has fundamentally failed or been denied in its developmental drive, either because of centrifugal internal developments or centripetal forces from the outside, and thus is left with 'directional frustrations' that make it an unpredictable actor in a world of rapid change. Whatever the result, China will remain a catalyst in global and, particularly, Asian international relations.

NOTES

1. Parts of this essay appeared as an article in the *International Journal*, XXXVIII:2, Spring 1983.
2. I am indebted to Professors Wang Gungwu and James Townsend for their thoughts on these issues.
3. See e.g. Robert A. Scalapino, 'China and the Balance of Power', *Foreign Affairs*, LII:2, January 1974, pp. 349–85.
4. An example is Franz Michael, 'Communist China's Foreign Policy toward the West', in Adam Bronke and Philip E. Uren (eds.), *The Communist States and the West*, Praeger, New York, 1967, pp. 128–36.
5. A similar view is found in A. Doak Barnett, *Communist China and Asia*, Random House, New York, 1959.
6. Kenneth Lieberthal, 'China and the Soviet Union: the Background in Chinese Politics', in Herbert J. Ellison (ed.), *The Sino-Soviet Conflict: A Global Perspective*, Washington University Press, Seattle, 1982, pp. 5–6.
7. See e.g. *Beijing Review*, 42, 18 October 1982, pp. 16–22. For the Chinese, the term 'superpower' itself is one of opprobrium, and whether or not a state is one depends upon its international aims and how it uses its power. China has promised never to become a superpower, nor does it seek to lead the Third World (or any other bloc). *Renmin ribao*, 12 January 1983.
8. Donald H. McMillen, 'China and the Central Balance: "Controlling Barbarians with Barbarians"', *World Review*, 20, October 1982, pp. 39–50.
9. Ren Guping, 'Repulse the Wolf at the Gate, Guard Against the Tiger at the Back Door', *Renmin ribao* (People's Daily), 29 July 1975.
10. Hua Guofeng, 'Political Report' to the 11th Party Congress, 12 August 1977, in *The Eleventh National Congress of the Communist Party of China*, Foreign Languages Press, Beijing, 1977, p. 41.
11. Editorial Department of *Renmin ribao*, 'Chairman Mao's Theory of the Differentiation of the Three Worlds is a Major Contribution to Marxism–Leninism', in *Beijing Review*, 45, 4 November 1977, pp. 10–41.
12. *Beijing Review*, 35–6, 7 September 1973, p. 22; and *Beijing Review*, 26, 30 June 1980, pp. 8–9.
13. See also, Jonathan Pollack, 'Chinese Global Strategy and Soviet Power', *Problems of Communism*, XXX:1, January–February 1981, p. 61.
14. *Beijing Review*, 25, 22 June 1981, pp. 22–5, outlines the Chinese view on Soviet global strategy at the time.
15. See e.g. Pei Monong, 'A Brief Discussion of the Strategic Relationships

'Opposing Soviet Hegemonism', *Renmin ribao*, 8 July 1981; and *Xinhua* (New China News Agency), 23 December 1982. At an early February 1982 meeting of top Chinese leaders it was apparently decided to seek a renewed dialogue with Moscow: *Far Eastern Economic Review*, cxix:13, 31 March 1983, p. 21. It might be added that a similar shift in policy has occurred under US Secretary of State George Shultz.
16. These are agriculture, industry, science and technology, and national defence.
17. See especially 'Hu Yaobang's Speech at Beijing Rally in Commemoration of 70th Anniversary of 1911 Revolution', *Beijing Review*, 42, 19 October 1981, pp. 14–21. 'Anti-hegemonism', which has effectively replaced 'armed struggle of the world's revolutionary forces', is said to be one of China's three basic foreign policy principles. The other two are unity and cooperation among Third World countries and safeguarding world peace. See *Beijing Review*, 32, 9 August 1982, p. 3. A Chinese definition and discussion of 'hegemonism' can be found in *Renmin ribao*, 5 January 1983 and *Beijing Review*, 6, 7 February 1983, pp. 17–19. An interesting caveat to China's promise never to practise 'hegemonism' itself was made when Ji Pengfei said: 'there is no way we can predict or guarantee that the second, third or fourth generations of successors will not guide China on to the wrong road.' *Zhongbao*, Hong Kong, 10–15 March 1980, in *Foreign Broadcast Information Service, Daily Report – People's Republic of China*, (FBIS-PRC), 18 March 1980, p. U4.
18. *International Herald Tribune*, 19–20 March 1983.
19. *Xinhua*, 7 September and 23 December 1982.
20. *Renmin ribao*, 9 October 1982; and *Beijing Review*, 44, 1 November 1982, pp. 18–20.
21. While condemning the superpowers' war of words over disarmament, Beijing has concurrently expressed support for the maintenance of US military bases in such places as Southern Europe. See, *Xinhua*, 23 June 1982; and *Renmin ribao*, 23 June 1982.
22. China's foreign minister, Huang Hua, quipped that American technical assistance to China was like 'loud thunder but little rain', *Asian Wall Street Journal*, 13 October 1982. Of the fifty-five categories of weapons that visiting Chinese procurement officers arranged to buy in Washington, the Reagan administration has approved only seven: *The Times* (London), 3 December 1982. See also, *Xinhua*, 2 January 1983. So perturbed was China, that on 7 April 1983 Beijing announced that nineteen planned cultural exchanges with the US for the remainder of the year were to be suspended. *The Australian*, 8 April 1983.
23. This was reaffirmed by Hu Yaobang in a meeting with Thailand's Prime Minister, Prem Tinsulanonda, in November 1982. *The Australian*, 24 November 1982.
24. A Chinese definition and discussion of 'national interest' can be found in *Hongqi* (Red Flag), 1 November 1982, in British Broadcasting Corporation, *Summary of World Broadcasts/Far East* (SWB/FE), 7187, 19 November 1982, pp. A1/1–6.
25. Deng Xiaoping, 'Opening Speech' to the 12th Party Congress, cited in *Beijing Review*, 44, 1 November 1982, pp. 18–19.

26. China also has made constitutional provision for 'special economic zones and administrative regions' to accommodate the reunification of Taiwan and Hong Kong. In 1981, it also proposed a Nine-Point Plan for this process. See e.g. Michel Oksenberg, 'A Decade of Sino-American Relations', *Foreign Affairs*, 61, Fall 1982, pp. 175–95.
27. *Beijing Review*, 13, 28 March 1983, pp. 13–16, 25.
28. *Beijing Radio*, 4 October 1982, in *SWB/FE*, 7151, 8 October 1982, pp. BII/1–2; and *The Age*, Melbourne, 2 September 1982. That there was some debate over the opening to the West was reflected by Shen Chuanjing, 'Zuo Zongtang Was the Successor to Lin Zexu and Wei Yuan', *Guangming ribao* (Enlightenment Daily), 6 October 1982, in *SWB/FE*, 7166, 26 October 1982, pp. BII/15–16. Premier Zhao Ziyang put forward four principles in China's economic and technical cooperation with other countries while on a tour of Africa in January 1983. These were equality and mutual benefit, emphasis on practical results, diversity in form, and common development: *Xinhua*, 10 February 1983. China has had enough experience in dealing with foreigners to be more resistant to corrosive influences from abroad. Moreover, its more broadly-based diplomacy and contacts gives it a scope of choice which it previously lacked. It is reasonable to assume that China's socioeconomic problems are a result of internal factors rather than external ones, despite what the official media alleges.
29. V. G. Kulkarni, *Far Eastern Economic Review*, CXIX:13, 31 March 1983, pp. 31–6.
30. Beijing has recently spelled out four principles governing relations between communist parties, namely independence, equality and cooperation, mutual respect, and non-interference in each other's internal affairs. See *Banyuetan* (Fortnightly Conversations), Beijing, 25 July 1982, in *SWB/FE*, 7100, 10 August 1982, pp. A1/1–2.
31. The other two are a decrease in Soviet troops along the Sino-Soviet borders (including those in the Mongolian People's Republic) to 1963 levels, a matter on which Deng has said there will be no compromise, and the withdrawal of all troops from Afghanistan.
32. *Liaowang*, 20 December 1982, in *SWB/FE*, 7213, 20 December 1982, p. A2/2. US analysts have claimed that seven divisions were added to the forty-five already stationed along the Sino-Soviet borders over the past two years. *Soviet Military Power*, Department of Defense, Washington, DC, 1983, pp. 51–5; and *Asian Wall Street Journal*, 11–12 March 1983. It is likely that leaders on both sides realise the potential benefits of lowered tension and fewer border troops, including the ability to allocate greater capital and manpower resources to more pressing domestic socioeconomic development programmes. One could even speculate that if China continues to feel perturbed about unresolved political problems in its relations with the US and is spurned in its attempts to obtain Western technology transfers it might turn for assistance to Eastern Europe or the Soviet Union, who have techonomic systems that are in many ways more compatible with Chinese needs and realities.
33. *Asiaweek*, 21 November 1980.
34. Ibid., 21 August 1981.

35. Ibid., 4 September 1981.
36. See e.g. Liao Chengzhi's speech to a January 1983 conference on overseas Chinese affairs, in *Xinhua*, 2 January 1983.
37. *Sydney Morning Herald*, 23 December 1982.
38. There are also domestic constraints on China's activities abroad including problems of remnant radicalism in the military and that institution's decline in prestige, tensions over economic and cultural liberalisation policies, continuing political and generational factionalism, discontent amongst ethnic and religious groups, and uncertainty about future leadership succession and policy direction. I have discussed these problems in 'China's Political Battlefront: Deng Xiaoping and the Military', *Asia Pacific Community*, 18, Fall 1982. Details of China's military strength and deployment can be found in *Military Balance 1982–83*, International Institute for Strategic Studies, London, 1982, pp. 78–81.
39. 'A Tentative Analysis of the "Debate (in the 1870s) on Coastal Defence Versus Land Border Defence"', *Guangming ribao*, 20 February 1981; *Guangming ribao*, 6 October 1982; and *Beijing wanbao* (Beijing Evening News), 7 October 1982, in *SWB/FE*, 7166, 26 October 1982, pp. BII/1–5.
40. For example, China is reportedly adding ten new missile-launching bases to the four it now has. These will become operational by mid-1984. See *Far Eastern Economic Review*, cxx:23, 9 June 1983, p. 11. See also my article, 'The Urumqi Military Region: Defence and Security in China's West', *Asian Survey*, xxii:8, August, 1982, pp. 705–31.
41. See, Richard Breeze, *Far Eastern Economic Review*, cxviii:25, June 1982, pp. 21–8, and Pei Monong, *Beijing Review*, 16, 18 April 1983, pp. 15–19.
42. *Asian Wall Street Journal*, 12 November 1982.
43. In fact, China cannot afford to bring its defence forces up to advanced world standards given their comparative backwardness. It has been estimated that it would cost Beijing US$41–63 billion just to obtain a 'confident capability' to deter a Soviet conventional attack: Drew Middleton, *International Herald Tribune*, 17 April 1981. Defence Minister Zhang Aiping has stated recently that China would not make any major weapons purchases abroad and would rely instead on its own efforts in this undertaking. *Hongqi*, 1 March 1983, in *SWB/FE*, 7272, 3 March 1983, pp. BII/1–2. China apparently decided in late March 1983 to cancel its purchase of the Sea Dart missiles; *Far Eastern Economic Review*, cxx:14, 7 April 1983, p. 21. Despite this, pressures for PLA modernisation will remain, including continuing petitions from within the Deng leadership group itself. It might be added that the sale of weapons to China by the US would be viewed with alarm by some Asian states, particularly in Southeast Asia where it is feared that such arms might be passed on to regional insurgents.
44. *The Australian*, 24 May 1983.
45. Sun Tzu, *The Art of War*, translated by Lionel Giles, Luzac, London, 1910, pp. 46, 50–1.

11 The Soviet Union's Security Outlook

PAUL DIBB

> ... there is a certain similarity between the present and the events of the 1930s.
>
> Marshal N. Ogarkov[1]

The Brezhnev era has come to an end at a particularly harsh time for the new Soviet leadership. At home, the USSR faces serious economic difficulties whilst abroad the Kremlin perceives a series of defence policy choices and dilemmas as difficult as those at any time since the end of World War II. How will the new leadership in Moscow react to these perceived challenges? Will they judge that time is not on the USSR's side and that now is the moment to seize the military initiative? Or is it more likely that they will concentrate on solving the USSR's domestic problems and erecting a defensive barrier against the outside world – a sort of fortress USSR?

These are momentous questions, which for policy-makers in the West require sober and objective assessments. However, the Western intelligence community does not have a particularly good record in analysing the USSR and there have been numerous cases of both 'overestimates' and 'underestimates' of the Soviet military build-up.[2] A number of factors account for mistaken intelligence, including preconceived notions, 'mirror-imagery', misjudgement of Soviet strategic priorities, political and bureaucratic pressures, and a failure to use Soviet sources.[3] At present, the intelligence debate rages around such crucial questions as: has the USSR attained military superiority over the West, do the Soviets have more military forces than they need for defensive purposes, and what are the chances of the USSR actually using its military power given the risks of nuclear escalation?

In this chapter an attempt will be made to contribute to this debate by presenting a perception of the world as seen from Moscow. This is *not* to endorse the Marxist-Leninist view of the world nor, most emphatically, is it to deprecate the threat to Western interests posed by recent Soviet force improvements. But if we are to understand the Soviet Union we should avoid trying to impose on it a Western policy perspective. The focus of our enquiry is the next decade or so. This is a convenient time-frame because, in general, the weapons systems that the USSR is now deploying or developing will determine the characteristics of its force structure in the early 1990s. The analysis will examine the USSR's global strategic perspectives before turning to its particular concerns with the Asian region.

PERCEPTIONS AND THE SOVIET STATE

First, however, let us turn to the question of *perceptions* as applied to the Soviet state. At first glance, the concept of perceptions seems to belong more in the realm of psychological research than in strategic studies, where we are accustomed to dealing with positive facts and observable phenomena. But the approach of the positivist school of thought in strategic studies runs the danger of being overly preoccupied with raw military data.

There is now a respectable body of literature on the subject of perceptions in international relations.[4] It argues that the *images* policy-makers have of other nations and of their government's intentions and actions are the crucial aspects of the international environment, not the 'objective' conditions. Even in this age of highly capable technical intelligence, the most well-informed government cannot know *all* the relevant factors in a particular situation. Thus, any country's perception of reality will always be different from reality. These differences relate to differences in the perceptions of that country's strategic situation traceable to differences in pre-existing images of other nations or general views of the world, differences in specific historical experiences or geopolitical circumstances, or differences in ways of processing incoming information. An understanding of these matters is essential if we are to probe the 'why' questions underlying Soviet state actions.

We frequently assume that the way we see the world is the only possible one and thus believe that the other side sees our actions as we do. In the words of Robert Jervis:

Actors frequently assume that their intentions, especially peaceful ones, are clear to others. Failing to realize that others may see the actor as a threat to their security, the actor concludes that others' arms increases can only indicate unprovoked aggressiveness.[5]

This accusation can be directed against both superpowers at present, who in their implacable hostility towards each other perceive the opposition in exaggerated images. Their mutual fear of the other's military capabilities is driving them to ever higher and more dangerous levels of nuclear armament.

The Soviet leadership, for example, seems to overestimate the ease with which they can show to the US that the USSR does not seek expansionism. The Soviet perceptual system sees the US view of the world as inaccurate and dishonest. In Washington, so the Soviet argument goes, there are dissimulators who know the truth, but who for ulterior motives pretend to have a different perception of, for instance, the question of Soviet military superiority. The USSR's disbelief in its superiority in this regard is deeply rooted in its past experience of arms races with the US and its assessment that the Soviet Union faces an enormous defence problem of its own, which in turn leads it to believe that equality really requires a margin of safety in case of miscalculation.

Russian emotions about the outside world are deeply coloured by a sense of inadequacy in many fields of endeavour. For a long time, the USSR was militarily inferior to the US and even now the Soviet Union is an 'incomplete superpower' lacking much economic or technical impact in most of the world. Ever since Peter the Great, the Russians have been trying to catch up with somebody – and they are still trying. Three other Russian emotions should be mentioned. The first is a persecution complex which derives from successive waves of invasion of the Russian homeland, culminating in the death of 20 million people in the 'Great Patriotic War' against Hitler's Germany. Second is a feeling of uncertainty about Russia's proper spiritual identity in the world. On the one hand, the Russians want to be recognised as the greatest of the European powers, yet they have little in common with the cultural and spiritual heritage of the West. On the other hand, they have Asian pretensions based on their Mongol inheritance and their occupation of large territories in Asia, and yet no significant Asian power accepts the USSR as an Asian country. The third emotion is, despite being the largest country in the world, a feeling of being territorially vulnerable. The ethnic Russians, who form scarcely one half of the total population of the USSR, are surrounded by other Soviet nationalities – some of whom may be of doubtful reliability in wartime. Moreover, the confluence of history and geography confronts the Soviet Union with the sobering reality that military operations begin at its borders. Fifteen foreign countries surround the USSR and roughly 85 per cent of the world's population lies within 5,000 kilometres of the Soviet homeland.[6] No other country, except possibly China, faces such a potentially threatening physical environment.

How important is ideology in determining Soviet security perceptions? This is a vexed question, with some observers arguing that ideological imperatives are the paramount consideration in forming the Soviet Union's external policies and others emphasising the persistence of purely national Russian themes. Both are partially valid, as Moscow's view of the international system, and the Soviet state's position within that environment, is a combination of Russian national interests and communist ideological principles.

Marxism-Leninism establishes the intellectual framework through which Soviet policy-makers observe reality. Thus the contemporary world is seen as largely unjust and threatening to the USSR. Only the military strength of the Soviet state prevents renewed aggression from the capitalist world. Ideology defines the long-range goals of the USSR, which envisages that eventually the revolutionary forces of socialism under the leadership of the USSR will triumph in the world. But experience tells the Soviet leadership that this will not occur any time soon. Marxism-Leninism also provides general outlines for defining the basic characteristics of a given era within which specific foreign policy strategies can be enunciated. For example, once the USSR had reached a certain level of strategic nuclear development it was able to move away from the concept of inevitability of war to 'peaceful coexistence'.

The relevance of ideology in day-to-day decision-making in the Kremlin, however, may only be slight and in these areas the Soviet government probably acts like any other. It is, of course, convenient to be able to justify particular actions under the rubric of protecting the gains of socialism. But where there is inconsistency, as often there is, between promoting purely communist objectives and defending national interests, the latter usually prevail. It is one of the advantages of the flexibility of Marxism-Leninism that when such situations arise some ideological principle can be conjured up to justify the choice of national over doctrinal imperatives.[7] Despite the invocation of 'fraternal' socialist considerations, it was strategic imperatives that played the pre-eminent role in dictating the Soviet invasions of Afghanistan, Czechoslovakia and Hungary.

Is there a Soviet grand design for domination of the world? This seems unlikely given the USSR's failure to do a number of things: since World War II, for example, removing China's nuclear installations, taking a more flexible stance towards allies of the United States – such as Japan – who might have been wooed away from the alliance, and asserting control over Romania, Albania and Yugoslavia. As Jerry Hough has noted, 'those who believe that the Soviet leadership have some master plan on how to take over the world on the basis of rigid ideological prescriptions simply do not understand the contemporary Soviet Union'.[8] A more realistic view is that while the USSR is not planning to take over the world by military conquest, it is none the less eager to extend its influence at the expense of the capitalist West when no serious risks of military confrontation are incurred.

This raises the question, is the USSR a revolutionary rather than a status quo power? The answer is that it is both. Whilst seeking actively to expand its influence abroad, it also has to exercise self-restraint in the use of its power in order to preserve the gains it has won. As Soviet global power and influence grow, the USSR has more to preserve in the status quo because it is one of the two global powers at the apex of the international system. This does not mean that the USSR has abandoned its revolutionary goals, but it does mean that it has more carefully to weigh the chances of improving its situation against the risks of losing existing positions. Ultimately, the levels of risk perceived will depend upon Soviet perceptions of the balance of power and the expected responses to Soviet behaviour, especially those of the US.

Some Domestic Considerations

How important are domestic considerations in formulating Soviet foreign and defence policies? Some analysts claim that the Soviet leadership is increasingly preoccupied with trying to solve the USSR's domestic problems. This school of thought suggests that Andropov, who is an innovative leader, is most concerned to give priority to the Soviet Union's economic problems and is eager to avoid an expensive arms race with the US, which would harm the Soviet economy. Some US analysts believe that the best course for America is to force the

Russians into an all-out arms race in order to 'out-spend' them. This latter view seems to be rather simplistic because it underestimates the resolve of the Soviet leadership. Even so, there are some indications that Andropov would like to give priority to attending to the USSR's pressing economic difficulties, but there are limits to what he can do very soon.

How influential will the armed forces be with the new leadership? Andropov seems to have obligated himself to the military by promising 'that the Army and the Navy will be provided with everything they need, especially in the present international situation'. This was reinforced by his statement that the 'aggressive machinations of imperialism force us ... to be concerned, and seriously concerned, about maintaining our defence capability at the required level'.[9] Andropov's cultivation of the military's support is important because there are many signs that the armed forces are second only to the party apparatus in national security decision-making. In an important article in *Kommunist*, the Chief of Staff of the Soviet Armed Forces, Marshal Ogarkov, warned in 1981 against an 'underestimation of the threat of war' and demanded that the press 'more deeply tell the Soviet people the truth about the existing threat of military danger'.[10] Ogarkov's complaint came at a time when defence spending in the USSR had been cut from a growth rate of 3 per cent to 2 per cent a year and the production of tanks, warships, military aircraft and ballistic missiles had all been reduced from their previous levels.[11] As the Soviet economy continues to slow down in the 1980s, the question of defence spending will become an even more contentious issue among the Soviet leadership, and would only be alleviated if Andropov's advocacy of a policy of arms control were to succeed.[12] Diversion of part of the military budget to investment and consumption would greatly ease the strain on the Soviet economy. By contrast, any increase in military expenditure – which already accounts for about 15 per cent of GNP – would seriously exacerbate existing economic problems.[13]

We can expect to see Andropov support a general Soviet foreign policy approach committed to the pursuit of reduction of international tension (*razryadka*).[14] In fact, Andropov has lost no time in making diplomatic overtures to China as well as to Western Europe and the US. He has also indicated a disposition to engage in serious discussions with Western countries about arms control.[15] At the same time, Andropov has quickly put the Reagan Administration on the defensive, challenging the Americans to demonstrate a similar commitment to arms control.[16] He also has gone out of his way to stress that under his leadership the USSR will not be pushed around. In his speech to the joint session of the Central Committee and the USSR Supreme Soviet in December 1982, the General Secretary promised 'to counter the challenge of the American side by deploying corresponding systems of our own' and asserted that 'any policy directed towards securing military superiority over the USSR has no future and can only heighten the threat of war'.[17] At the time of writing, Andropov has only been in power for some five months, but the initial impression is of a certain flexibility combined with pragmatic toughness in the conduct of Soviet foreign policy.

THE SOVIET GLOBAL STRATEGIC OUTLOOK

There are distinct limits, however, to what any Soviet leader can do to change the USSR's external strategic environment. At its most basic level, the view from the Kremlin is informed by a perception of the contemporary international situation that is tense and potentially threatening to Soviet state interests. Militarily stronger than ever before, the USSR does not necessarily feel more secure. Although the Soviet Union has attained broad nuclear parity, or in Soviet parlance 'equal security', with the US, it does not feel confident of its position.

Of course, the strategic situation has improved immeasurably for the USSR since the 1950s, when the US had nuclear superiority, and the early 1960s, when Moscow suffered the humiliation of the Cuban Missile Crisis. Indeed, in the 1970s the tide of history seemed to be flowing in the USSR's favour. Detente brought a lessening of tension with the US, a series of arms agreements (SALT I, SALT II and the ABM Treaty) which stabilised the military relationship, a dramatic improvement in Soviet access to Western goods and technology, and a recognition in the Helsinki Accords of the USSR's legitimate security interests in Europe. Moreover, the American defeat in Vietnam in 1975 opened up the prospect of a fundamental shift in the situation in the Third World, in which the risks for the USSR of military confrontation with the US were significantly lowered. For Moscow, this latter assessment was confirmed by its military operations in Angola (1975) and the Ogaden War (1977), as well as its support for Vietnam's invasion of Kampuchea (1979).

Much of this has now changed. The USSR's invasion of Afghanistan in 1980 (which with hindsight is probably perceived in Moscow as a costly mistake), Soviet interference in Poland, and the evidence of an unremitting build-up of Soviet military power have effectively spelt the end of the era of detente. The USSR now faces the prospect of prolonged tension with the US and of a new Cold War period in which there will be a renewed arms race. Geopolitically, the Soviet Union observes that the US is now pursuing a neo-containment policy against it. All this is occurring at a time when the Soviet economy, as mentioned earlier, is immutably slowing down and presenting the Soviet leadership with a resource decision crunch, which could well involve pressures for lower defence spending.

At the same time, Moscow's rule over some of its East European satellites is shaky. Tight control over Eastern Europe, which provides a buffer between the Russian heartland and the powerful countries of Western Europe, especially Germany, is a vital concern for the Soviet Union. But the USSR has been shaken by a series of rebellions in its East European empire – in East Germany in 1953, Hungary 1956, Czechoslovakia 1968 and, most recently, Poland. Because of Poland's 35 million population and the strength of its anti-Russian feeling, the prospect of an invasion fills the Soviet leadership with apprehension. Current events in Poland, however they turn out, have weakened the Warsaw Pact. There is a natural evolution of the East European states away from the Soviet socialist model and Soviet military power seems incapable of coping with this fact.

Not everything, of course, is seen in terms of unremitting gloom from the Kremlin. The West itself faces formidable economic problems that are adversely affecting defence budgets. Moscow also observes the differences of opinion on security matters between the US on the one hand and NATO Europe and Japan on the other and it seeks to drive wedges between the Alliance, which in Europe it is doing with some success. On its eastern flank, Moscow believes that now is the best time in 20 years to improve its relations with China. Even so, the Soviet leadership know that the outlook for any substantial breakthrough in their relations with Beijing is not good. Soviet officials acknowledge that any improvement in relations with China 'will be slow and not easy'.[18] The USSR also perceives the new conservative governments in Japan and West Germany as unwelcome developments for its relations with those countries. As for the West's economic difficulties, from Moscow's point of view the last time capitalism went through such a crisis it ended in World War II. In the Third World, too, the USSR has experienced a number of setbacks over the years, in Somalia, Egypt, Sudan, Chile, China and Indonesia – and it knows from experience that friendship with such countries as Cuba, Vietnam and Ethiopia can be extremely expensive.

At the heart of the USSR's strategic concerns over the next decade, however, is its relations with the United States. The USSR perceives America as its most dangerous adversary for the foreseeable future. Soviet officials emphasise that there is no alternative to seeking a normalisation of relations and, if possible, cooperation with the US. But they express pessimism about what can be accomplished as long as present American attitudes persist, and they oppose modification in Soviet behaviour in order to satisfy US terms.[19] The Soviet view is that US policy at the beginning of the 1980s is 'posing a serious threat to peace and international security'.[20] Not that the Soviets think that the US will easily go to war, but they observe that increased tension between the US and the USSR may lead to higher risks of miscalculation – which could lead to conflict by accident rather than by design. In the event of military conflict with America, the Soviet leadership would seek to prevent it from escalating to general war. But they have little faith in the concept of the limited use of nuclear weapons and they see escalation as highly likely once a war has begun.[21]

The main preoccupation of Soviet military strategists is the nuclear balance with the US. They perceive two worrisome trends: the first is the counter-force capability of the new generation of US strategic weapons (the MX-ICBM, the Trident D-5 SLBM, and the cruise missile); and the second concern is the problem of verifying these forces in any arms control agreement. The Soviets claim that these developments will be difficult to reverse because, of course, the USSR will have to respond in like manner:[22]

> We will be compelled to counter the challenge of the American side by deploying corresponding weapons systems of our own, an analogous missile to counter the MX missile, and our own long-range cruise missile, which we are already testing, to counter the US long-range cruise missile.[23]

Similar concerns are expressed about US planned deployments of Pershing II intermediate range missiles in Europe. The Soviets see this missile as much more threatening than the ground-launched cruise missile because of its much higher speed combined with the fact that planned deployments of Pershing II in West Germany would allegedly give the Soviet leadership only about five to eight minutes' warning of a nuclear attack. In Moscow, the planned Pershing II deployments are seen as a sort of Cuban Missile Crisis in reverse and are described as 'the fourth arm' of America's strategic triad.

Soviet authorities also claim that the US is actively developing an anti-ballistic missile (ABM) system, the Low Altitude Defence System (LOADS), which together with renewed interest in civil defence measures, is creating serious grounds for pessimism about the continuation of the ABM Treaty.[24] Soviet concerns in this regard will have been heightened by President Reagan's announcement in March 1983 that the US intends to develop an operational space-based US ABM system by the year 2000. General Secretary Andropov's response was that the development of ABM systems 'would actually open the floodgates of a runaway race of all types of strategic arms, both offensive and defensive'.[25] And yet Soviet authorities talk about the 'objective limitations' which exist, including the fact that even if there is an arms race approximate parity will still prevail, but at a higher and more unstable level.[26] These people also point to the economic factors which are forcing President Reagan to reduce his defence budgets and the pressure that is being applied on the US by its allies. It is also made clear by Moscow that the USSR 'will do everything necessary' to match the US in the arms race. This is generally argued in the context that whilst it is not necessary for the USSR to match the US missile for missile, the counter-force capabilities of the US weapons systems will require 'a certain mode of counter-force development on the Soviet side'. In particular, the USSR implies that it can offset the MX ICBM with 'less investment and strategic effort than the US'.[27] There is evidence that two new Soviet ICBM's were flight-tested in late 1982 and early 1983, one of which may be a mobile, solid-fuel missile similar in size and payload to the MX.[28]

Still there is an underlying sense of apprehension in Moscow that perhaps the US is capable of running ahead, once again, with its superior technology.[29] This may be particularly so if Soviet weapons systems are not so capable as US authorities allege they are. It has been suggested, for example, that the Soviet ICBM force is not nearly accurate or reliable enough to destroy American missile silos in a first strike, contrary to US official estimates.[30] As seen from Moscow, by the early 1990s US technological advances may give America a margin of strategic nuclear superiority over the USSR. Such an advantage would be unlikely to be usable in military terms, but it could have political utility in terms of the perceptions that the USSR's friends and allies have of the relative strengths of the two superpowers. It is unlikely that, in the time frame of this study, either side will achieve a fundamental technical breakthrough that could disarm the other side's retaliatory capabilities, but in the long haul the technological aspects of the arms race tend to favour the US – at least from a Soviet viewpoint.

ASIA IN SOVIET SECURITY PERSPECTIVES

Where does Asia fit into the USSR's security perceptions? The Soviet Union's strategic priorities are clearly elsewhere. First comes its nuclear confrontation with the United States, then there is the requirement to maintain control over its East European buffer zone, and, third, is its political, military and economic relations with Western Europe, which have been historically critical to the Soviet state's survival. Asia ranks only fourth in the Soviet world view. Yet, Asia is proximate to Soviet territory in a way that Africa, Latin America and Oceania are not. The USSR has vital interests in Asia that relate to the security of its own territory, maritime approaches and sea lanes of communication, which do not exist elsewhere in the Third World.

The USSR's Asian territories are extensive: they include Soviet Central Asia, Siberia, the Far East and, for the purposes of this book, the Transcaucasus. Together, these regions account for three-quarters of the Soviet state or some 17 million square kilometres. The population of Soviet Asia is about 70 million, with over 40 million indigenous Asians, most of whom are Muslims, living in the Soviet republics that border on China, Afghanistan, Iran and Turkey. There is considerable ethnic overspill across the borders of these neighbouring countries, and the USSR is concerned that its Asian populations will become infected by radical Muslim ideas. Political instability on the USSR's southern borders, in Afghanistan, Iran and Turkey, is worrisome to Moscow and the Muslim threat to the communist revolution in Afghanistan was the main reason for the USSR's invasion of that country in December 1979. In general, the USSR's Asian peoples have a higher standard of living and welfare than their brethren in neighbouring China, Afghanistan, Iran and Turkey, but they bear all the hallmarks of a colonial occupation. In Soviet Central Asia most important political positions are held by Russians. Local agricultural and mineral resources and cheap textiles are sent to European Russia in exchange for 'imported' industrial products and services. The Russian language and the atheist communist ideology are imposed from Moscow. This is not to predict rebellion in the USSR's Asian possessions, which would quickly be suppressed were it to occur, but events in Afghanistan and Iran have probably heightened the awareness of Soviet Muslims to changes in the outside world. For the leadership in the Kremlin, problems on the boundaries of the Soviet empire – whether in Central Asia or Eastern Europe – will ensure that foreign policy increasingly will be a continuum of domestic policy.

As resources in European Russia become exhausted or too expensive to work, the centre of gravity of the Soviet economy will shift eastwards towards Siberia and Central Asia where there are surpluses of minerals, energy, land and, in Central Asia, labour. These economic trends will reinforce Soviet concern to maintain a strong presence in Soviet Asia and will shape fundamentally Soviet perspectives toward neighbouring Asian countries.[31]

In Asia, the USSR does not have the protective territorial glacis that it has in Eastern Europe. Taking the sweep of Asia from Japan in the east to the Middle East in the west, Soviet territory abuts on, or is very close to, ten Asian countries having a combined population of some 2000 million. It is the Soviet Union's policy to try to develop a buffer zone of friendly, or preferably allied, states as its neighbours. Although this is the ideal Soviet aim, the reality is that Moscow is faced with a hostile China on its eastern flank, as well as a Japan and South Korea that are allied to its arch rival, the United States. Together, these three Asian countries have almost 5 million troops. In the west, Turkey and Greece are members of NATO, with armed forces in excess of three-quarters of a million. These members of the Western Alliance, together with China, control the Soviet Navy's exits to the Sea of Japan and the eastern Mediterranean.

To the south the situation is more favourable to the USSR. Mongolia and now Afghanistan are effectively satellites of the Soviet Union and, in war, Soviet military operations out of these two countries could be useful for supporting attacks on China and to a lesser extent northern Iran, as well as conceivably on the Persian Gulf oil fields and the Straits of Hormuz. Elsewhere, the USSR has treaties with Iraq, Syria, India and North Korea. But none of these countries could be counted on to support the USSR in the event of general war. Even North Korea would probably assess that if it attacked American forces in South Korea during a war between the US and USSR it would risk prompt nuclear devastation. The USSR's major friend in Asia, India, would almost certainly stand aloof from military involvement and maintain its non-aligned status.

Further afield, in Southeast Asia and the Arabian peninsula, the Soviet Union has security treaties with Vietnam and South Yemen.

Soviet access to dedicated sea and air facilities in Cam Ranh Bay and Aden provide it with useful forward deployments close to important Western sea lines of communication in Southeast Asia (the Malacca and Sunda Straits) and the northwest Indian Ocean (the Straits of Hormuz and Bab-el-Mandeb). Both bases, however, are very vulnerable to being destroyed in wartime by US forces based in the Philippines and Guam in the case of Vietnam, and Diego Garcia or possibly Egypt, Somalia or Oman in the case of Aden.

The Soviet military presence in Asia is primarily concentrated in the northeast, where the USSR perceives the main threat from China, the US and Japan. Along the Sino-Soviet border the USSR maintains 52 divisions, or about one-quarter of its ground forces. In addition, the USSR deploys about one-third of its SSBN force from bases in the Soviet Far East, as well as about one-third of the Soviet Navy's general purpose forces. Siberia and Central Asia provide the USSR with great strategic depth for the dispersed location of the major part of its ICBM force, including at least thirteen of the Soviet Union's twenty-two operational ICBM bases with probably about 650 SS-18 and SS-11 missiles, which are targeted mostly against the US. Perhaps 120 or so of these missiles are located in three SS-11 missile complexes in the Soviet Far East, and are aimed primarily at China. In addition, 100 SS-20 IRBMs are now deployed in Siberia, mainly east and west of Lake Baikal, which are targeted against China and US bases in Japan and the Philippines. These regional nuclear strike forces are complemented by some seventy Backfire bombers, of which forty are located at Belaya, west of Lake Baikal, where they can strike China.

In the southern parts of the Soviet Union, Moscow does not perceive the same threat and its forces are not so large. Here there are only twenty-seven divisions, or about half the numbers along the Sino-Soviet border, and some 60 per cent of them are at low levels of readiness (category 3 status). Most are deployed in the Trans-Caucasus and North Caucasus military districts opposite Turkey and Iran, where the USSR has twenty-one divisions. In the Turkestan Military district, along the border with Afghanistan and northeastern Iran, the USSR has only six divisions. If the USSR wanted to invade northern Iran it would probably use forces from the Trans-Caucasus military district rather than from Afghanistan.

Soviet forces abroad in Asia consist of five divisions in Mongolia, which is a large increase from the two divisions that were there in 1975, and the 40th Army in Afghanistan which probably consists of four divisions plus an enlarged airborne division. The USSR's combat presence in Afghanistan has grown only by about 25 000 troops, to about 105 000, since its invasion, mainly due to augmentation by MVD and KGB security forces, which have assumed protection and security missions, thus releasing combat units from those functions. Moscow intends to persevere in Afghanistan and probably has settled down for a long campaign. Casualties are tolerable, at 5000 dead and some 10 000 wounded over the last three years. It is difficult to envisage the Soviets agreeing to a negotiated withdrawal as long as the Muslim insurgents pose a serious threat to the security of the communist regime in Kabul.

Other Soviet forces overseas, other than military advisors, are the Indian Ocean squadron, which regularly consists of five submarines and six major surface combatants – of which one submarine and two destroyers are normally in the northern Arabian Sea shadowing US aircraft carrier forces, and the South China Sea squadron, which has levelled off at two submarines, three cruisers/destroyers and one landing craft. These are normally the only regular out-of-area Soviet naval formations in the Asian region. In general, the USSR's power projection capabilities – except in contiguous land areas such as Afghanistan or Iran – will remain limited over the next decade, especially when it comes to sustaining power in distant crises when opposed by strong defences. Soviet force structure developments – now and into the future – strongly suggest a heavy orientation toward supporting contingencies around the periphery of the USSR. The primary mission for Soviet resources for amphibious lift, naval, infantry and airborne assault appear to be related to wartime control of flanks, and theatres of operation in Europe and China; close to the Soviet homeland. Nevertheless, the steady development of the Soviet Union's power projection capabilities will allow it to operate in its contiguous security zone (and in the Middle East, the Indian subcontinent and the North African littoral, where Moscow will have a growing potential to operate militarily).[32] This will become a matter for concern for US defence planners, particularly with regard to Persian Gulf contingencies.

What of the USSR's foreign policy prospects in Asia? In general, the picture is a mixed one for the Soviets with no clearly favourable trends. Broadly, the USSR sees itself as being checked politically in East and Southeast Asia, as having made as much progress as it is likely to in Indochina and, probably, the Indian sub-continent, and as facing a difficult and unpredictable situation in the Middle East, where traditionally the USSR has not performed very well. By contrast, the

USSR sees the US as having outmanoeuvred it diplomatically in China, Japan, ASEAN and in the Middle East generally. Economically, the USSR counts for little in Asia. Its only close economic relationships are with Mongolia, Afghanistan, Vietnam and North Korea. Soviet trade with the whole of Asia accounts for less than 12 per cent of total Soviet trade turnover, and half of it is with just three countries – Japan, India and Mongolia. Except for the communist countries of North Korea, Vietnam, Mongolia and Afghanistan, Soviet military and economic aid has been mainly directed to India and a small number of Middle Eastern countries (primarily Iraq, Syria, Iran and Turkey). The USSR has not seen its economic investments in Asia translate into unquestioning influence. In the Middle East, for example, it has not been successful in uniting the Arab states into an anti-imperialist bloc of pro-Soviet states.

The countries where the new Soviet leadership will be most alert to improved relations are China and Iran, which are important neighbours. Regional security would be most threatened by the re-emergence of an alliance between the USSR and China, but this seems highly improbable.[33] A more likely prospect is for China eventually to take a more balanced position between the US and the USSR. This could be beneficial to regional security because it would avoid the present dangers of feeding Soviet paranoias about a China aligned with, and receiving modern arms and military technology from, the West.[34] Negotiations with China will demand considerable tact and subtlety from the Russians, attributes for which they are not noted. Whilst making conciliatory gestures, Soviet statements continue, for example, to warn China about the dangers of confrontation with the USSR and 'to what irreparable consequences it may lead in the age of nuclear missiles'.[35] If the USSR is able to improve its relations with China later in the decade this will inevitably have a direct impact on Vietnam's perception of where it stands in Soviet priorities. There are already some signs of tension in the Vietnam–Soviet relationship, which are probably containable only so long as Hanoi is certain that Moscow is aligned with it against China, its traditional enemy.

Although Moscow welcomed America's eviction from Iran, it is not too sure that events there will unfold to its advantage. The USSR would like to see a friendly and compliant Iran on its southern borders, but the nature of the Iranian regime makes that an unlikely probability. The continuing war between Iran and Iraq has also put the USSR in a difficult position because of its long-standing relations with Iraq. Moscow's attempts to stand largely aloof from the conflict have probably pleased neither country. The USSR has latent historical interests in Iran's Azerbaijan province, which adjoins Soviet Azerbaijan. Twice this century, in the 1920s and during World War II, the USSR has occupied Iranian territory. There is concern that if the USSR was invited into the northern provinces by secessionists, or civil war threatened the territorial integrity of Iran, the Soviet Union would move in. Whilst this is a possibility that cannot be dismissed, it seems unlikely. Iran is a large country, with 40 million people, and as Moscow has observed in the Iran-Iraq war, the Iranians are capable of fighting in a fearless and reckless manner. Moreover, the USSR could not be certain of the American response given the perceived threat that *any* Soviet military move into Iran could imply for the security of Middle East oil supplies. The US has signalled its vital interests in this regard, including by the formation of the Rapid Deployment Force. It is highly unlikely that the Soviets have plans to invade the Middle East oil fields, which they know could risk war with the United States.[36]

What then is the outlook for Soviet security initiatives in Asia? Past Soviet proposals for collective security arrangements in Asia, confidence-building measures in the Far East, and discussions on Persian Gulf and Middle East security have not drawn favourable responses. It seems unlikely that the new Soviet leadership will be able to achieve a diplomatic breakthrough either. In the near future, Andropov will be preoccupied with strategic and theatre nuclear arms negotiations with the US. Moreover, with the Soviet invasion of Afghanistan, its association with Vietnam's invasion of Kampuchea, and the increasing display of Soviet military power in the region, most Asian countries seem to be wary of the USSR. For several Asian countries, not least Japan and China, the threatened re-deployment of Soviet SS-20 missiles from Europe to Asia is seen as a threatening move by Moscow, particularly as Soviet Foreign Minister Gromyko has stated categorically that it is the USSR's right to do this if agreement is reached about the disposition of these missiles in Europe.[37]

Unlike Europe, there are no multilateral security discussions in Asia involving the USSR. Yet, in a way Asia presents more uncertainties for Soviet security policy than does Europe. Soviet power in the region must be planned for more widespread tasks than in Europe because it has to be directed not only against China, but contingently against US bases, Japan and South Korea as well as in support of its distant ally Vietnam. Moscow also worries about the political turmoil on its southern borders – that ethnically are its soft underbelly – which could erupt one day into a crisis involving the risk of direct confrontation between critical Soviet and Western interests.

IMPLICATIONS FOR ASIAN SECURITY

Several important points emerge from the preceding analysis. The first is that the 1980s are going to be a tense and difficult period for the Soviet Union. The prospect of an arms race with the United States is high and there is the likelihood of strategic encirclement looming ahead. Unless there is a radical change in Soviet military policy, there can be little doubt that the next decade will see a major attempt by the US to redress the balance of power and the probability of confrontation in Soviet-US relations. The USSR's strategic environment is deteriorating and war, although not imminent, is no longer such a remote contingency from a Soviet viewpoint. Second, the Soviet economy is in poor shape and likely to get worse. This will have important implications for the burden of defence spending, as well as the productivity of Soviet workers and the mood of the people. Third, the Soviet view is that the basic post-war alliances involving the US, Western Europe and Japan are unlikely to change, and that probably nothing much can be done about China. Fourth, there is the ever present danger of instability in Eastern Europe.

Elsewhere in the world, not least in Asia, there are relatively few easy targets of opportunity remaining that the USSR can exploit at relatively low cost. While Soviet military power in Asia is very much greater than it was thirty years ago, its political influence is considerably less. This striking anomaly stems from Moscow's heavy-handed diplomacy in the region, which has worked against it in countries as diverse as China, Japan and Indonesia. Certainly the USSR has little revolutionary appeal in Asia these days and for most Asian countries the Soviet Union does not have much to offer in terms of trade, investment and economic aid. Even Soviet military power has its limitations and its use against states like China, Japan, Pakistan or Iran is extremely doubtful because of the enormous risks involved measured against the dubious results.[38]

All in all, Soviet domestic, military and foreign policies are at a crossroads where the limits to Soviet power are quite apparent and where the way ahead seems less certain and more dangerous than before. The USSR is, of course, used to being a beleaguered state but the leadership must be beginning to wonder if the situation will ever improve. One answer is for the Soviet Union to reduce its military forces, to appear less threatening to the West. But this seems unlikely because military power is the only attribute the USSR has to underpin its claim of being a superpower.

Most Western assessments of the Soviet Union emphasise the USSR's military strengths. By contrast, this chapter has argued that Moscow does not see itself as having a very favourable strategic environment. The USSR confronts formidable opposing forces in the US, Western Europe, Japan and China, and it has no reliable allies of its own. The point needs to be made forcefully, however, that Moscow's insistence on forces capable of assuring absolute security for the Soviet homeland against all possible enemies necessarily implies a perception of insecurity for everybody else. One nation's security is its neighbour's insecurity. It is one thing to explain Soviet behaviour as a manifestation of security, as this essay has; it is something quite different to condone the Soviet military build-up. At the same time, it is important that the West does not exaggerate the Soviet Union's military strength, which is the fashion at present. Otherwise, Soviet leaders may be encouraged to believe that the risks of military action are low, and hence worth taking before they deteriorate later in the 1980s.

It has been a central part of our purpose to show how different the world looks when seen from Moscow. But this ignores Washington's perceptions. In the US view, the USSR cannot but be seen as expansionist. The Soviet Union is the new superpower seeking its place in the sun and it threatens to dislodge US positions by pressing outwards from its Asian heartland. The dangerous situation we are in at present is that America's perceptions of *its* insecurity are setting in train a major build-up of US military power, which the USSR can hardly ignore. It is commonly conceded today that the large lead which the US had in ICBMs in the 1960s was the main factor in the Soviet decision to build a missile force greater in numbers than that of the US. The 1980s promise to be a repeat performance of twenty years ago, and in ten year's time – if we are all here – the world will be at a much higher and more unstable level of nuclear overkill. The risks then of a general crisis slide in world order, or of global war by miscalculation, will be much greater. This is the central issue for Asian security in the decade ahead.

NOTES

1. Marshal N. V. Ogarkov, *Krasnaya Zvezda*, 9 May 1981, p. 2.
2. Overestimates include the size of the Soviet bomber forces and the initial deployment of ICBMs and more recently Soviet MIRV capability, ballistic missile defence capacity and the appearance of a new penetrating bomber. Intelligence underestimated the pace of the Soviet ICBM build-up in the late 1960s and SLBM construction in the 1970s. See John Prados, *The Soviet Estimate*, Dial Press, New York, 1982, pp. 294–5, and Lawrence Freedman, *US Intelligence and the Soviet Strategic Threat*, Macmillan, London, 1977, pp. 106 and 155.
3. Ibid.
4. See in particular Robert Jervis, *Perception and Misperception in International Politics*, Princeton University Press, Princeton, NJ, 1976; K. J. Holsti, *International Politics*, 2nd edn, Prentice-Hall, NJ, 1972, especially pp. 353–400; and Steven J. Rosen and Walter S. Jones, *The Logic of International Relations*, Winthrop Publishers, Cambridge, Massachusetts, 1977.
5. Jervis, op. cit., pp. 409–10.
6. Dennis M. Gormley, 'The Direction and Pace of Soviet Force Projection Capabilities', *Survival*, XXIV:6, November/December 1982, p. 275.
7. For a discussion of ideological influences in Soviet foreign policy, see Jan F. Triska and David D. Finley, *Soviet Foreign Policy*, Macmillan, New York, 1968, pp. 107–27.
8. Jerry F. Hough, *World Politics*, XXXII:4, July 1980, p. 529.
9. Speech at the Plenary Meeting of the CPSU, *Pravda*, 23 November 1982.
10. N. V. Ogarkov, 'Na strazhe mirnogo truda', *Kommunist*, 10, July 1981, pp. 90–1.
11. Between 1980 and 1982 the USSR's production of tanks was reduced by 19 per cent, of major warships (including submarines) by 33 per cent, of military aircraft by 11 per cent, and of intercontinental ballistic missiles by 22 per cent. *Soviet Military Power*, 2nd edn, US Department of Defense, March 1983, pp. 78–80.
12. Boris Meissner, 'Transition in the Kremlin', *Problems of Communism*, XXXII:1, January–February 1983, p. 14.
13. Jerry F. Hough, 'The World as Viewed from Moscow', *International Journal*, XXXVII:2, Spring 1982, p. 185.
14. Archie Brown, 'Andropov: Discipline *and* Reform?' *Problems of Communism*, XXXII:1, January–February 1983, p. 25.
15. Ibid., p. 30.
16. Dimitri K. Simes, 'National Security Under Andropov', *Problems of Communism*, XXXII:1, January–February 1983, p. 38.
17. *Pravda*, 22 December 1982.
18. Interviews in Moscow with the Foreign Ministry and the Institute of the Far East, November 1982.
19. Simes, op. cit., p. 38, from the transcript of a Moscow television programme, 6 December 1982, featuring Georgi Arbatov, Director of the Institute of the USA and Canada, and Aleksandr Bovin, *Izvestiya* political commentator.

20. Georgi Arbatov, 'US Foreign Policy at the Outset of the 1980s', *Peace and Disarmament* (*Mir i razoruzhenie, Nauchnie issledovaniya*), Progress Publishers, Moscow 1980, p. 65.
21. Joseph D. Douglass, *The Soviet Theater Nuclear Offensive*, United States Air Force, Washington, DC, 1982, p. 4.
22. Interview in Moscow with the Institute of the USA and Canada and the Institute of World Economy and International Relations, November 1982.
23. Yuri Andropov, *Pravda*, 22 December 1982.
24. Interview in the Institute of the USA and Canada, November 1982.
25. *Pravda*, 27 March 1983.
26. Interview in the Institute of World Economy and International Relations, November 1982.
27. Ibid.
28. The Soviet Defence Minister, Marshal Ustinov, has said that 'the Soviet Union will respond by deploying a new intercontinental ballistic missile of the same class, with its characteristics in no way inferior to those of the MX'. *Pravda*, 7 December 1982.
29. In a secret military guidance paper, the US Secretary of Defence has allegedly said: 'We and our allies cannot expect to match the Soviets in many quantitative measures of military power. But there are many qualitative dimensions wherein the US possesses compensating strengths and advantages.' From a Pentagon document entitled 'Defense Guidance', quoted in the *Canberra Times*, 19 March 1983.
30. *Chicago Tribune*, 2 March 1983, quoting US intelligence sources and Kosta Tsipsis of the Massachusetts Institute of Technology.
31. Paul Dibb, 'Soviet Capabilities, Interests and Strategies in East Asia in the 1980s', *Survival*, XXIV:4, July/August 1982, p. 158.
32. Gormley, op. cit., p. 275.
33. 'All in all, despite the pressures that may encourage new Soviet reconciliatory efforts, the overall configuration of the 1980s will make even a partial reconciliation unlikely.' Seweryn Bialer, 'The Soviet Perspective', in Herbert J. Ellison (ed.), *The Sino-Soviet Conflict: A Global Perspective*, Washington University Press, Seattle, 1982, p. 47.
34. Paul Dibb, 'The Soviet Union as a Pacific Power', *International Journal*, XXXVIII:2, Spring 1983.
35. *Pravda*, 20 May 1982. The Soviet government has delivered a stinging attack on China, denouncing the list of 'impediments' to improved relations advanced by Beijing, which include Soviet involvement in Afghanistan, the presence of Soviet troops in Mongolia and along the Sino-Soviet border, and Moscow's support for the Vietnamese occupation of Kampuchea. *Izvestiya*, 19 April 1983.
36. In the event of war with the US, the USSR could attack Middle East oil facilities with nuclear missiles (SS-20s) or Backfire bombers.
37. Press conference by Soviet Foreign Minister A. Gromyko, Moscow, 2 April 1983.
38. Robert A. Scalapino, 'The Case for Complexity', in Robert E. Osgood, *Containment, Soviet Behavior, and Grand Strategy*, University of California, Berkeley, 1981, p. 64.

12 Concluding Thoughts

DONALD HUGH McMILLEN

From the moment the themes for this volume were conceived, and through the conference proceedings and subsequent chapter revisions, it was realised that it would be no easy matter to prepare this conclusion. It is not my purpose here to recapitulate on the essays in detail, for they have generally provided an excellent overview of current Asian security interests and viewpoints. Far too often, however, they have *not* explored the factors which have shaped these concerns and perspectives. It is on this point that I wish to begin my remarks, which will then be devoted to identifying areas of commonality and difference amongst the perspectives.

However, these thoughts should be prefaced by saying that the essays are not meant to be the final word, descriptively or analytically, on Asian perspectives as written by Asians (or scholars who have an acknowledged understanding and experience of Asian viewpoints). Rather, they constitute a first step towards a fuller scholarly exposé that hopefully will contribute to a more balanced dialogue and a greater mutual appreciation of the complexity of non-Western views on the great issues of our times, including international security. It is in this context that we might remember the words of K. R. Minogue:

> The points at issue here are not merely verbal. The fate of words is frequently an accurate reflection of how people feel about themselves and the world they live in. Each word stands for a cluster of thoughts and sentiments which in each culture dissolve and recombine.[1]

Indeed, we have only just begun in these essays to grapple with the complexities of Asia writ large, and the diversity of perspectives on international security that exist within the region as a whole and within each sub-region and each of its constituent states. These beginnings are not without significance. Most of our essays have masterfully described *an* Asian perspective, or assessment, of current security issues *per se*. Unfortunately, we have not altogether moved much beyond these descriptions to *analyse* the factors, both constant and variable, that have been crucial to their evolution and might thus assist us in plotting their future course. Nor have we often moved into a discussion of any alternative perspectives that may be extant in these states. In fact, on occasion we have witnessed the mere defence of perspectives rather than an anatomy of them.

For the scholar, analyst or policy-maker in any observer-state it is absolutely imperative to know from whence these Asian perspectives (and those of other states and regions as well) come, as much as it is useful to know what they are. This, of course, is not to say that descriptions of current security perspectives and threat perceptions tell us nothing about their origins and content. They are, in themselves, useful expressions of a state's views, but they are hardly explanatory. Moreover, perspectives may vary over time, and thus it is necessary to vault beyond simple descriptions so as to obtain more viable implications for the future as far as security policies are concerned. Each state's perspectives have complex roots that are traceable over time and space, although they often reflect seemingly inexplicable incongruities between their normative and functional dimensions (and the frustrations that may derive from them). These historical and geopolitical antecedents are further coloured by demographic, ethnic, cultural and ideological factors. It may not matter whether a given perspective, however coloured, is right or wrong. A state's perspectives (or mis-perspectives) on international affairs is reality for that state, whether driven by strictly ideological or by power-oriented motives.[2]

One of the dynamic factors that we have too briefly touched upon in our essays is nationalism – both as a phenomenon (whether a state of mind or state of being) and as a process. While it is not our purpose here to attempt anything as exact as a definition of the term, which itself is – admittedly – a term of Western derivation, we might suggest that most 'national-ists' have demanded that the 'nation' should have some kind of pre-political unity, whether that unity be of religious belief, language, blood, or agreement on a set of values and customs. This 'national-ism' may or may not have achieved some political form in the context of a state structure with its own institutions and territorial boundaries. In Asia, it might be suggested, this process of nation-building and nationalism is strong and evolving. It provides

Concluding Thoughts

both the substance and the rhetoric for power-wielders, power-seekers, and power-contenders. It has an important, albeit not completely understood, place in the attitudinal-value and power framework of Asian perspectives over time.

But what kind of nationalisms are at work in the region, and at what societal and politico-ideological levels? How do these nationalisms compete with or complement one another within and between the states of the region and at the supra-regional level? What resources are or can be marshalled to support them, and what are the constraints on their future viability and evolution? Can we differentiate between national development (and security) and regime consolidation – policy continuity? Who will be seen to constitute the 'nation' or the 'people' in political, cultural and ethnic terms? What are the traumas of national construction and modernisation, and how will states and societies deal with both the costs and benefits of these processes? At what stage, if at all, will constructive nationalism evolve into assertive nationalism, or combine with revolutionary internationalism? And, will the perennial conflict between the desire for national integration, consensus and prosperity and the demands of the external environment ever be rationalised?

While these may appear to be purely academic questions, and ones which are nearly impossible to answer, it seems to me that they raise highly relevant and important issues for those analysts and policy-makers concerned with the study of security interests and perspectives. Thus, they should at least be addressed in more than a passing fashion, and linkages between them and security–insecurity issues should be identified and analysed with care. It may well be that studying questions such as those raised above concerning nationalism and modernisation could take the study of security and security perceptions further beyond the bean-counting stage of totalling troops and weapons.

Absolute consensus has not been achieved in this volume, nor was it expected that it would be. While there were some notable areas of general agreement, there was also considerable diversity among the essays. First, there was a common belief that security should be seen in its broader dimensions, that is, beyond the rather narrow military-only focus. Socioeconomic and cultural aspects, problems of development/modernisation and national integration, and issues of interdependence versus self-reliance were deemed important considerations as well. In other words, besides strictly military security threats and perceptions, it is necessary to identify other areas of insecurity and vulnerability, whether long extant or incipient. As several of our authors (Jusuf Wanandi, Don McMillen and Paul Dibb) conclude, national political consolidation, economic growth and prosperity, and social unity *are* seen to be priorities in the overall security objectives of Asian states. And here it is important to point out the difference between regimes viewing or treating international security problems purely in a security-only manner and seeing and handling them in a way that both recognises and addresses their socioeconomic causes and effects.

Second, the Asian perspectives outlined herein are nearly unanimous in their emphasis on national and then regional security issues. Jusuf Wanandi, for instance, stresses the concepts of 'national resiliency' and 'regional resiliency' in his remarks about the ASEAN states, while Robert Springborg suggests the paramountcy of the regional sub-system for both the Arabs and the Israelis. In the Gulf, as Mohammed Ayoob's cogent analysis has shown, the linkages between regime security and national (and even regional) security are of the utmost importance. Whether or not these various national and regional objectives are in fact compatible remains an important issue. Many essays also suggest that the rising national and developmental aspirations and expectations that have been generated by these state-centred concerns will require careful management and control by leaderships, since if they are seen to fail (or are denied in their efforts) the result might be instability and insecurity.

Third, there are differing assessments of the superpower balance and its influence at the regional and national levels. These varying perspectives are the result of such factors as geopolitical location, distance from areas of conflict and superpower confrontation, and the type and degree of internal problems of the particular states and the ideology of their governing elites. Most essays recognise that there has been a fundamental shift in the nature of the superpower military balance and that this has had a marked influence on most Asian perspectives over the past decade. A few authors suggest, as do Professors Rhee and Kamiya, that the growth of Soviet military power and its political presence in Asia, when coupled with the corresponding erosion of American military strength and will power, will be a major security issue for the 1980s – and no less important than concerns about internal developments. Jusuf Wanandi argues to the contrary, saying that the United States is 'comfortably ahead' in the Asian power race with the Soviet Union. In West Asia, Robert Springborg adds, the United States holds virtually all the cards, although he cautions that a 'metamorphosis' in the Arab and, particularly, the Israeli views may be in progress due to a growing distrust and antipathy towards American power, style and interests in the region. All authors show concern about bilateral superpower issues, such as the arms race and confrontationist attitudes held by Washington and Moscow, and the evolving state of relations between the two superpowers and the Asian great powers, such as the Sino-Soviet dialogue and various squabbles between the United States and its Asian friends and allies.

On the perspectives of the American role in Asia, it is held that in Washington's approach to the region, especially in its dealings with friendly or allied states, it must exhibit a greater willingness for mutuality, consultation and coordination. While the American military role is deemed to be of importance, so is its political and economic role held to be crucial. In all of this, the United States is expected to better harmonise its global interests with its Asian ones, and take into account Asian complexities, diversities and sensitivities. Such a view of 'comprehensive security' is held by Japan and Indonesia. On the other hand, it is recognised that in East and Southeast Asia in particular there is a need for greater 'burden-sharing' in regional security, particularly in regard to sea lines of communication. At the same time, it is admitted that in Asia security-defence issues raise prickly problems about the extent of burden-sharing and stir anxieties concerning the possible re-militarisation of the region (and, especially, of Japan). From the Asian viewpoint, it is not so much a question of 'could' as one of 'should'. There are also the equally vexing issues of technology transfer and economic cooperation and trade (and the potentially negative socio-cultural side-effects of them).

Fourth, the essays differ in the weight they give to the influence of ideology in the shaping of Asian security perspectives. K. Subrahmanyam plays down the role of ideology in the Indian view of security, whereas Professor Rhee portrays the South Korean viewpoint as being dominated by the desire to preserve its liberal democratic system from the incessant threat of communism from the north. For him, ideology is a shaper of elite and popular values and attitudes, and has considerable impact on a state's will, intentions and capabilities. Professor Cheema and Carl Thayer also point to the underlying mistrust and mutual fear amongst states that results from or is justified on the grounds of ideological-religious differences. While ideological-religious factors are seen to colour each state's perspectives, most authors none the less feel that it is power politics that more often than not prevail in their policies and in the pursuit of their interests.

In summary, each Asian state has been shown to have its own security perspectives, sometimes similar to but often quite distinct from those of other states in the larger region. Each has its own abiding interests, fundamental principles, and set objectives. But the views of each are also subject to change, whether evolutionary or revolutionary, with new continuities arising that are both shaped by and contrary to the older views. The impact of science and technology contributes enormously to this process, both in a material and intellectual sense as well as both negatively and positively. It will undoubtedly drive us beyond old geopolitical realities and models to newer, and as yet unknown, security vistas. In the very process, technological gaps may in some ways widen the distance between states just as in other ways it narrows them; and technological change may race far ahead of our collective abilities to create the new value systems and structures needed to manage and control it.

What will the 'heartland' and the 'pivot' be? How will the 'heartland' concept shape the contours of the mental maps of the world? Will the new frontiers, the world's oceans and space, move from the margins to the 'pivot'? How will the world system of dynamically interacting nation-states evolve, and where will it be *seen* to be moving? Obviously, these questions constitute some great mysteries of the future, and we should be concerned with them. But, there are also present realities that will also be relevant. As T. B. Millar noted in the opening essay of this volume, it is what happens at the margins, or junctions, of the contemporary world (and its maturing nationalisms) that counts for much. And, perhaps as a result of our endeavours here, we will be able to speculate with greater understanding about the implications for Asia (and indeed for the rest of the globe) of the effects of the various outward pressures stemming from the imperatives of power and the corruption and seduction of opportunity from wherever they may derive.

NOTES

1. K. R. Minogue, *Nationalism*, Penguin Books, Baltimore, 1970, p. 11.
2. It is not our aim here to define, discuss (or debate) the issue of perception in international relations. Such a discussion can be found in Robert Jervis, *Perception and Misperception in International Politics*, Princeton University Press, Princeton, NJ, 1976.

APPENDIX: MILITARY AND SOCIOECONOMIC PROFILE OF SELECTED ASIAN STATES

(1979 figures*; more recent figures or estimates, where available, are shown in brackets)

State	Area ('000 sq.km)	Population (million)	Population growth rate 1970–78[d] (& % under 15 yrs[a])	Literacy rate %	GNP ($US billion)	Per capita income ($US)	Agric/industry as % of GNP	Defence expenditure ($US million)	Defence as % of GNP	Defence/education as % of public expenditure[a]	Numbers in armed forces ('000)
Afghanistan	647	15.9(16.4[a])	2.2 [45]	12	2.9–3.7(3.5[a])	197(230[a])	55/26	64	1.7(3.0[a])	15/15	90(46[a])
China	9,567	971 (1,029[b])	1.6 [38.6]	70	245.7(259.9–276.5[a])	245(229[a])		(10.2–11.9[b])	(3.8[a])	15.7/11	4360(4238.2[a])
Egypt	1,001	40.9(43.2[b])	2.2	50	18.8(20.6[b])	462		1865(2103[b])	9.9(7.3[a])		395(452[b])
India	3,288	677 (713.8[b])	2.0 [41]	40	133.2(159.7[a])	204(237[a])	34/25	3870(5263[b])	2.9(3.3[a])	19/11	1096(1104[b])
Indonesia	1,919	148 (156[b])	1.8 [40.9]	65	47.2(84[a])	240(520[a])	26/41.2	1711(2692[b])	3.6(3.3[a])	28/20	239(269[b])
Iran	1,648	37.6(39.1[b])	2.9	49	73.2(112.1[b])	1946		4489(4402[b])	6.1(3.6[b])		200(235[b])
Iraq	435	12.7(13.6[b])	3.3	35	33.4(38.98[b])	2633		2675(2980[b])	8.0(7.7[b])		222(342.25[b])
Israel	21	3.7(4[b])	2.7	88	18.6(21.1[b])	4917		5540(6056[b])	29.8(28.7[b])		166(174[b])
Japan	377	115.8(118.6[b])	1.2 [23.55]	99	1019.3(1153[b])	8797(8999[a])	3.9/93.6	9632(10453[b])	0.9(0.93[a])	7.1/19.7	241(270[b])
Korea(Nth)	121.7	17.4(18.8[a])	2.6 [40]	85	19.7(19.9[b])	1132(1060[b])	24/76	1230(1681[b])	6.2(9.8–11[a])	21.5/9.5	672(784[b])
Korea (Sth)	99	39.1(41.1[a])	1.9 [38.3]	93	61.1(63.3[a])	1560(1636[a])	15.8/40.8	3354(3970[b])	5.5(6.3–6.6[a])	28/14.4	617(601.6[b])
Malaysia	330.4	13.6(14.7[a])	2.7 [39]	66	19.6(25.7[a])	1431(1797[b])	23.4/20.4	779(2055[b])	4.0(8.3[b])	16.7/18.9	64(99.1[b])
Pakistan	796	84 (93.0[a])	3.1	28	20.7(27.3[b])	247(302[a])	29.1/23	1054(1888[b])	5.1–6(6.98[b])	24.82/10	429(478.6[b])
Philippines	797	47.8(51.6[a])	2.7 [44]	87	29.8(39.5[b])	618(815[a])	/37.5	641(862[b])	2.2(2.2)	13.2/12.2	103(112.8[b])
Saudi Arabia	2,150	9.2(10.4[c])	3.5	16	76.2(119[b])	8205		17168(24467[b])	22.4(20.5[b])		44(52.2[c])
Singapore	0.619	2 (2.5[c])	2.3 [26.25]	77	8.9(12.4[b])	3780(4071[a])		458(707[b])	5.1(5.7–5.9[b])	19.9/12.5	36(42[b])
Thailand	513	46.6(49.8[a])	2.7	84	26.8(39.3[a])	573(816[a])		1126(1206[b])	4.2(3.8[b])	19.5/	216(233.1[b])
USA	9,363	221 (230[b])	0.8	99	2375.2(2925[b])	10554(12,717[b])	24.81/27.89	122279(176100[b])	5.2(6.1[b])		2022(2116.8[b])
USSR	22,402	258 (269.7[b])	0.9	99	1067.3(1587[b])	4052(5884[b])		114000(191500[b])	10.7(11–15[b])		3657(3705[b])
Vietnam	333	52.4(56.6[a])	2.9 [37]	80	8.5(9.5–16[b])	162(160[a])	45/26	900	9.4		1023(1029[b])

SOURCE: *Based upon Ruth Sivard, *World Military and Social Expenditures 1982*, World Priorities, Washington, DC, 1982, pp. 26–37. All figures cited in this table should be used with caution and considered as being approximate measures since there often is no consensus on exchange rates; definitions of terms and concepts vary significantly; statistical systems in developing states are in the early stages of development; and inaccurate figures may be given for the purposes of propaganda or 'mis-information'. In some cases, such as China, defence expenditures shown here do not include such items as pay and allowances.

NOTES:
[a] *Asia 1983 Yearbook*, Far Eastern Economic Review, Hong Kong, 1983, pp. 6–9.
[b] *The Military Balance 1982–1983*, The International Institute for Strategic Studies, London, 1982.
[c] Author's estimates based upon various sources.
[d] World Bank figures.

Index

Afghanistan, 6, 17, 51, 105, 113, 131–3, 145
   relations with Pakistan, 119, 138, 141–4
   relations with Soviet Union, 119–20, 123–35 *passim*, 161–2, 174, 201
   relations with United States, 118–20, 127–30
Amin, Hafizollah, 124–5
Andropov, Yuri, 199–201, 204, 214n
Arab–Israeli Conflict, 77–85 *passim*, 100, 113–14
Arabs, 77–8, 81, 87–8, 90–1, 97, 100, 104, 113
Asia, 7, 179
   in balance of power, 3, 8, 205
Assad, Hafiz-al, 79
Association of Southeast Asian Nations (ASEAN), 29, 41–4, 55–6, 182
Australia, 29

Balance of power, 168–71
   global, 1–3, 8, 11–15 *passim*, 25n, 50–1, 67–9, 80–4, 91, 110, 126, 136, 146, 154, 173–5, 201, 218
   regional, 11, 53, 80, 84, 91, 139, 140–6 *passim*, 148–9, 158, 163
Bhutto, Zulfikar Ali, 142
Bipolarism, 12, 14, 25n, 154, 175
British Empire, 3, 6, 152

Carter, President J., 21, 87, 127
Chinese Communist Party (CCP), 54, 182–3, 193n

Chinh, Truong, 58–60, 62, 64
Clausewitz, Karl von, 18
Cold war, 11, 29, 92, 136–9, 149, 152–61 *passim*, 202
Comintern, 67
Communism, 11, 66, 106, 170, 198
Council for Mutual Economic Aid (COMECON), 71, 74, 122
Cultural Revolution (China), 59, 159
Czechoslovakia, 31, 127, 173, 202

Daud, Mohammed, 118–21
Deng Xiaoping, 159–60, 173, 179, 182
Detente, 12–14, 51, 128, 140
Deterrence, 13, 18, 25, 188
Diego Garcia, 106, 156–7
Dong, Pham Van, 59, 64
Duan, Le, 58–72 *passim*

East Asia, 11
   in balance of power, 11–21 *passim*, 24, 29
Egypt, 78, 80, 104
Elites, 94–5, 98, 103, 108
European Economic Community (EEC), 79

Factionalism, 58–60, 94
Foreign policy, 58, 171
   decision-making models, 58–65, 172
   objectives, 177–9, 192n
   process, 64-5, 75n, 170–1, 194n, 199

Gandhi, Indira, 142–3
Giap, Vo Nguyen, 58–64 *passim*

Gulf Cooperation Council (GCC), 105
Gulf, Persian, 7, 50, 69, 83, 95, 114–15, 118, 126, 156, 174, 208

Haushofer, Karl, 4, 8,
Heartland, 1–5, 115, 220
Hoan, Hoang Van, 59, 61, 70
Honey, P.J., 58–9, 74n, 75n
Hussein, King Ibn. Talal, 86, 105
Hussein, Saddam, 93, 102–3, 109–10

Ideology, 52, 79
  and foreign policy, 10–12, 65–70 *passim*, 94–5, 113, 151–2, 170–1, 178–9, 198–9, 216, 218–19
Imperialism, 3–4, 70
India, 5, 68, 114
  relations with Pakistan, 6, 114
Indian Ocean, 153–8 *passim*
Indochina, 29, 45, 72, 74
Indonesia, 42, 44, 46, 55
Intermediate-range nuclear forces (INF), 30, 34
Iran, 80, 92, 112, 209–10
  war with Iraq, 93–6, 104–12 *passim*
Iranian Revolution (1978–9), 92–3, 101–12 *passim*
Iraq, 93, 102–11
Islam, 7, 86, 90–7, 100, 103, 106, 159, 206
Islamic Republican Party (Iran), 94–6, 106–8, 111
Israel, 7, 77–8, 86–8, 90–1, 147

Japan, 3–5, 15, 31, 33, 50
  defence and military policies, 32–8, 53, 185
  pacifism in, 4, 28, 31–9 *passim*
  relations with Soviet Union, 30, 33–4, 38
  relations with United States, 32, 37–9

Kampuchea, 29–30, 43–6, 62, 74, 179–85 *passim*

Karmal, Babrak, 125
Kashmir, 138, 141–2
Khalq, 121–5
Khmer Rouge, 44–6, 180
Khomeini, Ayatollah, 103
Kissinger, Henry, 13, 80
Korean peninsula, 6, 23, 29
Korean War (1950–3), 12, 21
Kremlinology, 58

Laos, 71, 73
Liberal Democratic Party (LDP), 28, 32–3
Libya, 104
Lebanon, 78, 85, 99, 157

Mackinder, H., 1–4, 8
Mahan, A.T., 1–3
Malacca, Straits of, 42, 174
Malaysia, 42, 44
Mao Zedong, 85, 179
Maoism, 70, 85, 170
Middle East, 7, 78, 88, 113
Military balance, 52, 152, 195, 221
  in Asia, 21–2, 27n, 80, 109, 207
  between superpowers, 16, 19, 31, 67, 126, 176
  see also Balance of power; Nuclear balance; Superpowers
Minh, Ho Chi, 58–63 *passim*, 66–7
Missiles, 31, 154, 160, 203–4
  see also Military balance; Nuclear balance
Modernisation, 98, 115n, 159–60, 169–70, 174–5, 178, 183–4, 187, 190, 217
Mujahedin, 96, 106, 111–12
Muslim, *see* Islam

Nakasone, Yasuhiro, 32–3, 37
Nasser, G.A., 80, 82, 97
National interest, 54, 168, 171, 177, 192n, 198
National resilience, 41, 43, 51, 56, 218
National reunification and integration, 177, 217
Nationalism, 8, 39, 82, 169–70, 184, 190, 216–17

Naval power, 1–8 *passim*, 18, 20, 22, 186–7
Nixon Doctrine, 13, 101, 126
Non-Aligned Movement, 68, 71, 74, 149
North Atlantic Treaty Organisation (NATO), 25, 38, 50, 69, 154, 175
North Korea, 10–11, 14–15, 21–2, 29, 184
Northeast Asia, 4–5, 14, 21–5, 184
Northern Territories (Japan), 30–2
Nuclear weapons, 142–3, 157, 160, 165
  balance, 16, 31, 126, 176, 201, 203–4
  control, 3, 6–7, 34, 156, 200
  strategy, 13, 25n, 34, 156
  see also Military balance; SALT; START; INF; Superpowers

Oil, *see* Petroleum
Organisation for Economic Cooperation and Development (OECD), 88–9
Organisation of Arab Petroleum Exporting Countries (OAPEC), 92–3
Organisation of Petroleum Exporting Countries (OPEC), 81, 92, 97, 111
Overseas Chinese, 54, 179, 183

Pakistan, 5, 114, 118, 146, 148–9
  relations with China, 139
  relations with India, 6, 137–8, 140, 146–9 *passim*, 162, 164
Palestine Liberation Organisation (PLO), 89, 110, 113
People's Liberation Army (China), 159, 185–8, 194n
People's Republic of China (PRC), 4–5, 7, 29, 188–91
  and Asia, 70–1, 130, 179–85
  foreign policies, 30, 120–3 *passim*, 176–9, 209
  perceived, 44, 54, 72, 148, 159–61, 180
  see also Sino-Soviet relations

Perceptions, 77–88 *passim*, 90–1, 93–100 *passim*, 108–12, 151, 170, 196–7, 213n, 220n
  gap, 23–4, 172
  of threat, 9–11, 31, 44, 55, 71–2, 95–6, 118, 135, 141, 146, *see also* Perspectives
Percham, 121–4
Perspectives, xiii, 49, 65, 67–70, 79–82 *passim*, 216
  see also Perceptions
Petroleum, 7, 82, 92–3, 97, 101, 111, 157–8, 184, 214n
Philippines, 42, 136
Pike, Douglas, 59, 64, 75n
Pivot, 2–3, 220
Pot, Pol, 29, 163

Rapid Deployment Force (RDF), 7, 17, 25, 69, 80, 109, 128, 154, 157–8
Reagan, President Ronald, 69
  foreign and defence policies of, 18, 32, 39, 87, 99, 129, 200
  perspectives of, 5
Regionalism, 41–4, 78–81, 135, 148, 165, 179–85 *passim*
Russia, *see* Soviet Union

Sadat, Anwar al, 79–80, 82, 85–6
Samrin, Heng, 29, 46, 74n
Saudi Arabia, 83, 93, 97–8, 115n, 128
Sea lanes/lines of communication (SLOC), 19–20, 25, 32, 39, 53, 137, 185, 219
Security, 94, 114, 135, 167–8, 177, 215–17
  comprehensive, 31, 37, 53, 56, 219
  internal, 54, 94–6, 107, 159
  national, 65, 71–2, 78, 81, 112, 146, 151
  of regime, 78, 93–108 *passim*, 112, 115n, 218
Shah of Iran (Pahlavi), 84, 93, 97, 101, 103, 106
Shatt-al-Arab, 93, 102, 104
Singapore, 42

Sino-Soviet relations, 5, 12, 26n, 29, 46, 59, 138, 140, 147, 160, 173, 181, 193n, 209, 214n
Socialist Republic of Vietnam (SRV), *see* Vietnam
South Korea, 9, 15, 24–5, 29, 185
South Yemen, 79, 101
Southeast Asia Treaty Organisation (SEATO), 136–9, 146
Soviet Union, 2, 5, 23, 48
  and Asia, 3, 6–7, 23, 82, 88–9, 109, 144, 180, 205–12 *passim*
  foreign policies, 5, 48, 154, 197–212 *passim*
  perceived, 30–4, 44, 49–51, 111, 146, 174–6, 211–12
  power of, 2–8 *passim*, 14, 31, 203, 207–8
  see also Superpowers
Spheres of influence, 11, 17, 32, 44
Strategic Arms Limitation Treaties (SALT), 13, 48, 201
  see also Nuclear weapons
Strategic Arms Reduction Treaty (START), 16, 30, 49
  see also Nuclear weapons
Sun Zi (Sun Tzu), 17, 188
Superpowers, 12–15, 153–9 *passim*, 172, 191n
  balance of power between, xiii, 15, 31, 47, 51–2, 67, 82, 136–9, 154, 218–19
  perceived, 79, 96, 108–12, 146, 153, 175
  relations between, 49, 80, 114
  see also balance of power; Military balance; Soviet Union; United States of America
Syria, 80, 83, 104, 109

Taiwan, 7, 176–8, 193n
Taraki, N.M., 124–6
Technology 50, 176
  gap, 8, 157–8, 166, 220
  transfer, 49–50, 54, 84, 110, 176, 178, 183, 192n, 218
Territorial disputes, 30–2, 138, 141–2, 183
Thailand, 29, 46, 73, 136, 182
Third World, 14, 17, 48–51, 81, 89–90, 154, 175, 179, 201
Tho, Le Duc, 58–62, 74n
Treaty of Amity and Cooperation (1976), 42–4
Tudeh Party (Iran), 111
Union of Soviet Socialist Republics (USSR), *see* Soviet Union
United States of America, 2–8 *passim*, 11, 13, 17, 87, 129
  and Asia, 11–21 *passim*, 23–4, 50, 80, 85–8, 109–12, 119, 157, 219
  perceived, 15, 17, 24, 27n, 32, 49, 69, 97, 109, 128, 137–40, 147–9, 176
  security interests and policies, 13, 18, 50, 52, 87
  see also Superpowers

Vietnam, 3, 29–31, 43–6, 65–7, 71–4, 162, 179–82
Vietnamese Communist Party, 58, 61–7 *passim*

West Bank (Jerusalem), 100

Zionism, 86, 88, 101, 106
Zone of Peace, Freedom and Neutrality (ZOPFAN), 40, 42–5, 56